The Archaeology of Ancient Arizona

The Archaeology of Ancient Arizona

JEFFERSON REID AND
STEPHANIE WHITTLESEY

The University of Arizona Press
Tucson

The University of Arizona Press
Copyright © 1997
The Arizona Board of Regents
All rights reserved
∞ This book is printed on acid-free, archival-quality paper.
Manufactured in the United States of America

11   10   09   08   07   06   8   7   6   5   4   3

Library of Congress Cataloging-in-Publication Data

Reid, James Jefferson, 1942–
The archaeology of ancient Arizona / Jefferson Reid and Stephanie
Whittlesey.
p.   cm.
Includes bibliographical references (p.) and index.
ISBN 13: 978-0-8165-1380-2 (cloth : acid-free paper)—
ISBN 10: 0-8165-1380-5
ISBN 13: 978-0-8165-1709-1 (pbk. : acid-free paper)—
ISBN 10: 0-8165-1709-6
1. Indians of North America—Arizona—Antiquities. 2. Pueblo
Indians—Antiquities. 3. Excavations (Archaeology)—Arizona—
History. 4. Arizona—Antiquities. I. Whittlesey, Stephanie
Michelle. II. Title.
E78.A7R46   1997
979.1'01—dc20   96-25188

Contents

Figures

Preface

This book—a collection of essays and pictures on Arizona's prehistoric past and the archaeologists who have made it come alive—is written for the general reader. We are not writing for our professional colleagues, though much of the information contained in these pages has been or shortly will be presented to them. We are attempting to share with non-archaeologists the excitement of the past and its discovery. As professional archaeologists, however, we bring to this enterprise special experience and insights that derive from well over a half century of combined field and laboratory research. Our knowledge of Arizona prehistory and archaeology is based on our daily involvement in research, some of which is so fresh that it is yet to be reported. We are not, therefore, simply summarizing the research of others, although we have sought a balance in those instances where our interpretations differ from those of our colleagues. In these pages we combine our personal experience and research interests with the efforts of concerned citizens and other archaeologists into a highly personal prehistory. The interpretation of the past that we present is uniquely ours, for we have personally shared in its discovery, with shovel and trowel, survey and computer, analysis and reporting.

Ours is not the last word or the only way to view Arizona's past. A major point of each chapter is the almost unimaginable extent to which new information is accumulating day by day at a rate far faster than it can be evaluated and synthesized. So much archaeological fieldwork is going on as we write that it will be years before all of it can be published. Also important is the highly personal nature of archaeological interpretation. It may not be true that there are as many different interpretations as there are archaeologists, but it is true that each individual brings to the past a unique perspective, a point that is demonstrated again and again in the chapters that follow.

We also are aware that Native Americans have their own accounts of their cultural development. These accounts are not necessarily contradictory to an archaeological perspective. The different ways that Earth's moon can be characterized is a case in point. The marvels of Western science made it possible for astronaut Neil Armstrong to exclaim, "One small step for man, one giant leap for mankind" on July 20, 1969, as he stepped upon the surface of the moon. A totally separate body of images and explanations, however, has developed through the importance of the moon in literature, art, and religion for thousands of years preceding Neil Armstrong's historic step. When looking up at the moon, we know that Western science and global religion are not at odds but that each addresses the same phenomenon from vastly different perspectives. We alert readers to the fact that our account of Arizona's past is not the only one available and that it is not necessary to have only one account of the past. There are many paths to the past, and there are many pasts.

Likewise, there are many archaeologists with different roles and responsibilities toward the past. Archaeologists are most conveniently grouped into three categories depending on their responsibilities. Academic archaeologists are employed by colleges and universities to teach and conduct research. Government archaeologists are employed by federal, state, and municipal agencies to manage cultural resources and archaeological activities on lands under their jurisdiction. Contract archaeologists are employed by private environmental consulting firms and do the bulk of the fieldwork and research in archaeology today.

As authors and archaeologists, we also bring different perspectives to this book. Jefferson Reid has taught archaeology and anthropology at the University of Arizona for more than twenty years and directed the field school at Grasshopper Pueblo on the White Mountain Apache Reservation. Stephanie Whittlesey is employed by Statistical Research, Inc., of Tucson, a private archaeological consulting firm. She brings to our joint narrative her wide-ranging experience in research and reporting on the Hohokam, Salado, Sinagua, Patayan, and Mogollon. Teaching southwestern archaeology to university undergraduate and graduate students, as well as to senior participants in Elderhostel, has given us both a valuable perspective for explaining Arizona's past to the public.

Our perspective has also been enhanced, enlivened, and at times put firmly back on track by the comments and suggestions of individuals whose opinions we value highly. Five people read the entire manuscript at various stages in its development. Hartman Lomawaima, Associate Director of the Arizona State Museum, helped us negotiate a scholarly path over the sometimes uncertain landscape of contemporary Native America. Carol Gifford shared the trained eye and expertise of her many years as editor of the Anthropology Papers of the University of Arizona. James McDonald gave us comments from his perspective as archaeologist for the Coronado National Forest and one much involved in public outreach. Barbara Klie Montgomery's experience as an instructor in southwestern archaeology at the junior-college level was the source of many invaluable suggestions; and Judi Burkhardt—nurse, wife, mother, and student of Arizona's fascinating past—provided the confirmation that we had achieved the appropriate level of explanation.

Many other friends and colleagues assisted in reading individual chapters. We are especially grateful to George Michael Jacobs (chapter 1), C. Vance Haynes and Peter Hallman (chapter 2), Arthur DeFazio (chapter 3), Suzanne and Paul Fish (chapter 4), Julian Hayden (chapter 5), Kerry Lynn Sagebiel (chapter 6), and Jeffrey S. Dean and Emory Sekaquaptewa (chapter 7).

Joseph Wilder, Director of the Southwest Center at the University of Arizona, deserves special thanks for his support of David Burckhalter's photographic work and Charles R. Riggs's cartography for this book. Kathy Hubenschmidt and Ted Bundy made it possible to access the Arizona State Museum's vast photographic archives.

Our deepest thanks go to all of the people who made this book possible. The stories in these pages could not have been told without the federal and state agencies that support cultural resource preservation, and the archaeologists who excavate and analyze the remains of the past. Linda Mayro, the Pima County Archaeologist, has been especially tireless in her support of and dedication to historic preservation. Jeffrey Altschul, President of Statistical Research, Inc., has provided a model of enlightened public outreach, and we appreciate his enthusiasm for this project. We acknowledge the productive collaboration of our colleagues; many of their ideas appear in these pages. Our editors, Christine Szuter and Alan M. Schroder, believed in our concept and helped it come to fruition. We also acknowledge the students and staff of the University of Arizona Archaeological Field School, whose hard work uncovered the story of the Mogollon at Grasshopper, Kinishba, Forestdale, and Point of Pines; the White Mountain Apache, who were our hosts and friends; the Native Americans and their descendants whose experiences we recount here; and all of the interested and enthusiastic people who have ever wondered about Arizona's past. We hope to have served you well.

Jefferson Reid
Stephanie Whittlesey

The Archaeology of Ancient Arizona

1 FROM CLOVIS TO CORONADO

The American Southwest is like no other place on earth. It is the living mirror of a vivid and untamed era in our nation's history. Every town and city has a tale to tell, a legend from the past hidden beneath the glittering mask of modern development. From Tubac to Tombstone, from Tucson to Teec Nos Pos, Arizona tells its story through ruin and chronicle. Places such as the OK Corral, Fort Bowie, and Mission San Xavier del Bac are familiar from Arizona history. No less a part of our history, however, are those unnamed ruined villages of the Native Americans who settled this difficult, sometimes hostile land long before Columbus discovered the continent. The unique natural landscape of Arizona is impossible to ignore; giant, ungainly cactus, torrid summers, and the bareboned spires of volcanic mountains command our attention. Also unique is the state's cultural landscape.

Arizona, unlike any other state in the contiguous United States, is an American Indian state. There are more Native Americans in Arizona today than when the first Europeans—Spaniards under the command of Francisco Vásquez de Coronado—marched northward through present-day Arizona to Zuni in the early summer of 1540. A romanticized, cinematic western view casts Indians either as the fearsome horsemen of the Great Plains or as the breechclout-clad, black-haired Apaches against a backdrop of buttes and mesas. In Arizona the truth is much different from—and far more interesting than—the fiction.

Arizona remained Indian country for many years following Coronado's fateful march. Except for the ill-fated Franciscan missions established at Hopi in 1629 and abandoned during the Pueblo Revolt of 1680, the Spanish colonial settlement of Arizona extended no farther north than Mission San Xavier del Bac and the presidio at Tucson. By contrast, Spaniards settled the full length of New Mexico's Río Grande Valley and established Santa Fe as a colonial capital. Although the Gadsden Purchase of 1854 completed the transfer of ownership from Mexico to the United States, the land north of the Mexican town of Tucson nevertheless remained under the control of Indian tribes. Wars with the Apache continued until Geronimo surrendered for the last time on September 5, 1886. Fort Apache, which housed the famous Apache Scouts who helped to end this conflict, finally closed as a military post in the early 1920s.

Today Arizona has a population of more than 200,000 Native Americans among twenty-one federally recognized Indian tribes:

Ak-chin
Camp Verde Yavapai-Apache
Cocopah
Colorado River
Fort McDowell Yavapai-Apache
Fort Mojave
Gila River Pima-Maricopa
Havasupai
Hopi
Hualapai
Kaibab Paiute
Navajo
Pascua Yaqui
Quechan
Salt River Pima-Maricopa
San Carlos Apache
San Juan Paiute
Tohono O'odham
Tonto Apache
White Mountain Apache
Yavapai-Prescott

These people speak different languages, hold various distinct beliefs, and lead diverse lives. It is through their prehistory that the story of Arizona's Indian people unfolds, a rich and complicated tapestry as matchless as the land they call home.

Arizona: Land and People

Arizonans, new and old alike, never fail to marvel at the stark beauty of Arizona's many landscapes and the way that variations in light and season create subtle changes at each moment in time. Although visitors may find it difficult to imagine a single state ranging from desert cactus through alpine meadows to monuments in rough-hewn stone and red mesas, this is precisely what travelers experience as they journey from south to north in Arizona. This variability is the result of geological processes operating over millions of years, of topographic features like the Mogollon Rim, and most especially of water. The scarcity of water created and maintains the deserts. Water was the force that gouged the Grand Canyon, and rivers are the lifeblood of irrigation farmers. So, too, water was a major factor in prehistory.

Twelve thousand years ago when Paleoindian Clovis hunters entered Arizona, there was much more water than today. Well-watered valleys rich in grass and forage were the range for elephants (*Mammuthus columbi*, or mammoths), horses, camels, bison, and lurking predators such as the dire wolf and the saber-toothed tiger. This prehistoric zoo parade even included a ground sloth that could grow to twelve feet tall but that was, thankfully, a vegetarian. At the end of this geological period that geologists call the Pleistocene, the climate shifted to become more like it is today, the large animals disappeared, and the Clovis hunting culture gave way to sparse populations of Archaic hunting-and-gathering people. People of the Cochise Culture, the Archaic people of southern and central Arizona, hunted smaller game such as deer, turkeys, and rabbits, and invested much time in gathering wild plants. By the middle of the first millennium before the Christian era, they began to grow corn they had acquired from people to the south in present-day Mexico. Soon beans and squash were added. Farming villages sprang up wherever land and water were sufficient to make a living. In areas ill-suited to farming, however, the people continued to rely on hunting and gathering.

Some time around A.D. 200 and perhaps as early as A.D. 1 in some parts of Arizona, the art of manufacturing pottery containers was introduced. Soon after, we begin to recognize major differences in architecture, lifestyles, and ceramics that mark the divisions archaeologists recognize as prehistoric cultures. Three physiographic divisions of Arizona present

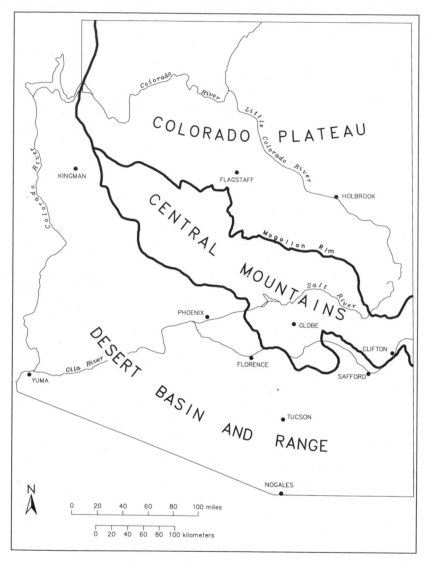

The three major environmental regions of Arizona.

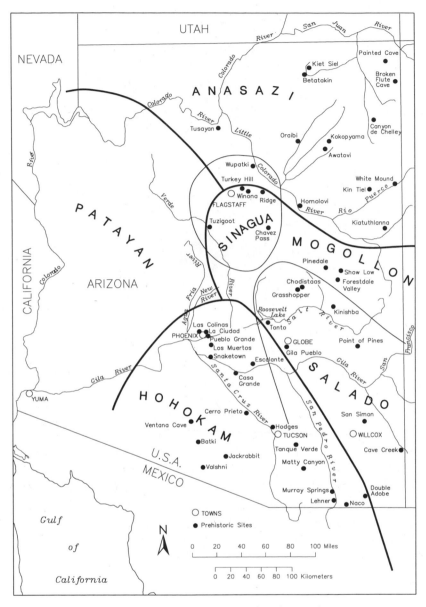

Principal culture areas and prehistoric sites of ancient Arizona.

Kokopelli dancers on a Santa Cruz red-on-buff
ceramic plate from the Colonial Period of the
Hohokam Culture.

radically different environments today, and in prehistory these environments played a critical role in distinguishing the major cultures on the basis of whether they earned a living by hunting and gathering or by farming. As you drive the highways and back roads of Arizona, consider what
the landscape around you could provide in the way of water, food, tools,
and shelter, and you will gain a heightened appreciation for the skill and
ingenuity of the Ancient Ones.

Southern and western Arizona are marked by Sonoran Desert basins,
mountain ranges, and Arizona's major rivers—the Colorado, Gila, Salt,
San Pedro, and Santa Cruz. The ancient Hohokam ("those who have gone
before"; "all used up" in the Piman language) drew water from the desert
rivers, especially the Gila and Salt, to irrigate their fields of corn, beans,
squash, and cotton. They also grew agave on the slopes of the foothills,
gathered wild plants such as cactus and mesquite, and hunted in the
nearby mountains. The Pima and the Tohono O'odham (formerly called

the Papago) believe themselves to be the descendants of the Hohokam.

The prehistoric Patayan people (the "old ones" in the Yuman language) pursued a more mobile lifestyle, shifting residence from their garden plots along the Colorado River to inland camps in the adjacent deserts and mountains. The Yuman peoples in this area today are probably their descendants.

The central highlands form a zone of heavily dissected topography, with steep canyons and mountains jutting above the tree line. The Mogollon Rim forms its northern boundary and is a principal feature, causing higher rainfall in the mountains than on the Colorado Plateau to the north. Here in the mountains the Mogollon people (named after the Mogollon Mountains of New Mexico, which were in turn named for the Spanish colonial governor Juan Ignacio Flores Mogollón) hunted deer and turkey; gathered pine nuts, acorns, and berries in season; and cultivated small gardens in isolated areas of fertile, moist soil. The Mogollon have no recognized descendants, although they undoubtedly are represented today among the Pueblo people such as the Hopi and Zuni. The Western Apache, on the other hand, are historical-period residents of the Southwest who provide the best example of how the prehistoric Mogollon adapted to the central mountains of Arizona.

Northern Arizona is the southernmost part of the vast Colorado Plateau, stretching from the Mogollon Rim into Wyoming. In this cold desert land of scant surface water, the Anasazi ("enemy ancestors" in the Navajo language) mastered dry farming. Their Arizona descendants, the Hopi, live there today along the southern edge of Black Mesa.

The prehistoric Sinagua ("without water" in Spanish), who were related to the Anasazi and Mogollon and who formed part of the Hopi's ancestry, were skilled farmers who lived around present-day Flagstaff and down through the Verde River valley. Late in prehistory the Salado people (named after the Salt River, the "Río Salado" in Spanish) adapted irrigation farming techniques to the river valleys of central and southeastern Arizona. Salado descendants remain to be identified as part of ongoing archaeological research and discovery.

As you read, you may be wondering how archaeologists know what the Hohokam and other ancient peoples called themselves. The answer is that we do not. The names of all the prehistoric cultures you will read about in

A horned lizard etched on the back of a *Cardium*
shell from the Sedentary Period of the Hohokam
Culture.

this book were assigned by archaeologists. We do not know what languages the Ancient Ones spoke, for they left no written records. We cannot know what they called themselves, although for many living native peoples it often is simply the words that mean "The People" in their own language. For similar reasons, we cannot draw precise genealogical connections between living Arizona Indians and those who came before or define them as "tribes," as modern Indians do. We tell here the story of Arizona's ancient people as it has been derived from excavation and survey, from artifact and ecofact, from inference, and, indeed, sometimes from guesses. Unfortunately, there are no pat answers, and we cannot always be sure that we are right.

In contrast to prehistory, the historical era stands in clear light. We have the luxury of written records; we know the languages people spoke, and we can associate names with individuals and the events of their lives.

Although less intellectual detective work is required to understand the past, history is no less fascinating than prehistory, nor is it less varied in the people who made it happen. Arizona history begins in the summer of 1540 with Francisco Vásquez de Coronado's march to present-day Zuni, though some might wish to reckon its beginning in the previous year. In 1539, Fray Marcos de Niza, guided by the intrepid Estevan—ex-slave and survivor, along with Álvar Núñez Cabeza de Vaca, of the ill-fated Narvaez expedition to Florida—claimed to have traveled to a place near Zuni and then returned to Mexico upon hearing of Estevan's death at the hands of the Zuni. De Niza carried the tales of the gold-rich Seven Cities of Cibola that convinced the viceroy of New Spain to send Coronado north. Coronado's failure to find riches did not deter the expansion of Spanish colonization, which was marked by missionary and military efforts to bring Arizona's land and people under Spanish control. The Spanish colonial period lasted until Mexico gained independence from Spain in 1821.

The period of Mexican control introduced a third element into the rich human tapestry of Arizona. Mexico stamped Arizona with her culture and her lifeways, and although the Mexican period formally ended with the Gadsden Purchase of 1854 and the abandonment of the Mexican garrison at Tucson in 1856, in many ways Arizona remained a Mexican state for many years after these events.

Still more variety in language, lifestyle, and culture was introduced during the subsequent American period. Many new ethnic groups, from Chinese to Greeks to peoples of African descent, joined the Arizona pageant. Statehood in 1912 marks the beginning of the modern period of Arizona history, when the state began to participate intensively in the national and international events sweeping the century. Today as then, Arizona is rich in human diversity, indelibly stamped by the Native American, Spanish, and Mexican peoples, and the peoples of many other heritages, all of whom call themselves Arizonans.

A Brief History of Arizona Archaeology

Arizona's prehistory is the special story of its unique Indian heritage as revealed by the archaeologists who dug it up and pieced it together. Untrained explorers of the nineteenth century paved the way for the first archaeologists trained as anthropologists, who in turn laid the foundation for the incredible expansion of archaeological research during the last half of the twentieth century. In universities and community colleges, in government agencies and private businesses, archaeologists work today to preserve the past for all Arizonans.

The spectacular growth and expanding importance of archaeology in the American Southwest parallels the growing interest people have in knowing about the past, both prehistory and history, throughout the world. The history of Arizona archaeology is part of this broader story, and in many ways it is as exciting as that of prehistory itself. We present here only a brief sketch of its history. In each chapter that follows, we amplify this outline to discuss its details more specifically, paint portraits of the major players on the archaeological stage, and present the discovery process as each major prehistoric culture emerged.

Our historical sketch of Arizona archaeology begins in 1879 with the founding of the Bureau of American Ethnology and ends with the Columbian Quincentenary of 1992. We divide it into three broad periods. The first period, from 1879 to 1920, was characterized by wilderness exploration, artifact collection, and site protection. The second period, from 1920 to 1960, was marked by the classification of artifacts, especially pottery, and the writing of culture histories. The third period, from 1960 to 1992, marked an elaboration of historical and scientific research combined with a growing concern for the rightful place of American Indians in the construction of their prehistory.

Exploring, Collecting, and Protecting Prehistory
1879 to 1920

Arizona began this period as a territory where merchants and highwaymen, church ladies and "sporting ladies," miners and cowboys, immigrants and Indians were major actors in the drama of frontier society. Into this land, seemingly uncharted and waiting to be explored, came men and women dispatched by the great museums of the East to bring back unusual things from the West. These people were not trained archaeologists, and many were interested less in prehistory than in contemporary Native Americans. These first explorers of the past were intent upon collecting artifacts for wealthy sponsors and grand exhibitions to fulfill a young nation's need for a visible, material history. Soon, however, professionally trained archaeologists appeared on the scene, and from their initial studies the outline of Arizona prehistory began to emerge. To the lasting credit of these first explorers, they also saw an immediate need to protect the prehistoric ruins of the Southwest through the passage of laws. The first Federal Antiquities Act was passed in 1906.

We begin in 1879 with the daring explorations of John Wesley Powell, the one-armed former major in the Union army who helped create and direct the U.S. Geological Survey (1881–1893) and the Bureau of American Ethnology (1879–1902). Shortly after Powell began his explorations, Adolph Bandelier, a naturalized American born in Switzerland, was the first to explore the ruins of the Verde Valley, the Phoenix Basin, and the White Mountains for the Archaeological Institute of America.

In Bandelier's footsteps followed pioneer archaeologists who had the unparalleled experience of excavating some of the major ruins of Arizona before they were vandalized or destroyed by farming and urban expansion. One of the first, in 1887, was Frank Hamilton Cushing, an eccentric character who had been studying Zuni Pueblo for the Bureau of American Ethnology and who now turned to excavating the ruins of Los Muertos and Pueblo Grande near Phoenix for the Hemenway Southwestern Archaeological Expedition. Shortly thereafter, Jesse Walter Fewkes began exploring pueblo ruins in northern Arizona, excavating at the ruined towns of Awat'ovi and Sityatki on the Hopi Reservation, at Homol'ovi and Chevelon ruins outside modern Winslow, and at the Chavez Pass ruin south of Meteor Crater. Between 1906 and 1908, he excavated at Casa Grande, which now is a national monument. Today's archaeologists, working at the same sites, often turn to the work of these pioneers to learn details impossible to reconstruct in any other way.

Some of the fundamental techniques of systematic archaeological excavation were established during this period. For example, Nels C. Nelson is credited with conducting the first stratigraphic excavations in the Southwest, at Tano Ruins in New Mexico in 1912.

This was also the era in which Arizona's educational institutions were founded and public interest in history and archaeology was formalized. Tempe Normal School (later Arizona State University) was the first, open-

Byron Cummings, one of the founding fathers of Arizona archaeology, at Rainbow Bridge in 1935.

ing in 1886 with thirty-three students. The University of Arizona was founded in 1891, and in 1893 the Arizona Territorial Museum (Arizona State Museum) was established there. Dr. Byron Cummings became the head of the Department of Archaeology and the director of the Arizona State Museum in 1915. He instituted Arizona's first formal archaeological field schools, offering a "Summer Course among the Cliff Dwellers" in 1919.

Societies like the Arizona Pioneers' Historical Society and the Arizona Archaeological and Historical Society were organized to foster public and professional interest in archaeology. Several of Arizona's numerous national monuments featuring archaeological sites were designated during this period. These include Montezuma Castle (a Sinagua cliff dwelling in the middle Verde Valley) in 1906 and Tonto Ruins (a Salado cliff dwelling near Globe) in 1907. The spectacular Navajo National Monument, including the Anasazi cliff dwellings of Betatakin and Kiet Siel, was designated in 1909. Walnut Canyon outside Flagstaff joined the list of Arizona national monuments in 1915, and Casa Grande Ruins in 1918.

Tracing the History of Past People and Culture, 1920 to 1960

Over the next forty years, archaeologists outlined Arizona prehistory and made significant contributions to the developing discipline of archaeology. Each decade brought major new advancements in knowledge and technique. Although each decade was distinct from the others, together these years can be combined under the theme of understanding time, space, and culture history. By the 1950s the culture history approach to southwestern archaeology had been firmly established. Culture history focused on classification and description, and its goal was to document variability in material culture in time and space. Space was divided into branches, and time into periods and phases.

The 1920s. These must have been exciting years for Arizona archaeologists, for during the 1920s they gained control of time. The framework of the Anasazi cultural sequence was outlined during the first Pecos Conference. Organized by the leading archaeologist of the time, A. V. Kidder, the historic achievement of this conference—held in 1927 at Pecos Pueblo, New Mexico—was to agree upon the diagnostic features for the Anasazi Basketmaker-Pueblo cultural sequence, which is still widely used by archaeologists. They divided the sequence into periods called Basketmaker II, Basketmaker III, Pueblo I, Pueblo II, Pueblo III, and Pueblo IV.

The coexistence of people and extinct animals also was established firmly. The most famous site, acknowledged as the first conclusive evidence for people in North America at the time of extinct animals, was near Folsom, New Mexico. At this site, which was discovered by the Black cowboy George McJunkin, spear points were found in the ribs of an extinct bison. In Arizona, Byron Cummings excavated artifacts associated with elephant bones at Double Adobe near Douglas.

By the end of the decade, Dr. Andrew E. Douglass's method for tree-ring dating of prehistoric ruins had been perfected. It would alter forever archaeologists' conceptions of time in prehistory.

Alfred Vincent Kidder (left), the premier southwestern archaeologist of his time, and Emil Haury, his successor, at the Point of Pines Pueblo in 1948.

Also during this decade, Wupatki National Monument north of Flagstaff was added to Arizona's growing list, and in 1927 the first Arizona Antiquities Act was passed to regulate archaeology on State lands.

The 1930s. While the United States was suffering from the Great Depression of the 1930s, Arizona was experiencing a burst of archaeological accomplishment sponsored by two private institutions established late in the previous decade: the Museum of Northern Arizona in Flagstaff and the Gila Pueblo Archaeological Foundation in Globe. Gila Pueblo defined the Hohokam, Mogollon, Salado, and Cochise Cultures; and the Museum of Northern Arizona identified Sinagua and Patayan Cultures and dated the eruption of Sunset Crater Volcano. Also during this decade a third private institution, the Amerind Foundation, was founded in Dragoon. In addition to designating cultures and their variations, archaeologists began to formalize artifact classification systems.

This decade also witnessed the designation of new national monuments, the development of important organizations and journals for disseminating the results of archaeological research, and additional legislation for historic preservation. Canyon de Chelly, outside Chinle, and Tuzigoot, on the middle Verde River, were designated as national monuments. In 1934 the national organization for archaeology, the Society for American Archaeology, was founded. In 1935 *American Antiquity*, the journal of the Society for American Archaeology, and *The Kiva*, the journal of the Arizona Archaeological and Historical Society, were first published. In the same year, the federal Historic Sites Act called for the preservation of significant national, historical, and archaeological properties, the designation and acquisition of national historic landmarks, and a survey of valuable historic and prehistoric sites.

The 1930s also saw the emergence of the University of Arizona as a premier research institution. In 1937 the Laboratory of Tree-Ring Research was established there. Dr. Emil W. Haury left Gila Pueblo to replace Byron Cummings as head of the Department of Archaeology at the University of Arizona, and in the following year he was appointed to the position of director of the Arizona State Museum. Haury held both positions until 1964. One of his most significant acts was to launch the Archaeological Field School in the Forestdale Valley south of Show Low. We will learn much more about Doc Haury in the pages to come.

The 1940s. American entry into World War II in 1941 disrupted archaeological research as faculty and students rallied behind the war effort. The University of Arizona Anthropology Club newsletter, *Atlatl*, was started to keep servicemen, alumni, and friends current on the activities of the Anthropology Department. The postwar 1940s saw the beginning of new field projects to fill in the gaps in the outline of prehistory sketched during the 1930s. Blank spots on the map and gaps in the chronologies were explored through survey and excavation.

The 1940s witnessed the definition of the Cochise Culture by E. B. Sayles and Ernst Antevs, working for Gila Pueblo; the publication of the first textbook on southwestern prehistory, *Southwestern Archaeology*, by John C. McGregor; and the establishment of the University of Arizona Archaeological Field School at Point of Pines on the San Carlos Apache

Gila Pueblo Archaeological Foundation staff in 1930. Seated, left to right, are Harold S. Gladwin, Winifred Jones MacCurdy (Gladwin), Nora MacCurdy, Hulda Haury, Emil Haury, and Russell Hastings. Standing, left to right, are Edith Sangster, Evelyn Dennis, and George Dennis.

Reservation. Young archaeologists would be trained at Point of Pines until 1960.

The 1950s. Called the "American Decade" by journalist David Halberstam, the 1950s were highly productive years for archaeology in Arizona. New regions were explored, prehistory was extended further back in time, and old disputes were resolved. By the middle of the decade, the culture history approach had become firmly established.

There were landmark events in archaeological method and theory as well. *Radiocarbon Dating,* by Willard F. Libby, was published, and the radiocarbon dating technique revolutionized the archaeology of those places and times beyond the reach of tree-ring dating. The Southwestern Archaeological Expedition of the Chicago Field Museum of Natural History moved to Vernon, Arizona, where it would become a major research center for the development of new concepts of archaeological science.

Charles Di Peso, Director of the Amerind Foundation, began excavation at the monumental site of Casas Grandes in Chihuahua, Mexico, and the Museum of Anthropology was established at Arizona State University. An era in southwestern archaeology ended in 1951 when the Gila Pueblo Archaeological Foundation was dissolved and its collections donated to the Arizona State Museum.

The Transformation of American Archaeology, 1960 to 1992

Since 1960, archaeology throughout the United States has been transformed by radical changes in the orientation and economics of research. The simple culture-history method made way for the challenge of processual archaeology, which in turn was amplified by behavioral archaeology and challenged by post-processual archaeology. The low-budget, long-term research habits of university archaeologists were transformed by federal funds and construction deadlines into efforts simply to recover prehistoric remains before they would be destroyed by urban expansion and highway and dam construction. Cultural resource management was born. It was a time of university growth, the movement of archaeologists into government agencies, and the establishment of private businesses for doing archaeology.

The 1960s. The sixties saw the rise of processual archaeology. This revolution in archaeological science sought to go beyond the simple description of material remains to reconstruct and explain nonmaterial behavior, emphasizing ecological and sociological processes—how ancient people related to their environment and to other people. Researchers who followed this view saw archaeology as anthropology and also believed it to be more science than art. They emphasized the deductive nature of archaeology and were concerned with testing hypotheses and theories about the past.

The paper entitled "Archaeology as Anthropology," by Lewis R. Binford, presented the principal concepts of processual archaeology. The Chicago Field Museum's archaeological field school at Vernon, Arizona, played a key role in developing new ways to reconstruct prehistoric ecology and sociology.

On the national level, the passage of three laws strengthened preservation efforts. These were the Reservoir Salvage Act, which extended historical and archaeological preservation specifically to remains that would be disturbed or destroyed through dam construction; the National Historic Preservation Act, which strengthened site protection through the National Register of Historic Places; and the National Environmental Policy Act, which called for the preparation of environmental impact assessments for all federal projects that would significantly affect the environment including archaeological resources.

Important events of this decade include the conclusion of fifteen years of research and teaching at Point of Pines and the moving of the University of Arizona Archaeological Field School to Grasshopper Pueblo on the White Mountain Apache Reservation, where it would continue for thirty years. The Department of Anthropology was established at Arizona State University, and it conducted its first archaeological field school.

The 1970s. This decade witnessed the expansion of archaeology beyond its traditional university base to include a growing cadre of government and private-sector professionals. Processual archaeology was enhanced by the development of behavioral archaeology, which expanded the domain of archaeology to include modern material culture. Behavioral archaeology was defined in 1975 by Jefferson Reid, Michael Schiffer, and William Rathje as the study of material objects in the past and the present in order to describe and explain human behavior. As part of this movement, Rathje began the Garbage Project at the University of Arizona to explore modern culture through, literally, its garbage.

The most dramatic development of this decade was the establishment of cultural resource management programs by federal and state agencies, by universities, and by private consulting companies. This was in response to the passage in 1974 of the Archaeological and Historic Preservation Act, which required all federal agencies to conduct archaeological investiga-

tions prior to initiating any project that would disturb or destroy significant cultural remains. In 1979 the Archaeological Resources Protection Act
(ARPA) strengthened the protection of archaeological resources on federal lands by clarifying and expanding the Federal Antiquities Act of 1906.

The 1980s. The 1980s were characterized by increased cultural resource
management activity and public involvement in many facets of archaeology. Processual archaeology's ecology, sociology, and empirical science
were challenged by post-processual archaeology. This newest development sought to go beyond the ecological and sociological to deal with the
ideological, exploring the extent to which ideological aspects of human
behavior could be reconstructed. It emphasized concepts such as gender
issues, Marxist perspectives, politically and socially biased presentations,
and the reconstruction of meaning. Women began to enter the field of archaeology in ever-increasing numbers, contributing unique perspectives
on the past.

In Arizona this decade was marked by major, often long-term, archaeological projects sponsored by federal agencies, such as the archaeology of
the Central Arizona Project. Great strides were made in understanding
Hohokam prehistory as a result of this work. At the same time, desert archaeology, which for reasons we will discuss in chapter 4 is not amenable
to tree-ring or radiocarbon dating, was revolutionized by the new concept
of archaeomagnetic dating.

The 1990s. The remarkable development of the nineties was the growing
voice of Native Americans concerning issues of archaeology, prehistory,
and the proper treatment of human remains and sacred objects. In 1990
President George Bush signed into law the Native American Graves Protection and Repatriation Act, which specified procedures for determining
cultural affinity for the purposes of reburying Native American human
remains and returning burial artifacts and sacred objects to the tribes.
The 500th anniversary of the European discovery of the New World provided numerous public occasions on which to commemorate the legacy
of Arizona's twenty-one recognized Indian tribes. The 1990s saw a growing partnership between Native Americans and archaeologists, which
surely was a healthy sign for the future.

The Importance of Arizona's Past

It is difficult to know which has changed more over the past century—archaeology or Arizona. Archaeology began in the late 1800s as a means of acquiring curios for display in museums and exhibitions, moved quickly through the classification and description stages of a beginning science to the development of alternative theoretical approaches, and expanded far beyond the universities into government agencies and private businesses. The American public kept pace with all of this expansion through their increased support for archaeology and their involvement in protecting the past. What is so intrinsically important to the future of Arizona archaeology is the growing leadership role of Arizona's Indian tribes in directing and preserving an appreciation for their individual and very different histories, written as well as unwritten. The future of the past is more exciting today than ever before.

Wherever we go, we discover that people are interested in archaeology, the past, American Indians, and especially Arizona prehistory. But there is more to the past than its value as an entertaining story. There is the important commitment by people of different cultures to understanding more about one another. Arizona Indians are an integral part of today's economic, political, and social fabric. They have raised their voices in recent decades to assert themselves as people concerned with preserving their special identity, their native culture, and their unique environment. We hope our book contributes to their purpose as well.

2 CLOVIS HUNTERS DISCOVER AMERICA

In celebrating the discovery of the Americas, the Columbian Quincentenary of 1992 drew all the world's attention to the significance of the events that doubled the size of the known earth and opened the New World to European colonization. Here in Arizona, the Quincentenary sensitized people more than ever to the historical role and contemporary significance of our Native American heritage. The events that were celebrated around the world as the beginning of New World history were, for the Native American people, only the final chapter in their own long and rich history. The story of the American Indian begins with the first discovery of the New World thousands of years before Columbus set sail to discover it once more. In bringing people into the New World from the icy, brutal wastes of Siberia, we begin the tale of Clovis, which will unfold and elaborate throughout the chapters that follow as Native American prehistory.

Clovis mammoth hunters were the first to cross the land bridge linking the continents of Asia and North America. Archaeologists call these first Americans the Paleoindians. Paleoindians were skilled and intrepid hunters of the huge animals that populated the land in the final centuries of the Ice Age. The Clovis pioneers were not only the first people to see the new land, they also are the ancestors of most Native Americans. As we will see, their blood, spirit, and history remain alive some 10,000 years after they hunted here for the last time.

The Environmental Background to Discovery

The stage for the initial discovery of the New World encompasses the entire globe during a time of extreme environmental fluctuation—the Ice

Age. This time is called the Pleistocene epoch, a geological period beginning almost two million years ago and concluding with the retreat of the
last glacier by 8,000 B.C. During the Pleistocene, giant bodies of ice in the
form of glaciers covered much of the northern hemisphere and then retreated, creating dramatic fluctuations in climate every hundred thousand years or so. In North America, glacial advances covered most of
Canada and extended into the northern Midwest of the United States. It
was during the incredible environmental fluctuations of the Pleistocene
that the evolution of modern people took place. By 40,000 years ago, modern humans (*Homo sapiens sapiens*) had become the sole survivors of the
selective process to produce the smartest animal on earth.

Making a glacier requires vast quantities of water, and the oceans are
the only source. When a vast amount of water from the oceans is locked
up in glaciers on land, the sea level falls dramatically, and this was precisely the situation during the last glacial advance of the Pleistocene. The
immense amounts of water locked up in glaciers lowered the sea level,
exposing land previously under the ocean. The Old World was connected
to the New World by a wide land bridge called Beringia linking present-
day Siberia to Alaska. The first discovery of America required none of the
sponsorship needed to outfit a fleet of ships, little in the way of naviga-
tional skills, and probably less of the fighting, bickering, fear, and self-
doubt that characterized Columbus's expedition. In fact, the actual discovery of America probably went unrecognized, as mobile hunters followed
the movement of large game animals from Siberia into Alaska and then to
Arizona and beyond.

After they crossed into present-day Alaska, their most convenient route
south would have been down the eastern slope of the Canadian Rockies
along an ice-free corridor between the two large glacial masses that covered Canada. Essentially the same route was traveled many thousands of
years later in much warmer times by the ancestors of the contemporary
Apache and Navajo, who moved from northern Canada into Arizona and
New Mexico about 400 years ago.

An alternative route south for these first Americans has been proposed
along the coast, where people who were adapted to earning a living from
marine resources, perhaps even with boats, would have found a rich environment for expansion. The likelihood of this alternative route is high,

but it is difficult to verify because the ancient coastline became submerged when the glaciers again melted. The campsites and game kill sites that mark this route now would be under water and layers of silt. Perhaps both routes were used by the first Americans. We may never have conclusive evidence for the coastal route, though we certainly will understand much more about possible trails south after future exploration of the continental shelf.

New information on the peopling of the Americas recently came from the unusual and unexpected sources of language and human teeth. Without going into detail, we can summarize the research of Joseph Greenberg, a linguist, and two Arizona biological anthropologists, Christy Turner and Stephen Zegura. Their interpretation of linguistic, dental, and genetic evidence points to three migrations from the Old World into the New World. The first migration was of people archaeologists label the Clovis Culture. These initial settlers of the New World apparently spoke a single language. From this original population developed much of the amazing variety we see in native North America today. The other migrations, which brought two additional language groups into the New World, occurred many thousands of years after the Clovis people spread throughout the North and South American continents. The date of the first discovery of the New World by Clovis people is the subject of a hotly contested debate in American archaeology. It is to this issue that we now turn.

People before Clovis

Were there people in Arizona before Clovis? Was there a stage of hunter-gatherer adaptation in which people used only chopping and scraping tools and no spear points, and which has been difficult to recognize because of the scarcity of remains and the crude character of the tools? Questions about the peopling of America certainly have inspired research to push back the date of entry into the New World. Currently there are numerous claims for the existence of pre-Clovis people at many locations throughout the Americas, from Meadowcroft, Pennsylvania, and Oro Grande, New Mexico, to Pedra Furada, Brazil, and Monte Verde, Chile.

Back in Arizona—or more precisely, just over the border in the Sierra Pinacate of northern Mexico—Julian Hayden has been searching for

Julian Hayden demonstrating how to make a Malpais tool.

evidence of Clovis precursors and building a case for the Malpais people as the initial human occupants of western Arizona. Since 1958 Hayden has made well over a hundred trips to the Pinacates. You will learn more of the man and his archaeology when we discuss the Patayan Culture in chapter 5, but for now it will be useful to outline some of his findings about the Malpais.

The Sierra Pinacate is unusually forbidding among the present deserts of North America—cinder cones jut 4,500 feet above basaltic lava flows, and desert pavement spreads over 600 square miles of unforgiving land-scape. On this barren ground, according to Hayden, all nonperishable re-mains—from the earliest stone tools to the tin cans left by cowboys—are preserved directly on the surface upon which they were deposited, undis-turbed by erosion.

Stone tools, like any rock on the ground exposed to conditions of the desert surface, develop a "desert varnish"—a dark, glossy coating much like a thick veneer of plastic. A double layer of varnish on stone tools is in-terpreted by Hayden as being formed during the dry, desert conditions preceding the wetter climate of Clovis times. Because human occupation of the Sierra Pinacate when desert conditions conducive to varnish for-mation prevailed is unlikely, Hayden reasons, the Malpais use of the area must have been during a wet period many thousands of years earlier than Clovis. Recent developments in techniques for extracting datable material from desert varnish has permitted Hayden to get radiocarbon support for his dating of Malpais tools.

The Malpais tool kit is typified by stone choppers and scrapers mini-mally shaped by hard-hammer percussion, that is, by striking flakes using another stone as a hammer. Shell from the nearby Gulf of California was similarly shaped into small knives, scrapers, and gouges. Other Malpais remains include sleeping circles, shrines, and intaglio figures. Hayden has also recognized Malpais trails connecting waterholes and extending be-yond the Sierra Pinacate.

Stone implements typical of the Malpais and lying below the Clovis level have been recovered from the conglomerate layer at Ventana Cave, a rockshelter in the Castle Mountains west of Tucson on the Tohono O'od-ham Indian Reservation. Excavated in the 1940s by archaeologists from the University of Arizona, including Julian Hayden, Ventana Cave pro-duced unparalleled evidence for continuity in human occupation from pre-Clovis times to the historical period.

In spite of Hayden's mastery of the desert and his established repu-tation as a consummate field archaeologist, his Malpais model of a pre-Clovis occupation remains highly controversial. For example, Vance Haynes and Arthur Jelinek, his long-time friends and colleagues, are openly skeptical of Hayden's claims for a Malpais Culture predating Clo-vis. As an Old World paleolithic archaeologist, Jelinek takes a global per-spective. He compares the North American situation to that of Australia,

Malpais stone choppers and scrapers found by Julian Hayden in the Sierra Pinacate of northern Mexico.

where in less than thirty years a handful of archaeologists produced conclusive evidence of human presence more than 30,000 years ago in a number of widely spaced regions. In addition, the Australian archaeologists uncovered strong indications of human presence 10,000 to 20,000 years earlier than that. The upshot of Jelinek's comparison is that, if humans were present in North America prior to Clovis, then all the searching and digging by archaeologists and the extensive earthmoving through construction and land modification in the area during the sixty years since the Folsom discovery in 1926 (see chapter 1) should have revealed conclusive proof.

Julian Hayden, no stranger to controversy, nevertheless has intriguing evidence for human-made stone tools he calls Malpais. His hypotheses and suppositions must be examined closely and tested further in the field through survey and excavation. The extreme deserts of western Arizona and northern Mexico do not beckon the university professor limited to summer fieldwork, so future work on the Malpais may await another intrepid researcher in the Hayden tradition.

Regardless of these debates, some of which we will take up in a moment, the bare truth of the matter is that the Clovis people moved relatively rapidly from their point of entry into North America and were hunting elephants in southern Arizona along the San Pedro River and its tributaries by 9,000 B.C. And what we take for granted today—that there was elephant hunting in Arizona—was unimaginable before the middle 1920s, when evidence for the association of human beings with now-extinct large animals was unearthed at the Double Adobe site.

Discovering Clovis

In 1926 Byron Cummings, the head of archaeology and director of the Arizona State Museum and soon to be president of the University of Arizona, received a call from the schoolteacher at Double Adobe, a tiny town between Bisbee and Douglas, informing him that elephant bones were washing out of an arroyo bank there. Always prepared to take a field trip in pursuit of an archaeological discovery, Cummings went to Double Adobe with his students Emil Haury and Lyndon Hargrave. Excavation into the bank revealed remains of mammoth, including a large lower jaw, above a layer of artifacts. The finding of artifacts in proximity to extinct elephant remains would have been a major discovery except for the fact that the relationship was uncertain and the artifacts were grinding tools used for processing plant foods, not elephant carcasses. In addition, Cummings may have been overly cautious for other reasons, most notably the atmosphere of extreme skepticism that surrounded all claims at that time about an association between people and Pleistocene animals.

The American public, as well as the academic community, had been plagued by frauds of all types and descriptions, and the requirements of scientific evidence had risen in response. Archaeologists, as we saw in chapter 1, had become more rigorously scientific than in the previous period of exploration and collection. Furthermore, the 66-year-old Cummings, though still energetic, probably was overworked by the university bureaucracy and certainly was closely involved in a more public, and perhaps to him more important, discovery. This was the unearthing on the outskirts of Tucson of lead crosses, swords, and spear points bearing inscriptions in Latin and Hebrew and dated to the eighth century A.D. In the shadow of the possibility that Tucson was originally founded as a Roman-Jewish settlement, the major discovery of human artifacts with elephant bones at Double Adobe was not given banner headlines. Further, it was soon eclipsed by the discovery that same year in Folsom, New Mexico, of a spear point lying convincingly among the ribs of an extinct form of bison. Major discoveries began to appear throughout the United States, and it was not long before the antiquity of people in the New World would be demonstrated conclusively to even the harshest skeptic. And, perhaps sadly for Cummings, the lead artifacts found near Tucson were determined to be fakes.

New Mexico became the focus of a flurry of efforts by amateur and professional archaeologists to define more precisely the association between people and extinct animals. The mammoth-hunting culture now called Clovis was first discovered in 1932 near the New Mexico town for which the culture was named. Considerable work took place in the general locality of the discovery, which subsequently led to the finding, at a site near Blackwater Draw south of the town of Clovis, of clear evidence for the stratification of Clovis materials below deposits with Folsom remains. As we now know, the Folsom Culture represents the immediate post-Pleistocene bison hunters of the high plains. The evidence for stratification clearly indicated that Clovis was the older culture.

After Cummings's discoveries at Double Adobe, few finds related to the early hunting people in Arizona were reported. Paleoindian archaeology languished until the 1950s, when things changed dramatically. The discovery of Clovis remains in southeastern Arizona was made by alert local people who were concerned enough to call in professional archaeologists. The great discoveries in Arizona, which rank among the most exciting in North America, continue to be made by nonprofessionals joining forces with archaeologists. Two stories of the discovery of Clovis in Arizona illustrate the critical and essential role of nonprofessionals in furthering everyone's understanding of the past.

The first story involves two ranchers from southeastern Arizona, Fred Navarrete and his son Marc, who discovered the Naco mammoth in 1952. Fred happened across some bones washing out of Greenbush Creek, an arroyo near the town of Naco on the international border between Arizona and Mexico. In digging around, he soon uncovered a spear point,

Emil Haury (right) and paleontologist John Lance excavating the Naco mammoth.

and Marc found a second one. They quickly realized the significance of their discovery and called Emil Haury, who, along with a team from the University of Arizona, excavated the bones of an adult male mammoth whose death was almost certainly the result of the eight spear points found among the bones. This discovery was so special that Haury and his team encased a block of ribs, vertebrae, and scapulae that contained five points in a plaster jacket about three feet square for shipment to the university, where it remains on display for all to see and marvel at. We should marvel also at the Navarretes' presence of mind in notifying professional archaeologists so that their discovery would be shared by countless future generations.

The same thing happened again not long after the Naco discovery and not far away, near Hereford along the San Pedro River. Local rancher Edward Lehner had visited the diggings at Naco to invite Haury to inspect a draw behind his house where animal bones were washing out of the bank. A quick visit by Haury verified that animal bones were indeed eroding out of the wall, but no signs of human presence were visible. Several years later, however, according to Haury, Ed Lehner appeared at the Haury home in Tucson with a box containing elephant teeth and a prediction that if something was not done soon, the bone bed would be washed away in the next heavy rain. Upon excavation in 1955, the Lehner Ranch Mammoth Kill Site, as it is now known, would reveal nine elephants slaughtered by Clovis hunters. An enlightened public, as illustrated so vividly by Ed Lehner and the Navarretes, is valuable both for the desire to share discoveries and for an unselfish dedication to preserving the past.

The Clovis Way of Life: Elephants and Wild Plants

We turn now to Clovis lifeways as they have been reconstructed from excavations at Naco, Lehner, and other sites in southeastern Arizona. The environment today along the middle San Pedro River valley near Sierra Vista is Chihuahuan Desert grassland and scrub, where the creosote bush is dominant, the saguaro is absent, and all manner of birds and bird-watchers flock by the thousands. This arid land today lends no clue about its distinct history. Far back in the Pleistocene, immediately prior to the arrival of people, the San Pedro Valley was a wooded parkland of ponds, marshes, and sufficient grassland to support herds of elephants and other huge grazing animals and the predators such as saber-toothed tigers who preyed on them. When the first people arrived in the valley a little before 9,000 B.C., they found a drought in full swing. Evidently the problem was so severe for the larger animals that elephants dug shallow wells to get at buried water, as they do today in Africa.

Arizona is fortunate to have within its borders a full range of sites created by Clovis people as they moved across the landscape in search of food and shelter. The evidence for Clovis occupation of the San Pedro Valley is unparalleled. The valley has yielded the largest single concentration of Clovis sites in North America. Kill sites range from Naco, the isolated kill of a bull elephant, to sites where many animals were killed, such as at Lehner Ranch and Murray Springs, where multiple elephant, bison, horse, and camel remains were found along with evidence of a small hunting camp. There is even testimony for the ones that got away, such as the Escapule site, where a large, mature bull elephant wounded by Clovis hunters apparently died. There also is evidence for the base camps of Clovis people, such as the volcanic debris level at Ventana Cave, from which were recovered the artifacts that we would expect to find in a Clovis base camp used repeatedly throughout the year and for many years. Through Arizona Clovis sites we can reconstruct the lifeways of these mobile hunting-and-gathering people.

We can imagine how Clovis hunters may have ambushed large game using only human intelligence, physical prowess, and a hand-held spear tipped with a flaked stone point. Indians would not use the bow and arrow until thousands of years later. Clovis points and the later, smaller Folsom points used to hunt an extinct form of bison are unique in that they have thinning flakes, or flutes, struck from the base on each side, thus the general label "fluted point." Clovis points are made from high-quality stone in a wide variety of sizes. The points from the Lehner Ranch range from a clear quartz point 31 mm (slightly over one inch) in length to a gray-brown chert point 97 mm (about four inches) long. Point size depended on the kind of stone that was used, the number of times points were resharpened, and the individual preference of the point maker. The weight of the point would not have been a critical factor in the performance of a weapon used as a thrusting spear that was jabbed into the animal from close range rather than thrown.

How do we know Clovis points were used on thrusting spears when common sense suggests it would be safer to hurl a spear from a distance? We do not know for certain, and in all likelihood there were numerous occasions when a thrusting spear was hurled in terror or panic or simply to get a last shot at a fleeing prey. The technology of the points themselves and the characteristics of the prey—in this case elephants—do provide clues to their use, however.

Clovis points are thinned at the base and are ground along the edge of the basal third of the point, indicating a deep haft and a secure binding to withstand impact as well as lateral stress. Hafting points into a foreshaft that could be inserted into a mainshaft permitted a hunter to carry a number of foreshafts and only one mainshaft. But this "reload" feature works only when used on a thrusting spear. Otherwise the hunter, having thrown away his mainshaft, is left with a handful of stubby foreshafts, each about a foot long, insufficient for a sustained attack upon large, powerful, and presumably angry prey.

Experiments conducted by Bruce Huckell on an elephant that died of natural causes confirmed that a replicated Clovis point hafted onto a foreshaft used as a thrusting spear was the only way to penetrate the elephant's thick hide. Furthermore, this experiment produced broken points similar to those found in archaeological sites. Being armed with a thrusting spear, however, is not quite the same as having a high-powered elephant gun. Even skilled Clovis hunters had to have a plan.

Vance Haynes, who has spent his professional career studying Clovis and is considered by many to be the pre-eminent Clovis archaeologist, thinks that the evidence indicates that Clovis hunters had a sophisticated knowledge of elephant behavior, which allowed them to target particularly vulnerable individuals as they were watering. Most of the western Clovis elephant kills are associated with streams or springs. As any western rancher or horseman can tell you, herbivores require large quantities of water daily to stay alive, and this is especially true of large elephants. Waiting at waterholes would have been a certain way for Clovis hunters to observe large numbers of animals from which to choose a target. Although the general pattern was to kill individuals, there appears to have been no selection for a specific age or sex category. As Haynes notes, the age-sex profile of the combined Clovis kills mirrors rather closely that normally found in a small herd.

Archaeological sites in southern Arizona also present a picture of the Clovis settlement pattern. Naco, which we introduced earlier, was an isolated kill site where a bull elephant died on the gravelly sand of a stream with at least eight spear points embedded in his chest area. The hindquarters were not recovered in the excavation and were either carried away by the hunters or by erosion, as a modern arroyo has cut deeply to expose the site. Although some archaeologists speculate that this particular mam-

Vance Haynes (a) fitting a Clovis spear point to a hardwood fore-shaft, (b) examining parts of a Clovis hunting spear, and (c) demonstrating the use of an atlatl, or spear thrower.

a

b

c

Clovis spear points found in the Naco mammoth.

moth escaped the butcher's blade to die alone on the bank, the evidence is clear that eight fatal hits by Clovis hunters must count as a kill. Hunting clearly was not limited to young or weak animals.

Lehner Ranch and Murray Springs give us more information on the behavior associated with multiple kills. Both sites, in contrast to Naco, were used repeatedly to ambush animals along creeks that ran into the San Pedro River. At Lehner Ranch, the recovery of flaked stone tools that were probably used in butchering and the presence of two hearths indicate that the site was used as a temporary camp for processing the meat. The original excavation at Lehner uncovered nine mammoths, mostly juveniles and one young adult, and at least one each of bison, horse, and tapir. The remains at Lehner Ranch may represent a mammoth family that was killed at one time. It is assumed that the tapir and the bison also were killed for food.

At Murray Springs, excavated by Vance Haynes, there was clear evidence for killing elephants and bison, and some evidence that horses also were killed. Near the kill areas on a piece of flat ground sheltered from the wind was a hunting camp where broken spear points were discarded, stone tools were made and sharpened, and scraping, probably of hides, took place.

Lehner Ranch and Murray Springs, then, represent temporary hunting camps for processing large animal kills. As every hunter knows, it is difficult to transport a large animal, or even sections of one, for any distance. It is much better to enlist other members of the group to help the hunter process as much meat as could be carried back to a base camp. Remains of these base camps, where Clovis people would have spent much of their time during any season, are tantalizingly ambiguous, but the evidence is no doubt there, awaiting discovery by another Julian Hayden or Ed Lehner, or a Navarrete.

Traces of human occupation also have been found along the shores of old lakes in Arizona. Along a buried shore of ancient Lake Cochise, now Willcox Playa, Emil Haury found a spear point, stone chips, and plant-grinding stones that suggested to him the possibility of a Clovis base camp.

Ventana Cave provides hints of what a Clovis base camp may have looked like. The volcanic debris level of the cave contained a crude spear point resembling a Clovis point, numerous chopping and scraping tools, and a plant-grinding stone—a tool kit we would expect to find at the base camp of people who lived by both hunting and plant gathering. Although horse and tapir bones were found at this bottom level, they probably were brought back to camp, not actually killed in the rockshelter. If we accept the possibility that Ventana Cave, with evidence of plant gathering as well as hunting, could have served as a Clovis base camp, then we gain insight into the Clovis people's capacity to change their means of livelihood when the large animals, especially elephants, became extinct at the end of the Pleistocene.

Pleistocene Extinction: Clovis or Mother Nature?

By everyone's evaluation, there was a catastrophe at the end of the Pleistocene when the glaciers that covered most of Canada retreated and the Arizona climate became more like it is today. A number of large herbivores such as elephants, horses, and camels, along with the carnivorous saber-toothed tiger and dire wolf, all disappeared. Disagreement about the reason for their becoming extinct has polarized researchers into two opposing camps. One group maintains that the increased temperatures, decreased water, and reduced forage that typified the end of the Pleistocene were by themselves sufficient to cause the disappearance of the large animals and their predators. The other group, led by the geoscientist Paul S. Martin, believes that human agents, namely Clovis hunters, were responsible for the demise of these animals. Martin labels his view the Overkill Hypothesis.

Let us look more closely at the debate surrounding the intriguing case of Pleistocene extinction. Throughout geological time, animals native to North America became extinct. The most popular examples are the dinosaurs and giant reptiles that became extinct 65 million years ago. Extinction is neither a novel nor a particularly unnatural phenomenon, though the list of endangered species today is a roster of animals nearing extinction because of human disruption of nature.

The Pleistocene animals of North America are collectively labeled the Rancho La Brean fauna after the La Brea tar pits in Los Angeles, where so many of these animals were trapped and preserved. This group included the animals that Clovis hunters preyed upon: a bison much larger than those of today, ground sloths, dire wolves, and many more. The facts surrounding their disappearance are well established. Almost two-thirds of the Rancho La Brean fauna disappeared, and the large animals, called megafauna, were the hardest hit. There was no comparable loss of small animals or plants.

Those scientists who think Mother Nature acted alone in this affair argue that it is the large animals that were most stressed when the environment became warmer and drier because they needed the most water, food, and cover. Deny them the essentials of life in such large quantities and they will die by natural causes.

Paul Martin, arguing his Overkill Hypothesis, interprets the facts differently. Yes, the large animals were affected disproportionately, he says, but the terminal Pleistocene glacial retreat was only the last of numerous advances and retreats that characterized the Pleistocene over two million years, and no extinctions of this magnitude marked the earlier glacial retreats. The only factor unique to the terminal Pleistocene of North America are Clovis hunters. The Martin scenario pictures Clovis people entering North America close to 10,000 B.C. and moving rapidly southward in an ever-expanding wave of colonization. This movement was driven by high rates of population increase in a rich environment free of other human competitors. Combined with an effective hunting strategy, this increasing population was able to kill off the large herbivores and, indirectly, the carnivores and other animals that depended on them.

Vance Haynes also is convinced of a Clovis role in extinction, but not as the sole cause. He reasons that a severe drought at the end of the Pleistocene would have concentrated animals around the remaining watering places, making their behavior more predictable and thus extremely vulnerable to human predation. Because elephants require as much as forty gallons of water and 600 pounds of vegetation each day, Clovis hunters need not have killed every animal in order to have been the critical element upsetting the delicate balance in an ecosystem under stress. They certainly may have hastened the extinction of many of the Pleistocene animals by denying them access to water.

What Happened to Clovis?

As surely as there are no native elephants in Arizona today, there are also no Clovis hunters. Did they, too, become extinct? If not, where did they go? To answer these questions, we need to consider how people change their behavior and culture.

A number of factors influence rapid cultural change. Climate often plays a prominent role in societies with simple technologies and probably brought about the rapid change in the Clovis way of life. Climatic changes have occurred throughout time independently of people's activities or wishes. For example, rapid change in the prehistoric Southwest was prompted by catastrophic natural events such as the eruption of the Sunset Crater Volcano near Flagstaff (A.D. 1064), the Great Drought of the northern Southwest from A.D. 1276 to 1299, and the great floods that devastated irrigation systems in the central Arizona desert in A.D. 1358 and in the 1380s.

As we have seen with Clovis, people can directly and indirectly influence their own environment through actions with unintended consequences, such as the hastening of the demise of the mammoth through relentless hunting pressure during a time of environmental instability. Thousands of years later, agricultural communities in the Southwest would exhaust farmland and be forced to move on to new lands. Rapid change can also occur with contact between groups of people, as in the dramatic instance of Europeans introducing new plants, animals, and diseases into the Southwest beginning in the summer of 1540.

Cultural change also can occur gradually through the incremental addition or subtraction of behaviors that are so minuscule that they go unnoticed in societies without a written language or television reruns from the 1950s. Minute changes through small innovations, or major changes brought about by dramatic new ways of doing something, can produce long-term changes without the appearance of new environmental forces or contact with outside peoples. Many archaeologists believe that internal change in simple societies of the past quite often was a result of the population exceeding local food resources. In fact, a perennial problem of yesterday and today is balancing human population with food resources.

Thus, cultural change may be rapid or gradual. It may happen because of alteration in climate or environment, contact with other people, population increase, and the normal process of people thinking up better ways to do things. All of these processes contribute to cultural change and human diversity.

So what happened to Clovis? The standard Hopi response to the similar question "What happened to the Anasazi?" is "We are still here!" And, indeed, the Clovis are still here in spirit, though not in name. If we agree with the Greenberg-Turner-Zegura hypothesis on migrations into America, we may stretch their intent to propose that Clovis was the founding New World population from which developed all Native Americans other than speakers of the two language groups that followed them into the New World. If this is near the truth, then it follows that Clovis gave rise to subsequent Paleoindians such as the Folsom people, who continued the tradition of big-game hunting on the plains, and to Archaic peoples, who remained in the Southwest to hunt small game and gather wild plant foods (see chapter 3). Thus, while Paleoindian traditions continued until about 5,000 B.C. on the plains, in the Southwest the food quest was evolving to depend more and more on gathering wild plants. Evidence for Folsom occupation of Arizona is slim to nonexistent, suggesting both that Clovis hunters moved into the high plains and that plant foods became more important. We see this change take place at Ventana Cave, and this brings us back to our story and introduces the Archaic Period and its way of life, which changed only gradually over the next eight to nine thousand years. This was the time when Native Americans developed the special characteristics that would make them the worldwide centerpiece of story, legend, scientific study, and admiration.

3 ARCHAIC ANCESTORS

Imagine a cold winter night five thousand years ago. A fire flickers in the rear of Ventana Cave. Old men tell stories of a time long ago when the land was green, water was abundant, and large, dangerous animals were killed by brave hunters who brought home meat for everyone. The men reenact a hunt for a huge, strange beast with big ears, a long snout, and two horns protruding from its mouth. Young people are mesmerized by the drama but cannot imagine that such odd creatures could ever have existed in the desert world of their experience. None of the old men had ever seen one of these great animals, though one, who had once traveled many, many days to the east, had seen vast herds of large, furry, horned animals. Perhaps the stories of old men were true, the children wondered.

The world of southern Arizona had changed dramatically from the green land of mythical beasts in the old men's tales to the dry, thorny desert the people of the Archaic Period called home. So, too, had the lives of the people been altered. The Archaic Period brought vast transformations to Arizona and the Southwest, beyond even the dreams of the old men. We now direct our attention to this time and this landscape.

Archaic Period People and Trends

The Archaic Period is an interval of time and a way of life. It began in the Southwest sometime after 9,000 B.C., near the end of the Ice Age and the disappearance of the elephants and other megafauna, and it continued for almost nine thousand years until the appearance of pottery in the early centuries of the first millennium A.D. Archaeologists use pottery as a convenient, durable marker in the archaeological record, but its appearance did not mark a radical change in the Archaic way of life. In fact, the Archaic way of making a living was extremely conservative, remaining remarkably stable until the introduction of corn from Mexico a thousand years before pottery arrived from the same source.

The Archaic people's way of life centered on hunting wild animals and gathering wild plant foods, just as did that of the Clovis people. The difference was one of necessity and emphasis. As we have seen, the elephants, horses, and camels upon which Clovis hunters preyed became extinct, for whatever combination of reasons, about 11,000 years ago. Archaic hunters had no choice but to turn to deer, antelope, squirrels, rabbits, and rodents—small, fast game requiring new hunting techniques and providing less meat than the big game of the Ice Age. Of necessity, hunting took second place to plant food gathering, and as providers men probably contributed less to the diet than women. Plant food gathering and processing by women, so conspicuous in the seed-milling stones of the archaeological record, was the essential component of the Archaic economy. Most important, a long familiarity with plant gathering provided the know-how that later would permit the Archaic people to adopt plant cultivation as part of their subsistence routine.

Because of this emphasis on gathering and hunting, the Archaic people followed a seasonal round of movements across the landscape, stopping in places long enough to harvest wild plants, to hunt, and later to farm plots of land and harvest a crop. Their shelters, tools, equipment—indeed, all their material goods—were geared to this high degree of mobility, and accordingly, Archaic sites are relatively ephemeral compared to the later homes of more sedentary, pottery-producing folk.

The Archaic Period is remarkable for thousands of years of reliance on wild plants and animals and for the incredible diversification of language, ritual, and ideology that occurred—precisely those areas of human experience that leave at best only a faint trace in the archaeological record. Although unseen, this diversification in Native American language and culture must have taken place, for undoubtedly the rather homogeneous Clovis Culture gave rise to the marked differences recorded for the village farmers of later centuries. In the artifact record, this differentiation is seen partially in a bewildering variety of spear point forms. Some forms represent different hunting functions, whereas others must represent different groups of people. Archaeologists recognize considerable variability among Archaic Period cultures and label them accordingly. As we shall see, the Archaic Culture of southeastern Arizona is called the Cochise Culture; in the Great Basin, it is called the Desert Culture; on the Colorado Plateau, it is the Oshara Culture; and so on. This multiplicity of labels and the distinct associations of stone tools that the labels embody should not mask the unifying character of all Archaic Culture, which is the emphasis on plant foods and a highly mobile lifestyle.

Cultural change and differentiation did not occur rapidly but rather over the thousands of years available for the internal and external forces of change to have an effect. Thus the Archaic Period can be viewed as a time of archaeologically invisible cultural change hidden beneath a rather stable subsistence routine of hunting and plant gathering. It was a period of transformation during which, over the course of thousands of years, the culture of the elephant hunters of the Siberian tundra was altered irrevocably to become the diversified lifestyles we know as Hohokam, Mogollon, Anasazi, and other prehistoric farming cultures of Arizona.

Today we know far more about Archaic ancestors than ever before, but for many reasons understanding remains elusive. When the first remains were discovered by Byron Cummings in 1926, the Archaic Period was virtually unknown.

Discovering Archaic Ancestors

The Cochise Culture in Southern Arizona

The first discovery of Archaic remains in Arizona took place at the site of Double Adobe, where Byron Cummings and his students unearthed grinding stones belonging to an early culture in a layer below elephant bones. As we have seen, the elephant bones were not accorded much attention by the archaeological community, nor were the grinding tools. Just as it was unparalleled territory for Clovis Culture sites, however, southeastern Arizona held a treasure of Archaic sites, and it soon drew other archaeologists. In the 1930s Ted Sayles, working in the region for Gila Pueblo along with Emil Haury, discovered surface artifacts and buried sites of a culture that did not hunt big game and did not have pottery—a culture as unlike Mogollon, Hohokam, and Anasazi as it was unlike the Clovis Culture. By 1941 enough field work had been carried out so that Sayles and the geologist Ernst Antevs were able to define the Cochise Culture and to identify three stages of development that they called the Sulphur Spring, Chiricahua, and San Pedro. In later classification schemes, these would be labeled as the Early, Middle, and Late Archaic Periods, terms that refer to intervals of time as well as patterns of material culture and lifeways.

The earliest, or Sulphur Spring stage, was defined by sites near Double Adobe where grinding tools were found without any associated spear points. In Sayles's mind, the absence of spears indicated a way of life devoted exclusively to plant gathering. Before radiocarbon dating had been discovered, dating of the associated geological deposits suggested that Sulphur Spring was as old as Clovis and thus that two different adaptations existed side by side. The idea that Clovis big-game hunters and Archaic gatherers were contemporaries pursuing vastly different ways of life is no longer considered valid, however. Modern dating tells us that the Clovis Culture clearly was earlier than the Cochise Culture. The beginning of the Sulphur Spring stage now is radiocarbon dated reliably to around 8,400 B.C., but the ending date is still unknown.

Many years after the original fieldwork had been carried out, Ted Sayles proposed a Cazador stage following the Sulphur Spring stage. The presence of spear points in the material remains attributed to the Cazador stage led Sayles to believe that it represented a change in lifeways to hunting, as indicated by the label Cazador, which means "hunter" in Spanish. Recent reevaluation of Cazador sites has led geologist Michael Waters to question the validity of this stage. It seems likely to him that at least some of the spear points attributed to Cazador belonged to the Sulphur Spring tool kit. In hindsight,the interpretation that the Sulphur Spring stage, as the immediate follower of the Clovis Culture in time, could have lacked spears with spear points seems unreasonable.

The other Cochise Culture stages have remained noncontroversial. The Middle Archaic Chiricahua stage, which followed the Sulphur Spring stage around 6,000 B.C., is rather loosely defined by shallow-basin milling stones, a variety of flaked stone tools, and small, side-notched spear points. The end of the Chiricahua stage is not well dated but is estimated to have been shortly after 1,500 B.C.

The Late Archaic San Pedro stage is well defined by grinding stones, flaked tools, and a number of large, distinctive spear points that archaeologists label as San Pedro, Cienega, and Cortaro points. The San Pedro stage ended with the introduction of pottery in the early centuries of the Christian era. It was during Late Archaic times all over the Southwest that the introduction and cultivation of corn propelled native cultures into radically new trajectories.

Today, many archaeologists have discarded the Cochise Culture label, preferring to use *Southwestern Archaic,* a broad term that applies to Archaic lifeways across the Southwest. Nevertheless, *Cochise Culture* remains a useful label for a particular expression of the Archaic lifestyle in the southern Southwest.

Ventana Cave, Desert Culture, and More

Sayles and Antevs were the first, but many others contributed their knowledge to our understanding of the Archaic Period. During these early years Malcolm Rogers, whom we will learn more about in chapter 5, combed the unforgiving deserts of western Arizona for scant traces of Archaic and earlier people. We have already been introduced to one of the most significant sites, however—Ventana Cave.

Haury had initiated a research program at the University of Arizona that focused on the history of the Papaguería, the western Arizona desert home of the Indian group called the Tohono O'odham (whom we will meet in chapter 4) from its earliest inhabitants to the modern Native Americans. A particularly important issue concerned the interval between the abandonment of the desert by the Hohokam around A.D. 1400 and the settlement of the area by Europeans, an interval that was then an archaeological blank. To study this time, Haury selected the site of Nuestra Señora de la Merced del Batki, a historical O'odham village west of Tucson visited by the Jesuit priest Padre Eusebio Francisco Kino in 1698. Excavations at Batki began in 1941 but were halted within an hour by a delegation of Tohono O'odham, who feared that the malignant influences of the Apaches, who had raided and burned Batki in 1850, would be released by the archaeological work. Haury chose another site for excava-

Ventana Cave. The layers of artifacts that accumulated in the cave over the 11,000 years of its occupation provided the key to understanding Archaic Culture in southern Arizona.

tion, and while en route to inspect the site he noticed a cave lying at the base of a hill. This cave was, Haury recalled, "the answer to a prayer." Excavated in 1941 and 1942, Ventana Cave would become the model for interpreting the Archaic Culture of the southern Arizona desert for many years to come. Ironically, it was not the close of prehistory for which Ventana Cave became famous but its beginning.

In Ventana Cave, archaeologists discovered a stratified series of deposits revealing a cultural sequence from the time of Clovis hunters and now-extinct megafauna up to the present. The excavations produced a wealth of perishable materials normally missing from open archaeological sites. Most important, the Ventana work provided good evidence for the development of the Hohokam Culture from an indigenous one.

The 1940s and 1950s were especially active decades for Archaic studies throughout North America. Herbert Dick's excavations at Bat Cave, New Mexico, in the late 1940s received critical attention because he identified

Excavating the lower level of Ventana Cave in 1941.

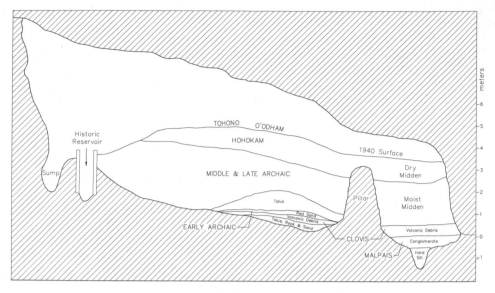

A cross section of the cultural and geological layers of Ventana Cave.

what at that time was the earliest-dated corn in North America, as determined by the revolutionary new radiocarbon dating technique. Radiocarbon dating made it possible to give an absolute date to the sites and events of the Archaic Period, and much later in the 1980s to redate the Bat Cave corn.

In the 1950s, Jesse Jennings explored rockshelters and caves in northern Utah and excavated Danger Cave, one of the most important sites discovered during this period. From evidence at Danger Cave, Jennings defined the Desert Culture, a concept that influenced the interpretation of Archaic life throughout most of arid western America. The Desert Culture was a widespread and long-lived expression of Archaic adaptation in the Great Basin, which remained essentially unchanged for many thousands of years. The parallels between the prehistoric Desert Culture lifeway and that of the Indians who lived in the Great Basin in historical times, lifeways marked by basketry and milling stones, were important parts of the Desert Culture concept.

In Arizona, Emil Haury excavated the Cienega Creek site during one season at the Point of Pines field school. Evidence from this site supported

Haury's earlier interpretation that the Hohokam and Mogollon developed from the Cochise Culture. The monumental discoveries of the Naco and Lehner Clovis sites in southeastern Arizona during the 1950s also helped define the early limits of the Archaic Period. By 1958 Julian Hayden, who had supervised the second year of excavation at Ventana Cave, had begun his exploration of the Sierra Pinacate of northern Sonora, and Ted Sayles was doggedly pursuing evidence of Archaic cultures in southeastern Arizona.

Archaic studies continued into the 1960s as the principal means of investigating two broad questions about the past. The first was when corn agriculture arrived in the Southwest, and the second concerned the nature of the relationship between Archaic hunter-gatherers and the later village farmer cultures—the Hohokam, Mogollon, and Anasazi. In the late 1960s the emphasis on studying living hunter-gatherers worldwide gave rise to ethnoarchaeological studies—studies of material culture and its use in contemporary societies to develop models for interpreting the past—and a stronger theoretical framework for investigating these questions.

In the 1970s important advances were made by Cynthia Irwin-Williams in defining the Oshara Culture, the Archaic predecessor of the Anasazi on the Colorado Plateau. Federally mandated contract archaeology during the 1970s and 1980s supplied funds for the expansion of fieldwork and analysis, especially of botanical remains. Equally important research was conducted on a shoestring and on weekends by archaeologists lured by the possibility of finding early farming villages.

Today the Archaic Period is a rapidly advancing area for archaeological discovery and research. Old ideas are confronted daily with fresh evidence and interpretations made possible by new discoveries and advances in analytical techniques. Although this recent research has yet to be synthesized, it adds highlights and details to the hallmark studies of the past and permits us to outline the basic features of the Archaic Culture in Arizona.

Early and Middle Archaic

It is difficult to imagine today, with our sprawling cities and congested freeways, but thousands of years ago there were few people in Arizona, especially during the Early and Middle portions of the Archaic Period.

Late Archaic dart points from the Cienega Creek site near Point of Pines. They show the variety of forms that people of the Cochise Culture used to hunt small game long after large animals like the mammoth disappeared from Arizona.

Picture small, isolated groups of people spread thinly across the landscape and constantly moving and you will have characterized the Early and Middle Archaic Periods. Each small group in its own creative way experimented with how best to make a living in the desert, mountains, and plateaus, and even along the shore of the Gulf of California.

Throughout the Southwest, Early and Middle Archaic sites are scarce, and the number of recovered spear points is low compared to the eastern woodlands of North America. Not only were there few people here but they also seem to have been distributed unevenly over the landscape. A family or a group of related families probably recognized a common territory separated from other territories by environmental features such as deserts or mountain ranges so that interaction between families of different territories was minimal. Isolated groups of people exploiting different environments would in time develop different ways of thinking about and doing things.

The people moved considerable distances within their territories in search of particular foods and other resources. Water, of course, was critical. It is possible that occasionally a territory was abandoned, at least for a time, during periods of extreme drought. It is likely that there were times when pockets of people were isolated in regions with relatively abundant resources or in regions far from their normal territory. As a result, vast areas may have been left unpopulated for lengthy periods.

Early and Middle Archaic people used all the available resources, even some we would not consider edible, including a variety of small animals and all types of plant foods. Nuts, berries, cactus fruit, and especially seeds of all types were harvested, prepared, and cooked by parching and grinding into flour.

What sorts of tools and equipment does such a lifestyle require? The ultimate requirement was that equipment be either portable and lightweight or capable of being securely cached when people were away from home. The hallmarks of the Archaic Period are baskets, milling stones, and spear points. Flat and basin-shaped milling stones and round cobble handstones were well adapted for processing the small seeds that were a common part of the Archaic diet. Seeds were placed in the basin and then ground in a circular motion with the handstone. Pottery was absent. Other ways of cooking food were used, perhaps boiling in perishable containers using fire-heated stones dropped into the container or roasting outdoors in pits. Food was stored in baskets, often inside pits for additional security.

The atlatl and the dart tipped with a variety of flaked stone points were the principal hunting tools. Pointed hardwood foreshafts without stone points also were used. Percussion flaking techniques—shaping stone tools by striking a stone with another object—predominated, along with the preferential use of large flakes and cores. There also were a number of specialized stone tools of crude appearance resembling Old World Paleolithic tools. The spear points, the stone debris left from fashioning them, and milling stones usually are the only evidence of Archaic occupation in open sites.

In dry caves, many other objects can be found. Along with baskets, archaeologists find cordage, tumplines or straps for carrying burdens, netting and matting, hides, skins, and sandals. At Danger Cave, Jesse Jennings also found wooden digging sticks, blunt dart points, curved wooden clubs, firedrills, horn shaft wrenches, tubular pipes, and shell beads from coastal California and Baja California.

Jennings observed that complete spear points were found in abundance, whereas items of ground stone, textiles, and basketry were fragmentary, apparently discarded only when they had become useless. Jennings makes an important point when he writes, "This discrepancy impressed me enough to make me suppose that flint was cheap, expendable and unimportant, whereas cordage, basketry, buckskin, bone, and horn tools, handles, and arrows all represented greater skill, a greater expenditure of effort, and had actually a higher practical and investment value than did the stone. If flint were thus cheap, one wonders how important it was. How valid are detailed reconstructions of culture history based on flint typology?"

And what of their shelters? Small family groups favored cave and rock-shelter locations for base camps, which were used for extended periods and year after year. Work camps and other temporary sites would be set up in areas where specific resources were available and occupied for only as long as it took to collect and process the resource. Certainly the people built shelters, but they were relatively impermanent and left few traces for archaeologists to find.

We think that the family probably was the basic social unit. Groups of related families often lived and traveled together, frequently joining with similar groups, called bands, when local resources were abundant, usually during the summer. There probably was little social inequality. Leaders may have been individuals with special skills such as hunting or basket making or an ability to deal with supernatural forces. We assume that positions of prestige and influence were not inherited but were achieved through the demonstration of competence. Social relations would have been similar to those found in families throughout the world where authority is vested in parents and the division of labor is according to age and gender. In an era without writing and books, the elderly were no doubt regarded highly for their knowledge and wisdom.

Although this picture suggests an uncomplicated, simple way of life, we do not mean to suggest that the people or their culture were simple. The Archaic people had trade connections with coastal California and Mexico; some bands traveled extraordinary distances to obtain particularly valued resources—no mean feat in the trackless desert. Near Picacho Reservoir northwest of Tucson, for example, archaeologists found evidence for at least two different groups of people, one of which ranged as far as what is today New Mexico. No doubt their social relationships, language, and oral history were rich, even complicated, in symbolism and meaning.

To understand the Archaic people fully, it is necessary to know the land where they lived and appreciate that they were totally dependent on the wild plants and animals found there. The only domesticated animal was the dog, probably brought over from the Old World with the Clovis people and not commonly a source of food. The animals on which we depend today for food—cattle, pigs, chickens—would not arrive in the New World until Europeans brought them thousands of years later. To make a living, plants had to be collected and processed and animals pursued, killed, butchered, and brought back to camp. One important feature of this way of life is that people must go to where the food resources are during the time they are available. Further, plants and animals were distributed unevenly over the various desert, mountain, and plateau environments of Arizona. Although no single family could range over all three zones in search of food, most desert dwellers would have traveled to nearby mountains for resources found only there.

We have found it useful to portray the Early and Middle Archaic food quest as though it were grocery shopping. We use a desert basin for our example because it contains the major environmental zones: river, foothills, and mountains.

Consider that you have no refrigerator and limited storage, so you must do some "shopping" every day. Specific food items are available only in certain areas at specific seasons of the year. And, of course, you must have water, although at some times during the year you might have to dig a well to get at it.

The nearby foothills have cactus with fruit that ripens in early to mid summer, but water is scarce there, so be sure to bring some on those hot June days. In fact, you might want to bring the whole family to set up camp and help collect the fruit. From this temporary work camp, parties may go into the mountain canyons to hunt deer or the elusive mountain sheep.

The river is a good place to be in the summer. There is water, shade and wood, dense stands of mesquite that provide beans to pick, and many animals that also are drawn to the water.

Acorns and pine nuts are available in the fall but are not to be found in the basin. The nearest stand would be up in the mountains, where there is ample water and good hunting, so again you will want to bring along some able-bodied family members to help carry the nuts home or bring the whole family to camp until it gets cold and it is time to return to the winter base camp in the basin.

Hopefully, over the summer and fall you will be able to store enough dried and smoked food and enough body fat to last you through the winter, because there is precious little fresh food available through the winter months. You are on your own to feed the family with what you were able to put away during the summer and early fall.

To be successful requires that you make a number of important decisions about scheduling hunting and plant gathering trips and assigning tasks to family members. Will everyone go along or only a couple of people? Will the trip be short or long? Can the children walk or must they be carried? All of these decisions must be made against a background of daily food requirements and cooperation with other family groups, to say nothing of social and religious obligations that may have little to do with getting groceries.

Consider further that this is the situation during the best of times. What happens when there are food shortages, droughts, or unexpected losses during the months when customary foods normally are available? Will starvation make people desperate, forcing some into robbery or murder to get food for themselves and their families? Although you might never resort to violent behavior, you know that others would, and you must protect your family. How do you make decisions about scheduling trips to hunt or collect plant foods when there are those who would take advantage of your absence to steal food or perhaps to kill or capture un-protected family members?

But planning is only a part of what concerns you as a responsible mem-ber of an Archaic family. There is no writing or any way to make notes, and there are no guidebooks to trails, plants, or animals, or to survival. Essential information for earning a living must be stored in the minds of group members and passed from generation to generation through pa-tient teaching and example—because survival depends on it.

These thoughts bring us to two views of hunter-gatherers. The older view is of people who scratch a meager living from an inhospitable envi-ronment. But the view that emerges from recent anthropological research on modern hunter-gatherers is that of people who spend less than twenty hours per week in the food quest and the remaining time in leisure pur-suits. Hunter-gatherers have been labeled the original "affluent society." Both pictures probably are true to some extent, depending on time and place, because hunter-gatherer life has been so variable throughout the world. For the Southwest, we believe the evidence leans toward the hard-times view of Archaic life, largely because of the uncertainty and harsh-ness of the southwestern environment.

Analysis of coprolites—human feces that have been preserved in the archaeological record—provides a picture of people who were eating everything edible, supporting our view that the Archaic life was often harsh. Insect parts, bones of small mammals and reptiles, assorted animal hairs, and egg shells are not uncommon. In dry caves, archaeologists occa-sionally find mouse quids—the remains of a mouse that was chewed whole and spit out—and the residue of mice that were pounded into a paste on a milling stone.

The important point to appreciate is that the price of ignorance or of a bad decision in the Archaic game of life could be severe. Sometimes it meant death. A true story illustrates this point vividly. A healthy young man—an anthropology graduate of a prestigious university—went to the backwoods of Alaska to live off the land. Armed with a .22-caliber semi-automatic rifle with a telescopic sight and a book on edible plants of the region, he should have been able to survive handily in the bush. Instead, he was unable to find enough food even through the summer months of greatest food abundance. Sadly, this young man, who thought he could live off the land as the Indians did, died of starvation after only four months.

Recognizing that their life was harsh must not detract from our appreciation of these past peoples. If anything, it should make us far more aware of the intelligence, energy, and skill it took to survive. Furthermore, it should increase our admiration for people who were able to overcome the demands and hardships of daily existence to perform those acts that are uniquely human—to tell stories, to dance, to sing, to express a vast range of emotions, and to give meaning to life, death, and the world around them. Our tale of the young man in Alaska also points up another uniquely human value characterizing Archaic people—the importance of family members, neighbors, and friends in coping with the uncertainties and hazards of life.

Late Archaic Beginnings of Corn Agriculture

The most significant event of the Late Archaic Period came with the introduction of corn, beans, and squash from Mexico. We facetiously refer to this as the invention of the tortilla, soon followed by refried beans. When placed in culinary perspective, the reasons for the acceptance of agriculture at first seem obvious and unworthy of scientific scrutiny, but that would be a false impression of agriculture's significance. The shift from hunting and gathering to food production brought profound changes wherever it occurred throughout the world. It has attracted considerable scientific attention and close examination as one of the major events in the long history of human development.

The origin of agriculture is less an event than a rather complicated process. Certainly the production of the first tortilla may be described as momentous, but it actually was one step in a prolonged and ongoing process of developing better foods and better production techniques to feed more people.

To investigate the origins of agriculture, we must distinguish between primary and secondary food production. Primary food production is the conversion of a wild food source into a domesticated food. For example, in the Old World wild sheep and goats were captured, tamed, and domesticated through selective breeding. After the Pleistocene extinction, North America lacked wild animals, such as horses and cattle, that could be domesticated profitably. But the Americas did have plenty of wild plants that could be cultivated and improved as food sources. Primary plant domestication took place in relatively few localities throughout the world and then spread from there. In the Americas, corn, beans, and squash were domesticated in what is today Mexico, although recent evidence suggests that a type of squash was domesticated independently in the eastern United States.

Corn, along with the other major plant crops, including cotton, came to the Southwest from Mexico. This transfer and acceptance is called secondary food production. In the Southwest, then, we are concerned with the process of acceptance, rather than domestication, of food plants.

Although the total conversion to settled village farming life did not happen overnight, the shift in subsistence to cultivated plant foods was a major change. What would make Archaic hunter-gatherers abandon a well-rehearsed way of life pursued for thousands of years to become settled village farmers? In familiarizing the reader with the Archaic way of life, we have emphasized the hardships, the severity and uncertainty of the food quest, and the insecurity of family groups during times of scarcity and social unrest. This is not a universal view of the Archaic Period in general or the Southwest in particular. In fact, quite a number of contemporary archaeologists believe that the acceptance of agriculture must have been by comfortable, prosperous hunter-gatherers, not people who were always on the brink of starvation.

To understand what actually happened requires that we cease to look for single causes and concentrate instead on the interaction of multiple variables affecting people living in different environments.

Residential stability may be the key to the transition to food production. If you are not at the right spot at the right time to plant corn, and later at the same spot to harvest it, you are not going to have tortillas for supper. Residential stability, in this sense, has two components, which vary according to circumstances. One is the repeated use of a location, and the other is the extended occupation of a campsite. One or the other must coincide with planting and harvesting to incorporate corn into the food quest.

Given that you have the seeds and the knowledge of how to plant, what might bring about an increase in residential stability? Let us look at a shift in the yield or diversity of a food resource. Suppose, for example, that as a hunter-gatherer you are able to expand the number of different kinds of foods gathered from an area or increase the yield of a particular food. You might be able to do this by adopting a new technology, such as replacing the spear with the spear-thrower (atlatl) and dart; or by gaining new information, such as new techniques for storage and preserving food; or by changing the organization of food-getting activities, such as organizing cooperative hunting rather than individual ventures.

Environmental changes also can bring about shifts in the availability of food resources by making them more or less abundant. A decreased abundance of traditional foods creates an imbalance between people and resources that, according to many archaeologists, is the critical step in the acceptance of agriculture.

Food production may well have been an unintended consequence of women experimenting with harvesting, storing, and cooking wild plant foods. As the ones responsible for plant gathering and processing, women would have had the essential knowledge about plants to facilitate accepting the technology—both information and activities—of food production. It probably did not take long to convince folks of the advantages of food production after a couple of crops came in.

Once a group begins to alter its hunting and gathering routine to incorporate food production, other aspects of life begin to change accordingly. Residential stability may increase to the point where the same location is used throughout the year, and food collecting and hunting activities that required a trip of several days away from the home camp would be carried out cooperatively by individuals from several families. Food production would encourage and make possible more families living together in the same location.

Population increase in an area caused by people coming together would be augmented by an increase in the number of children in each family. Among mobile hunter-gatherers, infant children must be carried everywhere and nursed until they can eat on their own. Children can contribute little to the food quest because of insufficient hunting skills or plant collecting knowledge. Among residentially stable cultivators, however, children do not need to be carried around by their mother because they can be fed at home by older siblings or their grandmother with the soft foods available to farmers. Thus, mothers can be freed from child care to pursue other activities in the field or in the home. Furthermore, children provide valuable help in the field by pulling weeds and scaring away birds and rodents.

Population increase and residential stability further reinforce people's dependence on cultivated foods by depleting local supplies of wild plants and animals. Eventually people must go farther and farther away from the village to find animals or plants to augment the food grown in the fields. At this point they have become fully committed to and totally dependent on cultivated foods as their dietary mainstay.

Psychological and social factors, which admittedly are difficult to identify in the archaeological record, also must play a factor in keeping people together once they have sufficient food resources to make it possible. We humans are social animals and prefer the security and companionship of others. It is because human beings do not usually wish to live alone that threats of being ostracized from the group function effectively as social control in small communities.

It is easier to understand the general process of shifting to food production than to identify the actual events of prehistory that led to making farmers out of Archaic hunter-gatherers. There are several facts we know for sure. Whereas evidence for Early and Middle Archaic people is scarce, Late Archaic sites dating between 1,000 B.C. and A.D. 200 are abundant, and most have yielded botanical evidence of corn. We turn now to Late Archaic Period farmers to see how life had changed from earlier times.

Late Archaic Farmers of the Tucson Basin

The river valleys of southern Arizona—with their rich farmland, reliable water, and riverine resources—were the home of Late Archaic people who built settlements of considerable size and permanence, and who coaxed the desert to produce fields of corn even before they had learned to make ceramic vessels and long before the Hohokam built their vast systems of canals.

Only a few short years ago, it was thought that the southern Arizona deserts were essentially unoccupied during the Late Archaic Period. The floodplain along the Santa Cruz River in the Tucson Basin was thought to be an "empty niche" waiting for Hohokam agriculturalists to fill it. Today we recognize that this picture was false, the product of limited archaeological research. Not only were there many more people living there than ever before, the most recent research suggests that the Sonoran Desert was the heartland from which the notion of corn agriculture spread throughout the rest of Arizona.

Emil Haury first proposed that corn was transmitted northward from Mexico along the Sierra Madre mountain corridor and that it spread from the Mogollon highlands into the Colorado Plateau and the Sonoran Desert, where it was adapted by Cochise Culture people. More recent work indicates that this path probably was reversed. The first varieties of corn grown in the Southwest probably were resistant neither to drought nor frost but were adapted to warm growing conditions at low elevations, which would make them ideally suited to the Sonoran Desert methods of planting fields in well-watered floodplains. R. G. Matson thinks that, because of these characteristics, corn agriculture developed first among Archaic populations in the Sonoran Desert and then spread widely.

The Late Archaic farmers of the Tucson Basin and adjacent river valleys practiced a seasonal round that required continued mobility in the quest for wild plant and animal foods but that also required residence for a considerable time near the fields during the planting and harvesting seasons. This lifestyle was not so much a dramatic change as it was an intensification of the traditional Archaic pattern, in which lowland base camps were occupied in the summer to allow their residents to take advantage of the plentiful harvests of wild resources. Agriculture permitted the Archaic folk to continue this way of life by allowing the necessary flexibility and providing storable foods to ameliorate scarcities in collected resources—a clever and productive strategy.

The riverine settlements, often including a dozen or more houses, consisted of clusters of round houses sometimes forming a loosely circular arrangement. Although the houses were simple compared to the elaborate homes of later ceramic-producing peoples, Late Archaic hamlets reflected a considerable increase in the complexity of material things compared to those of Middle Archaic Period people. Houses typically were round in shape and were constructed simply in shallow basins with brush and pole walls. Most were small, averaging about eight feet in diameter.

Numerous earthen pits located in the floors of houses or in the areas between houses served as secure storage for valuable tools and equipment, such as milling stones and flaked stone tools, as well as for foodstuffs. Many of the pits were large and bell-shaped. The floor area of houses was sometimes almost completely taken up with storage pits, and this—combined with the absence of hearths in many houses—suggests that they primarily served as storage areas, as well as indicating that these settlements could have been lived in only during the warm seasons. Other activities probably took place outdoors in the open or under simple shades (in Spanish, *ramadas*). Cooking was carried on outdoors in large, rock-filled roasting pits.

A fascinating discovery consists of the "big houses" found at some Late Archaic sites, which hint at a well-developed ritual life. These large structures, as much as thirty feet in diameter, are circular, with postholes around the perimeter and one or more posts supporting the roof. Like those of the dwelling houses, the roofs of these big houses probably were dome-shaped, and the walls were probably covered with grass, brush, mud, or hides. Unlike dwellings, however, the big houses did not have storage pits in the floor. The big house at the Coffee Camp site in the Santa Cruz Flats northwest of Tucson produced a variety of unusual objects, including a "baton" or "wand" made of phyllite, pigments, figurines, bone tubes, and worked shell pieces, suggesting nondomestic kinds of activities. A pair of deer antler racks graced the top of the house when it was in use; archaeologists found the antlers lying above charred roof beams and burned clay from the earthen covering.

Most likely the big houses were used for ceremonial activities in the same way as the much later Mogollon and Anasazi kivas. Their size suggests that many of the villagers could crowd inside to participate in rituals or perhaps to make important group decisions. Similar big houses occur at the earliest Mogollon and Hohokam sites, leading us to believe that there was a continuity in religious beliefs and to suspect that the Late Archaic folk were probably the ancestors of these later people.

Visualizing Late Archaic life as it must have been gives us a glimpse into how it had changed from earlier times. Corn agriculture provided a more stable food base and the freedom to play, tell tales, and develop the rich and sustaining ritual life that would characterize prehistoric Arizonans in times to come. Beneath the July sun the farmers weeded the corn, waiting for the monsoon rains that would fill the river and flood the fields. Children threw stones at crows and tried to catch rabbits. In the evening, smoke rose from cooking fires as the children raced around, shouting and giggling and chasing the dogs. Perhaps later there would be the insistent drumming that called their parents to the big house, where they would sing and dance and call down the gods from the sky. In the fall, with the plentiful harvest secure for the winter, the village would begin to break up as families left the summer encampment by the fields for their smaller campsites in the foothills. The newly married people who had found spouses in the summer encampment would leave to begin new lives. All would bring away with them fond memories of the summer by the river.

Dependence on Agriculture

We have come full circle in our ideas about the extent to which Late Archaic people relied on corn agriculture. Emil Haury proposed in 1962 that the arrival of agriculture in the Southwest had relatively little impact on the lifeways of Archaic hunter-gatherers. Following these ideas, Paul Minnis labeled the arrival of agriculture "a monumental nonevent." In the 1980s archaeologists began to emphasize the size of Late Archaic sites, the presence of houses and storage pits, and the quantity of corn. They suggested that, although lacking ceramics, the Late Archaic folk were settled village farmers who depended on corn.

We propose a notion more like that of Haury and Minnis: Late Archaic people certainly farmed and grew considerable quantities of corn, but they did not depend on it as the mainstay of their diet. Valuable though corn was to Late Archaic people, they did not give up their familiar wild plant resources. We infer these patterns from many categories of evidence.

Most Archaic sites have well-protected, often hidden storage pits containing caches of food, tools, and other valuable items. This emphasis on protecting food and tools indicates that the residents traveled between several different camps and did not live year-round in one place. In the Tucson Basin, people probably moved between the riverine area in the summer and higher elevations in the nearby foothills during the rest of the year. The absence of hearths in houses at the larger settlements supports this notion.

Although corn is found in abundance at Late Archaic settlements, other cultivated plants, such as beans and squash, are scarce. We do not know whether this is because of preservation factors—with tough kernels of corn preserving better archaeologically than softer-hulled squash seeds and beans—or because other cultigens were used to a lesser extent. The equipment used to process plant foods—small basin metates and handstones—tells us that the Late Archaic people continued to rely heavily on wild plant seeds.

Corn is not a particularly nutritious food, being deficient in certain amino acids, vitamins, calcium, and iron. Throughout the New World today, people who are dependent on corn soak it in limewater and grind it into flour to prepare mush, or in Spanish, *masa*. Soaking in limewater to remove the tough outer hull, grinding, and long boiling—steps necessary to prepare masa—also are processes that increase the nutritional value of corn. These steps, however, require essential tools that Late Archaic people lacked—ceramic containers and trough metates. Soaking and boiling corn kernels cannot be accomplished easily without ceramic vessels. To grind corn kernels effectively into flour—a backbreaking and rough job—requires the use of big, heavy metates with deep troughs on which corn is ground with large, rectangular manos in a back-and-forth motion. Archaic people also generally lacked these tools.

We think, therefore, that corn must have been prepared much like other plant foods, by roasting whole ears in pits. This way of preparing corn also is likely to leave lots of burned corn kernels for archaeologists to find, skewing our notions of corn's importance. The small-kerneled Archaic corn also could have been ground, parched, and prepared with cold water as bread or gruel. Corn, therefore, was not prepared in ways that enhance its nutritional value.

There also is the question of the corn itself. The first varieties of corn grown in the Southwest had small kernels and many rows, bearing little resemblance to modern corn. Not until much later did a more productive variety with big, floury kernels and fewer rows become common.

Pottery and the End of the Archaic

Yet another dramatic change awaited the Late Archaic folk. Sometime in the closing centuries B.C., a new idea that probably originated somewhere in what today is Mexico made its way across the Southwest. This was the notion of making and firing pottery containers that could be used to store, cook, and serve food. The Late Archaic people certainly understood what would happen to clay when it was baked at high temperatures. They modeled and fired human figurines, miniature objects, and beads from clay. They did not, however, use this material to make containers, suggesting to us that the idea was introduced from elsewhere.

Not so long ago it was thought that village life, farming, and ceramics appeared together as part of a new adaptive complex that was adopted rapidly across the Southwest. Today we think otherwise. People began to live more settled lives first; corn agriculture appeared next; and ceramics, it seems, came last on the scene.

The earliest ceramics we have found in southern Arizona come from the Coffee Camp site, which was occupied between 200 B.C. and A.D. 50. These ceramics are different from the finely made pottery that characterizes later sites. They are thick and tempered with fibers (perhaps grass or other organic materials) and do not seem to have been fired. Many fragments have impressions on the surface that suggest textiles or animal fur. These earliest ceramics may have been simple clay linings for containers made of other materials, such as hides or basketry. We cannot know whether the ceramics were fashioned deliberately as containers or were the accidental product of attempting to make perishable containers watertight by sealing them with mud.

We do know that a scant 50 to 150 years after the Coffee Camp site was first occupied the people living at settlements in the Tucson Basin, such as the Houghton Road site that we will learn more about in chapter 4, were making skillfully wrought, thin, well-polished, and well-fired ceramic vessels—little time to develop the necessary techniques without information from those already skilled in making pottery.

The transition from experimental ceramics to well-made ceramic containers took place around the same time across the Southwest. In the San Simon Valley of southeastern Arizona, where Ted Sayles defined one branch of the Mogollon Culture (see chapter 6), ceramics appeared around A.D. 200 at sites that otherwise resemble Late Archaic Period settlements. This was true in the mountains and on the Colorado Plateau as well. At Bluff Village, an early Mogollon site in the Forestdale Valley, finely made pottery has been tree-ring dated between A.D. 200 and 400. In the Petrified Forest area, ceramic containers may have been made slightly earlier. On the Colorado Plateau, ceramics appeared around A.D. 200 but are not abundant until around 400 to 500.

Wherever they occur, the first ceramics are simple, although well made, and their characteristics are similar. The pottery was not painted but was a plain ware that was gray to brown in color and lightly polished. Most of the first pots were small jars lacking a neck, called seed jars. There are few jars with necks that could have been used as cooking vessels and few bowls for serving food or for other purposes. The first ceramics are thin walled and lightweight—characteristics that are helpful in a mobile society but that preclude long cooking over hot fires. Cooking, water storage, and other functions were carried out using the kinds of perishable containers that the Late Archaic people employed. This suggests that the original function of ceramics was to protect valuable seed corn against dampness, mold, and pests. A farmer without seed will not survive long. The early seed jars have been found buried beneath the floors of houses in storage pits, a fact that reinforces the notion that they were used to store seed corn. The small size of seed jars indicates that storage pits and perhaps basketry, not ceramics, met people's bulk storage needs.

Ceramic container technology apparently had little impact, at least at first. As we will see in chapter 4, the earliest ceramic-making people continued the seasonal round that had characterized the Archaic way of life, settling along the rivers in the summertime to plant and harvest corn. They continued to prepare foods in traditional ways, and although corn surely was an important part of their diet and growing corn a significant aspect of their lives, many other foods were just as vital.

The intriguing possibility exists that the appearance of ceramic containers was the impetus for greater dependence on agriculture rather than the other way around. When ceramic technology had improved to the extent that corn could be cooked for a considerable time and could perhaps be treated with limewater before cooking, it was then possible to rely on corn as the dietary mainstay. Some archaeologists have suggested that ceramic containers also made possible the efficient cooking of beans. It may be no coincidence that beans, improved pottery containers, trough metates, and bigger and better corn arrived in southern Arizona at about the same time, completing the transformation of Late Archaic hunter-gatherer-farmers into settled village farmers.

This transformation took considerable time, however. Not overnight did ceramic containers, corn agriculture, and other inventions change Late Archaic people into Hohokam or Mogollon or Anasazi. The entire process probably took as much as a thousand years in some parts of the Southwest.

The Archaic in Retrospect

If you concluded that our view of the Archaic Culture in Arizona is a hazy picture, clear in places but fuzzy in others, you would be correct, but you would be missing some important lessons of archaeology and prehistory. The Archaic Period stands as a testament to the rapid rate at which archaeological knowledge can increase and the radical changes that increased knowledge can create in our understanding of the past. We know much more now than we did just twenty-five years ago, and far more than we did fifty years ago when Ted Sayles and Ernst Antevs first defined the Cochise Culture. In fact, the most remarkable strides in Late Archaic and early ceramic period archaeology were not made until the 1990s. Moreover, there is still so much more to discover that all of us—professional archaeologists and public supporters of archaeology alike—must be vigilant to preserve the fragile record of the Archaic past. The greatest advances in Archaic archaeology have come from sites threatened with destruction through modern development. Only through the concern and cooperation of all Arizona citizens can the past become better known and appreciated.

4 THE HOHOKAM

Today all that remains of the Hohokam lies buried and silent. Their pit houses left nothing on the surface. You may see the linear traces of what were adobe walls, now melted to dirt by centuries of rain and wind. Perhaps the grass grows a little differently along these walls, or you may note an upright stone or two that served to bolster the mud walls. No visible stone ruins mark where the Hohokam lived, only fragments of pottery vessels made by skilled hands more than 700 years ago. In the summer, the only sounds you hear are the shrill cries of locusts in the deep green mesquite and perhaps the howl of coyotes in the evening. Once the villages rang with the sound of barking dogs, children's laughter, and the ever-present scraping and pounding of mano on metate and pestle in mortar to produce the daily bread. Fill your mind's eye with the raucous turmoil of a ball game, and listen for the shouts of enthusiasm and despair. These were the people, the Hohokam, the ones who have gone. They laughed, they bartered with skill, they made flawless and beautiful things, they mourned their dead. Perhaps they live still in the blood of Pima and Tohono O'odham. Gila Pueblo found them, Emil Haury gave them substance and glory, and today's archaeologists amplify their history.

Today the forgotten people are well known, but this was not always so. We emphasize the Hohokam Culture in this book for several reasons. More than any other prehistoric culture, they were the original Arizonans. Mogollon, Anasazi, and Patayan peoples lived in many parts of the Southwest, but the Hohokam called the Sonoran Desert and it alone home. In contrast to the Anasazi, who are well represented in the archaeological literature and in ruins that can be visited and appreciated, little has been written of the Hohokam for the general reader, and there are few Hohokam sites that the public may visit. Moreover, archaeologists themselves gave the Hohokam short shrift until recent years, when a flood of cultural resource management projects filled in the gaps in our understanding of these people. Their story is exciting, and the tale is worthy of the telling.

Land and People

The Hohokam were the masters of the desert. The urban sprawl that today defines Phoenix and Tucson marks the areas once densely settled by the Hohokam, who farmed the fertile valleys of the Salt, Gila, and Santa Cruz Rivers. Their skill in adapting to and manipulating the desert enabled the Hohokam to develop a way of life based on riverine farming enriched by distinctive and elaborate crafts, supplemented by mercantile enthusiasm, and supported by an intricate and rich ceremonial complex.

The Sonoran Desert

The Sonoran Desert is vast, encompassing the mountains and valleys of southern Arizona, the western portion of Sonora, the Baja California peninsula, and a narrow strip of land on the California side of the Colorado River. This is a harsh land and, for those unschooled in desert learning, an unforgiving one. Extremes of temperature and precipitation are the norm, the resident creatures are armed with stinger and poison, and even the plants are unfriendly. Those who understand the desert, however, can coax from it a dependable and substantial supply of food, and the Hohokam understood the desert well.

Little rain falls on this land. In Tucson the average rainfall is between ten and twelve inches per year. Phoenix receives even less, around seven to nine inches. The desert has two rainy seasons. Rainfall is heaviest and most dependable during the summer monsoon season, when masses of warm, moist, and unstable air from the Gulf of Mexico collide with the hot, dry air rising above the mountain ranges. Intense and often severe thunderstorms result, bringing relief from the heat but also heavy rain accompanied by spectacular lightning displays and sometimes by destructive wind and hail. Sonoran tradition holds that the summer monsoons—*chubasco* in Spanish—begin on June 24, on the Feast Day of San Juan.

The Tucson Basin, looking toward the Santa Catalina Mountains.

Winter rains are created by cyclonic storms originating in the Pacific Ocean and typically are more widespread and less intense than summer rains. At other times of the year, the desert receives little rainfall. The late spring (May and June) and fall typically are the driest times.

Summer's intense heat can be likened to a furnace blast, with the average maximum July temperature in Tucson hovering around 100°F, and in Phoenix about 104°F. Winters, however, are typically mild as well as dry, and the many frost-free days provide an extended growing season for cultivated crops.

Most of the Sonoran Desert is characterized by basin-and-range topography. Broad alluvial valleys separate the mountain ranges, some of which reach between 8,000 and 11,000 feet above sea level. These "sky islands" offer in microcosm a complete range of climatic and environmental variables from desert floor to mountain peak.

Desert vegetation is adapted to conserve water. Plants have small leaves to reduce surface evaporation, and have developed many different ways of storing water. The Sonoran Desert is unique among the world's deserts in its trees, gigantic cacti, and succulents. Some of its most notorious plants can only be described as bizarre, such as the huge inverted carrot with the Lewis Carroll name of boojum. The higher-elevation foothill slopes (*bajadas* in Spanish) are the richest zone of useful plant life, and cactuses grow thickly there. The green belts or riparian zones along the rivers include the desert's only deciduous trees, such as the cottonwood, Arizona ash, and sycamore. Nearly impenetrable stands of mature mesquite trees (*bosques*) once stood in the river bottomland, but overgrazing and other kinds of environmental degradation in historical times have reduced these stands to mere remnants.

From cottontail to kangaroo rat, the animal denizens of the Sonoran Desert are as well adapted to its conditions as are its plants. The shy ringtail cat, the Gila monster with its colorful beaded skin, the javelina, and the western diamondback rattlesnake are some of its better-known residents. Plants and animals help each other survive the rigors of the desert. The bat that draws nourishment from the saguaro blooms, for example, also pollinates them.

The lifeblood of the desert is water. Today's dry riverbeds bear little resemblance to the wide, flowing rivers that the Hohokam knew. Rivers that once ran year-round have been dammed for modern uses, and water usually flows only after summer thundershowers or heavy winter storms. The Gila and Salt Rivers, which join near Phoenix, were perennial rivers with surface water along their entire lengths. The Santa Cruz River, which passes through Tucson, was somewhat different. That river ran underground along much of its course, with water flowing to the surface only in certain locations. Elsewhere, the river was more of a marshy area, or cienega, than a river. Canal irrigation therefore was much more important to the Phoenix-area Hohokam.

It is difficult to picture from the present dry riverbeds what these rich, green oases must have been like 800 years ago. It is still more difficult to imagine the power and destructive force of rivers in the desert. We learned a great deal from the 1983 and 1993 floods, which devastated Phoenix and Tucson, about the perils riverine dwellers must expect. Farmland, homes, office buildings, stables, and lives were lost as raging rivers swollen by the wettest storms in recent history swept away everything in their path. So too must the Hohokam have lost canals, villages, and fields in the most destructive floods.

Many of the characteristics of the Sonoran Desert have also affected Hohokam archaeology. Perhaps most important is the lack of trees that produce annual growth rings, which has hampered precise dating of Hohokam sites. These uncooperative desert trees are hardwoods that can survive for many years on the dry desert surface, so they may have been as much as a hundred years old when collected by a Hohokam householder for firewood. As a result, radiocarbon dates often are much older than the events that they appear to date. And not to be ignored is the fact that in the early years of southwestern archaeology the intense summer heat was shunned by archaeologists, who were instead drawn to the cool and wooded mountains.

Hohokam Territory

The distribution of the stately saguaro cactus conveniently marks the boundaries of the Sonoran Desert and the Hohokam world. The basins now occupied by the modern cities of Phoenix and Tucson, the southwestern Arizona desert (called the Papaguería), and the desert foothills of central Arizona north of Phoenix define the Hohokam culture area. Outposts of Hohokam settlement also were scattered deep in the home territory of other cultures, chiefly among the Sinagua of the Flagstaff region and along the Verde River (see chapter 8).

There are a number of ways to look at the regional distribution of Hohokam settlement and culture. One way was suggested by Emil Haury on the basis of his research at Ventana Cave. Haury divided the Hohokam into two groups based on where they lived and how they adapted to the landscape, and the resulting effects on their economic and social organization. The group he classified as the River Hohokam lived in the major river valleys and grew their crops by canal irrigation. Their villages were large and were often occupied for hundreds of years. The site of Snaketown is a well-known village of the River Hohokam.

The group Haury labeled the Desert Hohokam lived in the valleys and bajadas away from the river zones and relied on rainfall to water their crops. Their lifestyle was simpler than that of the River Hohokam. Their villages were smaller and were usually occupied for a shorter period of time, and their artifacts were less elaborate than those of the River Hohokam.

Another way of looking at the difference among Hohokam settlements is to define a core area or heartland flanked by peripheries or colonized areas. In this view, Hohokam colonies spread outward from the initial settlements in the Phoenix Basin and remained socially and economically tied to the heartland villages.

A third way of viewing Hohokam territory considers the distribution of the Hohokam cultural system. David Wilcox considers it pointless to argue about what constituted the Hohokam "core" area and to trace the patterns of Hohokam colonization. He suggests instead that archaeologists study the interactions and relationships among the Hohokam over their entire zone of occupation, referring to this and to the religious, political, and ideological ideas it embraced as the "Hohokam regional system." This is the most flexible way of viewing the Hohokam, for it permits us to consider that people living in different parts of Arizona, not all of whom may have been ethnically Hohokam, participated in the Hohokam Culture in various ways. Some people may have participated intensively, adopting the ballcourts and associated rituals. Others may have taken up only the outer trappings, such as pottery vessels. Still others seem to have adopted Hohokam family structure and borrowed material goods such as pottery but apparently eschewed the religious system. This view offers many possibilities for study.

The People Today

When the Spanish soldiers and priests arrived in what is today southern Arizona and northern Sonora, they found it inhabited by groups of Native Americans speaking different dialects of one language and occupying different areas. These Pimas Altos, or Upper Pimas, call themselves O'odham, meaning "we, the people." Their land is called in Spanish the Pimería Alta. In modern times the Pimas living along the Gila River called themselves Akimel O'odham, or "River People," and the desert Pimas referred to themselves as the Tohono O'odham, or "Desert People." The river-dwelling O'odham typically have been called Pimas by non-Indians, and the desert-dwelling O'odham were known previously as the Papagos.

We can learn much about the ways in which the Hohokam lived by studying the people who still flourish in the desert. The Piman people developed three different ways of adapting to the harsh desert land. One way of life was nomadic. The "No Villagers" were the Hia-Ced O'odham, who occupied the westernmost stretches of the desert near Yuma and in northwestern Sonora. By necessity, the No Villagers were food collectors rather than food producers. In addition to desert plants and animals, the No Villagers incorporated the marine resources of the Gulf of California into their diet. They traveled constantly over this harsh country in search of food and water, the vital lifeblood in this driest part of the Sonoran Desert. As a result, the No Villagers had only a few simple tools, made no pottery of their own, and lived in temporary brush shelters or windbreaks.

The "Two Villagers" are the Tohono O'odham, who live in the central Papaguería on both sides of the present international border. Although lacking permanent streams, the Papaguería is relatively well watered, and plant and animal life is abundant. The Two Villagers lived in winter camps located on the bajadas near permanent sources of water, such as springs, and moved down to the alluvial valleys in the summer, where they farmed. Because their lifeway was less mobile, the Two Villagers had a much richer inventory of tools and equipment than the No Villagers. They made pottery and lived in brush houses of simple but solid construction.

The "One Villagers" were the most settled of all the Pimans. These people lived along the Salt, Gila, and Santa Cruz Rivers. The riverine environment provided a ready and constant supply of water that could be tapped through the use of irrigation canals and ditches. Although the One Villagers often maintained agricultural fields a short distance from their villages, the summer-winter round of movement followed by the Two Villagers was unnecessary. Their villages were large and were occupied throughout the year.

Today the O'odham live in two main regions that correspond roughly to the One Villager and Two Villager homelands. The Pima occupy reservations along the Gila and Salt Rivers, and at the confluence of the two. The Tohono O'odham live in the reservation districts of San Xavier (Tucson), Sells, Ak Chin, and Gila Bend. Many O'odham live off the reservation in the metropolitan Tucson and Phoenix areas, and as they always have done, many still live in northern Sonora, Mexico.

Food and Farming

Under the capable hands of the Hohokam, the seemingly inhospitable Sonoran Desert yielded a rich harvest. Their way of life was based on bringing water to the desert, transforming the arid land into lush fields where they grew a variety of crops. The extensive networks of irrigation canals that watered the fields of the River Hohokam distinguish them, more than any other part of their culture, from the other prehistoric peoples who lived in Arizona. Moreover, as Jerry Howard reminds us, irrigation systems have played a significant role in the debate concerning Hohokam sociopolitical complexity and cultural development.

As early as 1929, irrigation systems were described by Omar Turney, whose maps often provide the only existing information concerning canals that have been destroyed by modern development. The Phoenix-area canal systems were many miles in total length and irrigated thousands of acres of land. For example, Turney's Canal System 2, located on the north side of the Salt River, consisted of fifty main canals constructed over a period of about 900 years. Canal networks included large main canals, smaller secondary canals, and numerous feeder ditches.

Constructing the irrigation networks required considerable effort. Canals were dug by hand using digging sticks and stone tools, and canals and gates had to be cleaned periodically and maintained. It may have been necessary to rebuild entire systems following destructive floods. Most important, labor had to be organized and directed, and decisions had to be made about whose fields would receive water, how much, and when. The relationship between social and political complexity and irrigation has long been noted by anthropologists.

With irrigation the River Hohokam were able to grow their staple crops—corn, beans, and squash—in this land of little rain. That the desert could be transformed into a paradise with the aid of irrigation also was recognized much later by the historical occupants of the Salt River valley. The Hohokam may have been able to grow two crops each year, first by utilizing runoff in the spring, and later with water from summer rains. Tobacco and cotton also were cultivated. The oil-rich cotton seeds were eaten, and the fiber was spun and woven. Cotton requires substantial water and a long, hot growing season, so it was an ideal crop along the Gila River.

The Desert Hohokam relied on floodwater farming. The Tohono O'odham still practice one type of floodwater farming, called *ak-chin* farming. *Ak-chin* is a Piman word for the alluvial fan at the mouth of an arroyo. Agricultural fields were located on these aprons of fertile soil and were watered only by rainfall runoff, sometimes directed by brush or stone dams and simple ditches. Fields also could be watered by flooding when streams overflowed their banks. Still other fields were watered solely by rainfall, a technique called dry farming.

The Desert and River Hohokam alike supplemented their diet by collecting the wild plant foods of the Sonoran Desert, which provided a nutritional boost and helped buffer against times when agricultural crops were poor. The thorny, scrubby desert plants that seem inedible at first glance actually are a rich and varied source of nutritious foods. Mesquite beans and cactus—especially cholla, saguaro, hedgehog, and prickly pear—were the two wild plant staples.

The Hohokam may have prepared desert foods in much the same way as the O'odham traditionally did. Mesquite bean pods were ground into slightly sweet flour that was made into unbaked breadlike cakes or mixed with water to make a refreshing drink called *atole*. As ethnobotanist Gary

Nabhan notes, mesquite foods are simple to prepare and require no cooking—important in an environment where fuel wood probably always was scarce. Hundreds of basin-shaped mortars ground into the living bedrock or the tops of boulders throughout the desert attest to the Hohokam use of mesquite beans.

Cactus products were used in many different ways. Fresh green cholla buds were collected and roasted in pits. Bright red saguaro cactus fruits were dried, boiled into syrup, patted into cakes, and fermented into mildly alcoholic wine. Sometimes the seeds were skimmed from boiling fruit, ground, and added to *pinole*, or gruel. One of the most frequently told stories about desert peoples and their food is the "second harvest" of the *pitahaya* or organ-pipe cactus. This euphemistically named food recycling practice is not one Europeans favor, but it points up the scarcity of food in the most arid reaches of the desert. When pitahaya fruit was abundant, the O'odham often stayed in one place for weeks to harvest and eat it. They would defecate in the same spot. When the feces were dry, they were collected and the seeds were winnowed out and cleaned meticulously and then ground and cooked before being eaten. As Gary Nabhan points out, the cactus seeds were a source of protein, oil, and calories that the people could not afford to waste in times of drought and hunger.

Weedy annual plants that favor disturbed ground, such as mustard and wild buckwheat, grew in the fields and along ditches. These plants provided useful seeds and greens, according to archaeologist and pollen analyst Suzanne Fish. Pimans prepared seeds by parching, grinding into flour, and preparing pinole. The greens of these plants were boiled, providing a natural spinach called *quelites*. Not only did annual greens fill in gaps in the O'odham diet, being one of the first foods to sprout, they also provided nutrients, such as calcium, that were not supplied by domesticated corn.

Hunting supplemented the Hohokam diet with protein and a dietary change of pace. Some of the important desert animals that were hunted included cottontail and jackrabbits, antelope, deer, and bighorn sheep. When other game was scarce, the Hohokam turned to rodents, reptiles, and even insects. Zooarchaeologist Christine Szuter calls our attention to the relationship between the farmer and the hunter. Clearing land for fields, as well as cutting wood for building purposes and fuel, modified the environment and made it attractive to certain kinds of animals. The Hohokam took advantage of this fact and adapted their hunting practices to include animals that preyed on crops. This practice of "garden hunting" had the added benefit of ridding the fields of pests.

Discovering the Hohokam

The concept of the Hohokam Culture is relatively new in the history of southwestern archaeology, and even after it was "discovered," many archaeologists viewed the idea with skepticism. Although it may seem odd that a prehistoric people would require "discovery" in much the same way as penicillin or the measles vaccine, recall that science develops continually through new discoveries and inventions.

The Hohokam Culture was discovered by the Gila Pueblo Archaeological Foundation. This private institution was the inspiration and life work of Harold S. Gladwin. A man described as having "great mental strength, style, and purposefulness," Gladwin also was unconventional. He often stressed theories over facts and occasionally manipulated facts in sometimes creative ways to fit his purposes. His often cavalier pursuit of prehistory and his lack of formal training in archaeology were disdained by many of Gladwin's better-educated colleagues.

Gladwin held a seat on the New York Stock Exchange, which he sold in 1922 to move to California. His friendship with the great southwestern archaeologist A. V. Kidder led Gladwin to reorient his life toward archaeology. Desert Arizona had not been studied systematically at that time. Little was known about the culture of the people who once lived there, beyond the obvious fact that it differed from that of the Anasazi. Kidder, who was the most learned and influential scholar of the time, urged Gladwin to investigate the desert.

Gladwin began working for the Southwest Museum in Los Angeles. His interest in the Hohokam was sparked by an expedition to Casa Grande National Monument in 1927, where he conducted stratigraphic excavations that indicated that two different peoples producing two kinds of pottery had lived there. Gladwin suspected that the red-on-buff pottery was earlier than the pottery decorated in red, black, and white. These investigations led him to conclude that the Phoenix Basin was "actually

Red-on-buff painted pottery of the Hohokam Culture.

invaded by a northern people" who made the polychrome pottery, buried their dead, and built houses of adobe. The local people, Gladwin believed, were different; they built houses of poles and mud, cremated their dead, and made the red-on-buff pottery.

The following year Gladwin founded the Gila Pueblo Archaeological Foundation to pursue his dream: to do archaeology and do it well. Gila Pueblo was built on a prehistoric site located in Sixshooter Canyon near Globe, Arizona. This Salado pueblo (see chapter 9) was reconstructed as it was excavated. The new building followed the spirit of a prehistoric pueblo in its multiple stories, adobe walls, and beamed ceilings. Here the Gladwins and the archaeologists who came to Gila Pueblo worked and lived. It was in some ways an ideal situation; those who worked there were free of many of the financial and theoretical constraints that can often hinder archaeologists.

We have come to associate the Hohokam Culture with Emil W. Haury, considered by many to be the single most important southwestern archaeologist of our time. In 1930 Haury joined Gila Pueblo as assistant director, readily fitting into the frenetic pace set by Gladwin. As Haury recalled, "There was no time to get bored and not enough time to get one's work done. Any archaeologist truly interested in what he or she was doing would find the schedule fulfilling one's wildest dreams."

Gladwin engaged the Gila Pueblo staff in an intensive effort to trace the "red-on-buff culture" (as it was then called for its distinctive pottery) across the Southwest. Archaeological survey then was vastly different from the way it is conducted today; the Gladwins and their staff traveled in a remodeled Pierce Arrow town car splendidly outfitted as a field vehicle. Gila Pueblo archaeologists followed the trail to California and Utah, Mexico and Texas. As Gladwin recounts it, however, "search as we would, we could not find a trace of them outside of the valley of the Gila and its tributaries."

Soon more obvious evidence of the "red-on-buff culture" was amassed. In 1931 Haury excavated Roosevelt 9:6, a Hohokam site located on the south shore of Roosevelt Lake in the Tonto Basin. This work led him to conclude that the "red-on-buff culture" clearly was distinct from the Anasazi Culture from its earliest stages onward.

In 1933 Gladwin and his wife, Winifred, formally presented the Hohokam as a new culture in a publication. This work gave a tentative chronology for the culture, a description of the pottery, and comparisons with other parts of the Southwest and other cultures. The name Hohokam was a Pima expression meaning "those who have gone" or "all used up."

Archaeologists resisted the idea of a new culture, especially one focused in the desert lands of central Arizona. Most archaeological investigations had concentrated on the Colorado Plateau, and other regions were known only sketchily. All archaeological remains were held up against the Anasazi standard for comparison, and they usually fared poorly. In the first synthesis of southwestern archaeology (published in 1924), A. V. Kidder noted that what was known simply as the "lower Gila valley culture" departed from the Pueblo pattern in significant ways. The archaeological remains of this area, he wrote, "are in some ways so aberrant that, were it not for the pottery, we should be forced to consider that we had overstepped the limits of the Southwestern culture area."

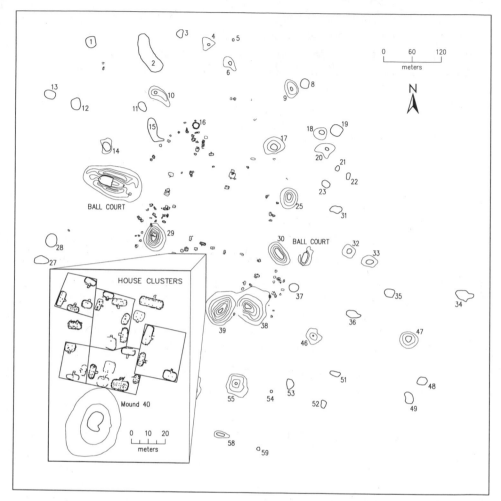

The major Hohokam site of Snaketown, which included mounds, pit houses, and ball-courts. The enlargement depicts five house clusters, which consisted of two to ten houses grouped around a central courtyard.

The most important work had yet to be done, however. Gladwin be-lieved that the only way to learn more about the Hohokam Culture was to excavate. Earlier he had recorded a huge "red-on-buff culture" site located along the Gila River a few miles downstream from the Pima community of Sacaton. The Pima families who lived there called the place by a Pima

Gila Pueblo staff at Snaketown in 1935. Left to right, they are Fisher Motz, Julian Hayden, Evelyn Dennis, E. B. Sayles, Erik Reed, Nancy Pinkley, Irwin Hayden, and Emil Haury.

term meaning "The Place of the Snakes" or "Many Rattlesnakes." The site was therefore called Snaketown. Gladwin selected this huge site, consisting of sixty mounds in an area more than a square mile in extent, as the best place to work because it lay in the center of the Hohokam area and it had not been spoiled by vandals. Work began at Snaketown in 1934 under Haury's direction.

The excavation of Snaketown was a monumental effort that became a landmark in southwestern archaeology, and the resulting scientific report (published in 1937) was the standard by which the Hohokam would be known for thirty years. The excavations produced a wealth of information about the Hohokam. Some forty houses, two ballcourts, an irrigation canal, numerous mounds, and more than 500 cremations were excavated. The rich and striking material complex of the Hohokam Culture, including red-on-buff pottery, carved stonework, and ornate shell jewelry, was described in detail. The pottery typology and stratigraphy presented in the Snaketown report, which Haury was responsible for, together provided

The Snaketown ballcourt in 1935, showing the excavated half.

the basis for the phase sequence and chronology that placed the Hohokam in prehistoric time. Perhaps most significant, the Snaketown publication settled the scientific controversy that had surrounded the Hohokam. From that point on, the idea of a Hohokam Culture gained acceptance in the archaeological community.

Haury left Gila Pueblo in 1937 to become the head of the Department of Archaeology at the University of Arizona and the director of the Arizona State Museum the following year, inaugurating another chapter in the history of Hohokam archaeology. The reasons for Haury's break with Gladwin will never be understood completely, but it was probably based on a controversy over intellectual issues. In 1942 and 1948 Gladwin published revisions of the Snaketown chronological sequence that collapsed it considerably in time. He based his revision on a detailed critique that cast obvious doubt on the validity of Haury's stratigraphic studies, which had established the original chronology. Gladwin's revisions affected Haury deeply.

While at the University of Arizona, Haury launched a series of studies that would affect conceptions of the Hohokam. One especially significant project was the excavation of Ventana Cave, as discussed in chapters 2 and 3.

During this time, other archaeologists also were tackling the Hohokam. New schemes of Hohokam cultural development emerged that conflicted with the original sequences and ideas. Little new information had been collected, however, in part because of the impact of World War II on archaeology. Without sufficient data to evaluate the competing theories, no progress could be made. Haury wrote that "This chaotic state of affairs convinced me that the only way to solve the dilemma was by launching new studies, that the only reasonable way to argue the points under contention was with the shovel."

Haury returned to Snaketown in 1964 and 1965 to conduct a second monumental study of the Hohokam Culture that would answer the questions raised by Gladwin in the 1940s (see Haury 1976). As with the original work, the return to Snaketown resulted in the discovery of a mass of material objects and information. More than 180 houses, a ballcourt, hundreds of cremations and outdoor facilities, and a platform mound were excavated. Information concerning farming and other subsistence pursuits was collected, and a number of radiocarbon dates were obtained—vital data missing from the earlier study, which antedated radiocarbon dating. Haury evaluated the stratigraphic and temporal information carefully and concluded that the original Snaketown chronology was valid. He revised his thinking concerning the origins of the Hohokam Culture, however. The work convinced Haury that the Hohokam were an immigrant group who had come from the south in what is today Mexico.

A new direction in Hohokam archaeology was initiated during the 1960s and 1970s. At this time, desert Arizona experienced a rapid increase in population, which resulted in a flurry of construction. Laws protecting cultural resources required that archaeological sites be excavated before any construction was initiated. The result was that millions of dollars were spent excavating dozens of Hohokam sites through cultural resource management, also called contract archaeology. Where before there had been little excavation—Snaketown being the sole large, well-documented Hohokam site—suddenly there was an overwhelming amount of new information from numerous excavated sites. The Hohokam Culture was revealed to be far more variable and complex than archaeologists had thought. Snaketown could no longer serve as the model for all the Hoho-kam Culture. This recent wave of archaeological research also expanded our knowledge, however, with new techniques not available to previous researchers. Consequently, we know much more about the Hohokam diet, farming practices, and social organization, as well as the past natural environment. Perhaps most important, we have amassed a substantial body of radiocarbon and archaeomagnetic dates.

There is still much to be learned about the Hohokam. Wide gaps in our understanding remain, and the wealth of new data has fostered compet-ing interpretations and theories. Fortunately, the pace of archaeological discovery continues unabated in southern Arizona today.

Hohokam Origins

The origins of the Hohokam Culture are shrouded in mystery. As we have learned, southern Arizona was inhabited by Clovis and Archaic people be-fore the Hohokam. Archaeologists are undecided about whether the Ho-hokam were descended from Archaic ancestors and developed their way of life by a long process of cultural evolution, or else migrated to southern Arizona from Mexico. Those who favor the first hypothesis seek continu-ity between the Cochise Culture and the earliest Hohokam, but the mech-anisms by which the relatively simple lifeway of the Archaic people may have been transformed into the complex and elaborate Hohokam Culture remain poorly understood. The second hypothesis implies that the Ho-hokam were unrelated to the local Archaic people but rather imposed their own, more complex systems of organization, irrigation agriculture, and ritual upon the indigenous people, who had a simpler way of life.

Haury initially favored the first theory. He believed that the Hohokam Culture was the product of a long sequence of cultural development be-ginning about 300 B.C. Haury's ideas were based on the initial excavations at Snaketown and the sequence through time of Hohokam cultural devel-opment that was derived from that work. The work at Ventana Cave pro-vided good evidence for an evolution of Hohokam Culture from that of the local Archaic Period people.

Charles Di Peso developed a similar opinion with a unique twist. He asserted that there were local people who developed from the Cochise

Culture but that they were not Hohokam. Di Peso, who studied with Haury at the University of Arizona, joined a private archaeological research institution, the Amerind Foundation, in 1948 and began to pursue a lifelong interest in the indigenous people of southern Arizona. Di Peso called these people the Ootam, after the Piman word for "people." The Ootam, he said, were descended from the indigenous Cochise Culture. Di Peso viewed the Ootam as a basic culture that was widespread across the Southwest and from which the Mogollon and other cultures developed subsequently. Although he included the earliest phases of the Hohokam Culture in his Ootam concept, Di Peso was convinced that the later phases were different. The Hohokam were not the same people as the Ootam but were immigrants arriving much later from Mexico.

After his work at Snaketown during the 1960s, Haury changed his mind and joined Di Peso in accepting the notion of the Hohokam as a migrant people. Haury held to this interpretation even as younger Hohokam archaeologists took up his earlier view.

Recent findings shed light on the controversy. During the early 1990s we discovered a previously unknown settled population whose members were making ceramics and growing corn in the Tucson Basin, the Phoenix Basin, and elsewhere in central Arizona between A.D. 200 and 400. The early sites appear to bridge the gap between the preceramic Cochise Culture and the earliest phases of the cultures that can be recognized as Hohokam and Mogollon.

The first such site to be excavated in the Tucson Basin was the Houghton Road site, investigated by archaeologists from Statistical Research, Inc., for the Pima County Department of Transportation. The site proved to have features that we now recognize as defining the earliest ceramic-making people, including plain ware pottery, Archaic-style grinding tools, and a reliance on gathering wild plant foods as well as farming. A distinctive pit house with a bean-shaped floor plan and flexed burials, much like those of contemporary Mogollon sites (see chapter 6), were present. An unusual feature, called a great house or communal house, was a large, deep house that we think was a communal ceremonial structure.

There is a great deal of similarity between these characteristics of the earliest ceramic-producing folk of the desert area and the Mogollon Culture. Apparently little except their geographic location distinguished the

Mogollon from the Hohokam at this early time. The similarity to Di Peso's Ootam concept is clear and requires archaeologists to rethink its usefulness.

Further, there is a distinct contrast between the early pottery-producing culture and the later Hohokam Culture. The distinct, recognizable aspects of the Hohokam Culture that we will learn about shortly—such as irrigation agriculture, a unique pottery tradition, and a complex ritual system centered on ballcourts and cremations—did not appear until hundreds of years after the appearance of pottery in the desert. Does this mean that the Hohokam were immigrants? Perhaps. It is also possible that both points of view are correct. The early people, such as those who lived at the Houghton Road site, may have been local folk descended from the Archaic people. Later, Hohokam immigrants arrived on the scene, bringing with them interesting new concepts and things. Further study definitely is needed to clarify this issue.

The Pioneer Period

Some time around A.D. 400 to 500, red-slipped pottery was added to the technological repertoire, marking the initial phase of the Pioneer Period and the first usually labeled as Hohokam. In the Phoenix area, the earliest phase is called the Vahki phase, and in the Tucson area it is called the Tortolita phase. Regional differences began to emerge at this time. Vahki phase settlements along the Gila River were characterized by intensive agriculture supported by canal irrigation and by permanently occupied villages. Along the Salt River and in the Tucson area, agriculture was based on floodwater farming, villages appear to have been less densely settled, and there were differences in architecture.

Decorated pottery, a red-on-gray or red-on-brown ware painted with broad lines, began to be made during the late 600s. Phases defined for the Gila River area at Snaketown include Estrella and Sweetwater. Equivalent phases have not been defined for the Tucson Basin and other parts of southern Arizona. At this time, there continued to be similarities between the peoples of the Arizona desert and the western mountains of New Mexico in architecture, pottery, and other lifeways. Little is known of this period, however, as few sites have been excavated.

During the 700s, in the last phase of the Pioneer Period, the Snaketown phase, a new constellation of material traits appeared. A unique hatched decoration was used on the pottery, and for the first time pottery was distributed across a vast region. The distinctive characteristics we identify with the Hohokam Culture emerged. Trash mounds capped with adobe appeared, and the large houses of the Vahki phase no longer were constructed, suggesting a change in ceremonial organization and the beginning of the Hohokam ceremonial complex focused on elevated structures. By the end of the period, the ballcourt ritual complex would be established and large-scale irrigation systems developed. The characteristics that emerged at this time occurred long after the appearance of permanent villages, ceramic vessels, and intensive agriculture in the region, as we have seen. These changes have been used by archaeologists to hypothesize the arrival of a new people who brought with them these unprecedented traits.

The interesting possibility exists that the Gila River area was the "motherland" of the Hohokam Culture. Many of the traits we associate with the Hohokam first appeared in this area, perhaps because of the Gila River itself. A broad, shallow river that periodically floods a wide area beyond its banks, the Gila River could be easily tapped with canals, and farming in the floodplain was possible when the waters receded. The Salt and Santa Cruz Rivers provide greater challenges to irrigation. The Gila River alone could support intensive agriculture at this time, and this may have been the necessary spark for population growth and the development of arts and crafts.

Pioneer Period Lifeways

Shelters for protection against winter storms and torrid summer heat were built from the materials that were available. Building stone is rare in desert country. Riverbeds are filled with rounded boulders and cobbles that are unsuitable for building coursed masonry houses. Hohokam houses were therefore built of poles, brush, and mud. The house was set in a shallow depression in the ground, and the flat or dome-shaped roof was supported by posts placed around the inside perimeter of the pit. This style of architecture is called a "house-in-a-pit," although archaeologists usually refer to the houses simply as pit houses. Typically there was a single covered entryway in the center of one wall, with a step down onto the house floor. Shallow, basin-shaped firepits lined with clay provided light and heat inside the houses. Because of the hot desert climate, much daily activity took place outdoors in open-air work areas. Roofed, open-sided ramadas sheltered cooking fires and provided a shaded work space. Houses probably were used primarily in rainy and cold weather, and for storage. Inside they were dark and smoky, and they probably housed scorpions, spiders, and other unfriendly pests.

Rectangular or square houses grouped in a scattered, loosely organized fashion formed the Pioneer Period villages, most of which were relatively small. Some of the Vahki phase houses at Snaketown were large, suggesting either that they sheltered large family groups or, more likely, were used for communal ceremonial purposes. These houses may be unique to the Gila River region, however, as few of them have been found in the Tucson Basin.

The desert was more sparsely settled during the Pioneer Period than in later times. Recent work has suggested, however, that Pioneer Period settlements were distributed over a broad area. Sites dating to the Snaketown phase have been excavated along the lower Verde River, in the Tucson Basin, and elsewhere. The population may have been concentrated in the Phoenix Basin at this time, however. Despite its apparently small size, the population nevertheless supported canal irrigation, the production of finely crafted artifacts, and by the end of the period, a ceremonial complex focused on platform mounds.

Carved stone bowls, stone palettes, figurines, and shell jewelry are among the elaborate craft items that appeared in the Pioneer Period. Figurines are a particular hallmark of this period. Although the decorated designs were simple, the pottery was well made and was produced in a variety of forms.

The elaborate Hohokam death ritual was based on cremation, which was a complicated process that may have involved several different steps. The deceased was cremated in large open areas devoted solely to this purpose. The ashes and calcined bone fragments were then placed in pits or trenches. Offerings of crushed and burned pottery sometimes accompanied the remains. Because the amount of burned bone is so small in most

Hohokam cremations, and mixing of individuals of different ages and sexes occurs, it is possible that the remains of the deceased were divided in some way, either before or after cremation. A few inhumations, simple burials within earth graves, also have been found at some sites. The mortuary ritual was associated with an unusual artifact complex, including stone censers, stone palettes, and ceramic figurines representing humans and animals. These items appear to reflect a strong connection with Mexican cultures.

Colonies and Traders of the Colonial Period

The Colonial Period was a time of cultural florescence, exploration, and development that followed the Pioneer Period in the late 700s and continued until the latter part of the 900s. The elaboration of all aspects of Hohokam life, from household structure to ceremonial organization, that occurred during this period indicates that the Hohokam had mastered the desert. With a secure and abundant food supply, the Hohokam could turn to tasks of wider scope. Hohokam Culture spread throughout desert areas distant from the Phoenix heartland, and trade appears to have been one impetus for its spread.

Hohokam villages developed an increasingly patterned structure that appears to reflect household organization and higher levels of organization crosscutting domestic life. According to Richard Ciolek-Torrello, Hohokam households typically occupied two or more houses. These were a large house used for habitation (identified by the presence of a hearth for light, heat, and cooking) and one or more special-purpose structures. Often the latter were storage rooms, identified by the lack of a hearth and the presence of storage pits and vessels.

Groups of two to ten houses representing household units were clustered around a central open area or courtyard. Courtyard groups tended to maintain their integrity over time, although some houses might be abandoned and new ones built. The houses forming a courtyard group probably were occupied by extended families—groups of related families often comprising two more generations. It is plausible that residence rules dictated the structure of courtyard groups. In many cultures, these are unwritten rules suggesting with whom—the bride's parents or the groom's parents—a newly married couple will live after marriage. A courtyard group may have consisted of an older couple, their unmarried children, and their married children and families. Archaeologists estimate that about sixteen to twenty individuals lived in a courtyard group. Often each group had its own cemetery, trash disposal areas, and communal cooking facilities such as outdoor ovens (*hornos*).

Clusters of courtyard groups formed villages. The largest villages were composed of village segments or precincts formed by several courtyard groups. These precincts may represent large groups of people related by kinship. Villages often had a loosely concentric arrangement of these segments grouped around a central public area. Public structures such as platform mounds and ballcourts were built at the edge of this village arrangement. The stability of Hohokam villages and the importance of family ties in residential organization suggest that kinship was an integral part of Hohokam life and culture, and that kinship-group identity was reinforced by village organization.

Religious life also structured the Hohokam world. A unique ritual system based on a public ball game with sacred connotations first appeared in the initial phase of the Colonial Period, the Gila Butte phase. Hohokam ballcourts are large earthen structures of an elongated oval form. The courts have low, rounded walls, entries at each end, and usually stone markers at the ends and center. These structures were not roofed, and the embankments presumably were used by spectators. Ballcourts vary in size, and some villages had more than one. The massive court at Snaketown measures more than 16 feet in height and more than 197 feet in length and could have accommodated 500 people on its embankments! We can only guess about the function of the ball game and the rules by which it was played. Balls made from *guayule,* a natural rubberlike substance from plants native to Chihuahua, have been recovered at Hohokam sites, along with human figurines made from clay and thought to represent ball players.

Hohokam ballcourts probably represent a borrowing of the enclosure used throughout Mesoamerica for a similar ball game, with modifications for desert construction materials. Played by the Aztecs, the Maya, and many other Mesoamerican peoples, the ball game always had sacred connotations, although the players, the rules of the game, and the associated religious symbolism may have varied. The ball game probably was associated with a religious cult and also may have served as a method of adjudicating disputes and integrating the social classes.

That the ball game concept was brought to the Hohokam through a Mexican connection, either directly by migration or through simple information exchange, seems indisputable. That new forms of religious ideology and social structure were brought to the Hohokam along with the ball game seems likely, but we lack evidence to support this theory.

The mortuary ritual became even more elaborate at this time. The great care taken with the treatment of the dead reflects a deep concern with preparation for an afterlife. Cremations began to be buried at the locale of burning, although the removal of the remains for burial elsewhere also continued. The crematory areas appear to have been associated with village segments. Offerings placed with the deceased included ceramic and stone vessels, palettes, stone axes, and arrow points. These artifacts often were burned along with the remains of the deceased and were warped and sooted by the crematory fire. Perhaps also associated with the death ritual were buried caches of deliberately destroyed stone effigies, ceramic figurines, and other objects. The house of the deceased person also may have been burned as part of the death ritual.

Carved, ground, and flaked stone artifacts; shell jewelry; and figurines were most skillfully made and decorated at this time. Carved stone bowls were fashioned in the shape of frogs, horned toads, and snakes. Marine shell from the Gulf of California was worked into elaborate ornaments—including bracelets and effigy pendants carved with birds, frogs, and snakes—beads, and pieces covered with turquoise mosaic. Shell also was intricately etched and painted. Craft specialization existed at the household and village level. Entire villages apparently specialized in making shell jewelry. At these manufacturing villages, such as the site of Shelltown northwest of Tucson, shell dust, other waste products, and unfinished ornaments indicate that the Hohokam did not simply import the finished shell jewelry.

Ceramic design was at its peak of artistry during the second phase of the Colonial Period, the Santa Cruz phase, with great attention paid to detail and linework. Hohokam pottery was made using a technique called paddle and anvil. Decorated pottery was painted with red designs on a

Hohokam stone palettes from the Colonial and Sedentary Periods.

buff-colored background—the "red-on-buff" pottery that Gladwin first traced in search of the Hohokam. The designs typically are composed of small, repeated elements forming spiral or circular bands of decoration. Many human and animal figures were used in these designs. Quail, herons, snakes, turtles, fish, lizards, scorpions, bugs, dancing figures, burden carriers, and flute players march en masse, appearing to move across the surface of the pot. Other designs are formed solely of geometric elements. Scoops, graceful bowls with flared rims, and globular jars with narrow necks were common forms. More exotic forms included human

Hohokam ceramic effigy vessels from the Sedentary Period.

and animal effigy vessels, thick-walled censers, rectangular bowls, and tripod plates.

Hohokam settlement intensified in the lands far beyond the Gila and Salt River Basins during the Colonial Period. Exchange may have been a driving force in this expansion. The Hohokam were energetic entrepreneurs and traders as well as craftspeople, procuring the necessary materials, producing the finished goods, and distributing the products widely. The Hohokam distributed shell jewelry to other people throughout Arizona. Red argillite was obtained from the Verde Valley and was fashioned into pendants and other ornaments. The Hohokam also were involved in distributing the copper bells and macaws that came into Arizona from Mexico.

The occurrence of Hohokam artifacts and ballcourts in areas far removed from the Phoenix Basin has been viewed either as migration or the incorporation of a wide region under Hohokam influence and control. In some cases, simple exchange rather than migration can account for the distribution of Hohokam artifacts, and it is clear that the magnitude of exchange was substantial. In other cases it appears that Hohokam settlements were established in areas where desirable resources were available, such as the argillite and salt of the middle Verde Valley. The Hohokam ritual system served to anchor, maintain, and control the long-distance exchange system. Ballcourts and cremations have been found at many non-Hohokam settlements in Arizona, including Wupatki near Flagstaff and Point of Pines in the mountains of east central Arizona. It may be that public ceremonies were associated with trading activity.

Hohokam settlements also were established in the lower Verde Valley, the Tonto Basin, and other areas lacking the sort of desirable resources Hohokam traders might seek. Along the lower Verde River, for example, numerous villages with ballcourts were built in the Horseshoe and Bartlett Lake areas. These regions probably witnessed something more like actual migration or colonization, in which Hohokam people moved in, bringing with them their entire complex of lifeways. In some of these regions, ballcourts are present, but other areas lack them. No ballcourts have been found so far in the Tonto Basin, for example.

Probably there were many different ways in which elements of the Hohokam lifestyle became broadly distributed. Whatever the relationships, it appears that the ballcourt occasion—be it game, dance, or simple social gathering—was a semisacred activity that helped to integrate Hohokam communities, cement ties with communities in other areas, and intensify Hohokam relationships with peoples living to the south in Mexico.

All of these developments of the Colonial Period—the territorial expansion, social development, and artistry—were supported by extension and development of the agricultural system. Irrigation canals were lengthened and deepened to reduce evaporation and bring more land under cultivation. The productivity of food plants probably increased, and less-productive land was made more efficient.

Times of Peace and Stability in the Sedentary Period

The Sedentary Period, between 975 and about 1150, consists of a single phase, named the Sacaton phase in the Phoenix area and the Rincon phase in the Tucson area. This was a time of consolidation and growth. It also was a favorable time for farming, with abundant rainfall at the appropriate seasons. In the Tucson and Tonto Basins, numerous new settlements were founded on the bajadas and along the secondary watercourses away from the major rivers in areas that previously would have been difficult to farm. New settlements were established as far away as the Flagstaff area, as we discuss in more detail in chapter 8. It also was a time of population movement. Some areas were depopulated, perhaps because their residents relocated to the Phoenix or Tucson areas.

As might be expected in a situation of population growth and movement, villages increased in size. In the Tucson Basin, large, permanently occupied villages were located along major watercourses. Smaller, seasonally occupied encampments were situated in a variety of environmental settings and included farmsteads and camps for gathering resources such as cactus and mesquite. William Doelle points out that in some areas site density is so high that it suggests almost continuous occupation along rivers and secondary streams.

Public religious rituals became increasingly important during this period. Ballcourts increased dramatically in number. Ballcourt locations shifted along with the changing location of Hohokam villages in the Tucson area; new courts were built as others were abandoned. Platform mounds became still more formalized in construction and location.

Let's take a closer look at platform mounds. They are artificial elevated areas formed by building up a fill of earth, trash, or rubble and then facing and flooring the surface of the structure with caliche plaster. In appearance like a truncated cone with a flat top, platform mounds apparently served as stagelike areas for performing ceremonies. That this custom was borrowed from Mexican peoples seems certain.

It was during the Sedentary Period that completely artificial, deliberately constructed mounds for religious purposes first began to be built. Many platform mounds dating to this time show evidence of repair and remodeling. Mound 16 at Snaketown, for example, was remodeled eight different times. Wooden palisades built around mounds isolated these structures from mundane activities and symbolized their ritual function.

There is evidence for other kinds of public construction during this period as well. Some sites display centrally located plazas with prepared

Hohokam dancers on a red-on-buff pottery bowl from the Sedentary Period.

caliche floors that may have served as dance areas. In the Gila Bend area, a possible specialized ceremonial center has been identified that contained few residential houses and unusually rich cremations.

At this time the common cremation practice was to bury the ashes of the deceased in a funerary urn, typically a red-on-buff jar, and to cover the urn with an inverted bowl. Additional vessels and other offerings might accompany the urn. All of these items were placed in a pit excavated in the ground. House clusters typically had formal cemetery areas, but at some villages cremations were scattered among the houses.

Changes in pottery that took place at this time include the appearance of jars with extremely sharp shoulders, marking the point where the potter joined the flat piece of clay that formed the base to the thick coils that formed the sides. Ceramic art appears to decline from its high point during the Colonial Period. Pottery was, however, produced in great quantities, suggesting there was mass production by artisans rather than artists. Potters in the Tucson area, however, were experimenting with different

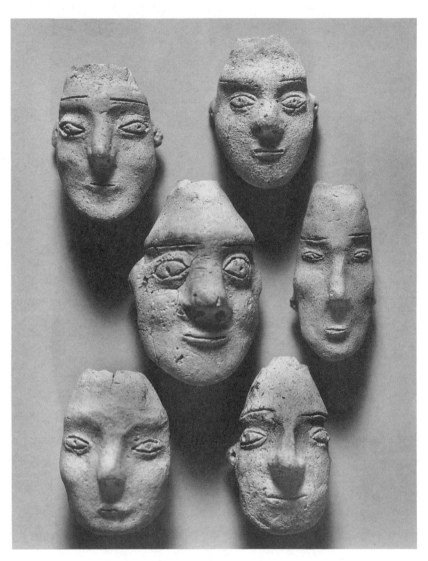

Hohokam ceramic figurines from the Sedentary Period.

color combinations and unique designs. Polychrome pottery, a pleasing combination painted with black designs on white and red, was developed at this time and is perhaps the earliest polychrome to be produced in the Southwest. Polished red ware also was made. At the West Branch site near Tucson, archaeologists have found evidence for the manufacture of poly-chrome and red ware pottery. Excavated houses produced tools and mate-rials for making pottery, including caches of stone anvils, highly polished and faceted stones that were used to smooth and polish pottery, balls of prepared red pigment used to color the red ware, and pottery vessels filled with the iron mineral crystals that were ground for paint. During investi-gations at this site directed by Stephanie Whittlesey, we discovered a prob-able reason for the emphasis on pottery manufacture at this village: it was located less than a quarter-mile from a large deposit of the best clay for making pottery that has yet been identified in the area.

Elsewhere in Hohokam country, other crafts were elaborated. New tech-niques for decorating shell jewelry were invented, more elaborate mosaic mirrors were produced, and copper bells were imported from Mexico.

Agricultural techniques and productivity were stable during the Seden-tary Period. Emil Haury suggested that the great size of storage jars at this time indicates greater agricultural productivity and a food surplus. Throughout the Southwest this was a time of good climate and plenty.

The Winds of Change in the Classic Period

Sometime late in the Sedentary Period, the seeds of change on a revolu-tionary scale were sown and the Hohokam Culture was altered irrevoca-bly. The Classic Period began sometime between 1150 and 1200 and intro-duced sweeping alterations in the fabric of Hohokam life. Whether the changes that took place can be attributed to the collapse of the culture, the migration of a different people into the Hohokam area, or a reorganiza-tion of lifeways remains one of the most burning issues of Hohokam pre-history and one of the most difficult to resolve.

Archaeologists divide the Classic Period into two phases, called the Soho and Civano phases in the Phoenix area and the Tanque Verde and Tucson phases in the Tucson Basin. The dramatic changes of this time are easiest to see in architecture, pottery, and funeral customs. Beginning at the end of the Sedentary Period, the Hohokam began to experiment with adobe construction and above-ground architecture. Some pit houses were built with walls of adobe, either solid or reinforced by wooden posts. Other structures were built on the ground surface, with walls of solid adobe or adobe reinforced by posts or cobbles. Later, most adobe structures were rectangular solid-adobe houses built on the ground surface. Simple rectangular doorways rather than covered entryways provided access.

An increasingly common practice during the Classic Period was the enclosing of houses within a wall to form a compound like those at Los Muertos. A thick adobe wall was built in a rectangle to surround several adobe houses. Often houses were built against the compound wall, and occasionally compounds were divided into one or more plaza areas by additional interior walls. Each compound probably housed one or more extended families.

At some villages, multistoried great houses—essentially apartment houses of adobe laid in blocks and courses—were built. One great house, roofed to prevent further deterioration, can be visited today at Casa Grande National Monument. It may have functioned as a type of astronomical observatory whose architectural features may have aligned with celestial events.

Although cremation burial continued, with the remains commonly placed in funerary urns, the number of inhumations increased greatly, particularly in the Phoenix Basin. The deceased was laid out in an extended position with the arms at the sides and the legs straight. Some graves were covered with roofs built much like those of dwelling rooms.

The production of red-on-buff pottery declined in the Phoenix area, and by the Civano phase it had almost completely disappeared. In the Tucson area, however, decorated pottery production increased. New designs completely unlike those of the previous periods were used. The flowing, curvilinear decoration and life forms of the Colonial and Sedentary Periods were replaced by linear designs emphasizing triangles and rectilinear scrolls. Many of these designs were repeated again and again on different vessels, suggesting the kind of standardization that might be expected if only a few villages were producing the pottery. In the Phoenix Basin, different kinds of pottery appeared, including polished, smudged red wares, and in the Civano phase beautifully decorated red, white, and

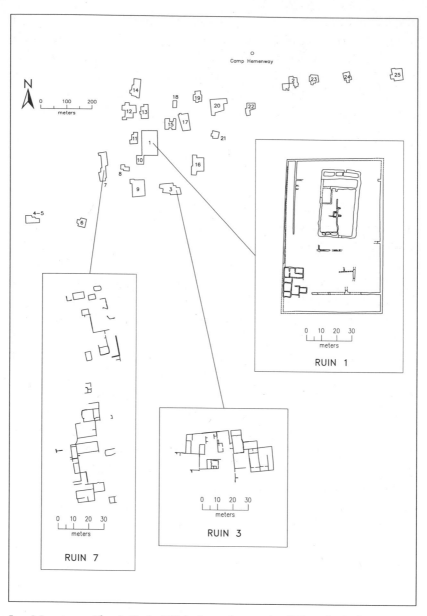

Los Muertos, a Classic Period Hohokam site south of Phoenix. Enlargements show details of compounds that form the site.

Casa Grande, one of the Classic Period Hohokam great houses. This photograph shows Casa Grande as it was in about 1902.

black polychrome pottery. The polychrome pottery also occurs in the Tucson area, but red ware pottery is rare. Vessel forms also changed, with the unique shapes of previous times being replaced by more utilitarian forms. The ornate craft items of the preceding periods—such as censers, shellwork, slate palettes, and elaborately carved stone bowls—became much simplified or disappeared entirely.

Less obvious but no less important changes took place in religious and social organization, and in the distribution of villages across the landscape. In all areas but Phoenix, ballcourts ceased to be constructed during the Classic Period, and platform mounds became the most important focus of Hohokam public ceremony. The construction of platform mounds also changed at this time. Instead of the truncated cones of earlier times, Classic Period mounds were rectangular in shape and resembled a flat-topped pyramid. Unlike earlier mounds, which were relatively solid on the interior, Classic Period mounds also contained interior retaining walls that resemble rubble-filled rooms to provide solidity and security for the construction. Some mounds also have rooms built on the top. The mound was enclosed within a massive rectangular compound wall of adobe or cobble masonry.

Platform mounds built during the Sedentary Period and the early Classic Period appear to have nonresidential functions. Even though some mounds were topped by pit houses or adobe-walled rooms, they apparently served functions other than as dwellings.

The area enclosed by the compound wall appears to have been formally structured for specific purposes. There is a ground area that could hold the audience for viewing ceremonies and a private area with restricted access. The walls and ground-floor rooms of the walls restricted the flow of traffic so that a counterclockwise circuit was required to gain access to the top of the mound. These patterns in architecture and the absence of dwelling rooms on most platform mounds suggest to Jerry Howard that the platform mounds were uninhabited ceremonial precincts.

Like irrigation canals, platform mounds required considerable human labor to build. The platform mound at the site of Escalante, near Florence, measured 118 by 79 feet and was about 10 feet high, for a total of nearly 2,500 cubic yards of fill. Because the Hohokam lacked useful dirt-moving metal equipment such as the shovel and wheelbarrow, all dirt was moved by hand with wooden tools and baskets.

Mounds were located with great regularity within compounds and with respect to ballcourts when these were present, suggesting uniform, perhaps inflexible, ideological symbolism. Platform mounds are regularly spaced along the desert drainages about three miles apart, and each one marks a Classic Period community.

During the late Classic Period, there is evidence for a new type of construction. The late platform mounds were surrounded by massive rectangular retaining walls that held a fill of trash and earth, the whole construction topped with plaster. At the same time there is evidence that people began living atop the mounds for the first time.

Who built the mounds and why? David Gregory argues that the political authority required to direct and organize mound construction probably also derived in large part from religious authority. It is possible that the highest-ranking Hohokam social group may have been symbolized and legitimized by residence on the mound itself, although there is little evidence to suggest that this happened. A platform mound of the type with retaining walls, once topped by structures, can be visited at Pueblo Grande. Under the direction of Todd Bostwick, Pueblo Grande is a National Landmark, a municipal park of the city of Phoenix, and a museum. This large site included several ballcourts and numerous houses along with the platform mound.

Another change evident during the Classic Period was a dramatic reduction in the dispersion of Hohokam people across the landscape. Many areas that had been populated heavily were abandoned, and the people clustered into a few large villages. Settlement location also changed; only rarely do Classic Period villages overlie earlier Sedentary Period villages. Most striking is the expansion of communities that previously had been small or nonexistent. This is most visible in the northern Tucson Basin near the town of Marana. There, a new community was forged between about 1100 and 1350 that encompassed earlier settlement clusters.

The Marana community incorporated multiple sites and environmental zones extending from the valley floor to the flanks of mountains. A central platform mound site, smaller compound sites, sites lacking compounds, large agricultural fields, and specialized activity locales form this large and highly differentiated community. Archaeologists Paul Fish and Suzanne Fish speculate that this community may be linked to increasing reliance upon, and perhaps specialized production of, agave. Huge complexes of agricultural features were found on the bajada slopes. Rock piles, cobble alignments, check dams, and enormous roasting pits where the agave hearts were baked cover more than two square miles. Knives used to harvest and trim the plants and abundant charred agave remains from the roasting pits leave little doubt that these fields were used for the cultivation of agave plants. The rocks helped to hold in moisture and protect the young plants from predators.

The Marana community was an extraordinarily short-lived phenomenon, emerging, flowering, and being abandoned wholly during the Tanque Verde phase. By the Tucson phase, only a handful of small sites were still occupied. Settlement may have shifted northward at this time and may have been associated with intensified agave exploitation.

Yet another change at this time that may have implications for some of these theories is the appearance of walled sites or *trincheras* (Spanish for "terraces") during the Classic Period. These walled masonry terraces found on the steeper foothill slopes served several purposes. Christian Downum has determined that some terraces were the foundations of houses and that others formed hillside garden plots. Long, high walls girdling steep slopes, on the other hand, strongly suggest a defensive purpose. These *cerros de trincheras*—terraced hills—are distributed widely in the Tucson area and the Papaguería but are most abundant in northern Sonora along the Altar and Magdalena Rivers. Although debate continues over whether the Trincheras Culture was a distinct and individual phenomenon or simply a variant of the Hohokam Culture, the differences in material culture, economy, and social organization are sufficient to suggest that the Trincheras people were distinct from the Hohokam. If so, the presence of walled defensive settlements in Hohokam territory may indicate the spread of a non-Hohokam people and resulting conflict.

Who or what was responsible for the dramatic changes in Hohokam Culture during the Classic Period? The first theory was the simplest and perhaps the most satisfying. In 1934 Haury hypothesized that the changes were the result of a migration of a pueblo people, the Salado, who left their homeland in the Tonto Basin to establish villages in the southern deserts. The Salado brought their own traditions of building pueblo villages, inhumating rather than cremating the dead, and making red ware and polychrome pottery. Haury theorized peaceful coexistence between the Hohokam and the Salado (see chapter 9). A variation on the theme of migrating people was suggested by Charles Di Peso, who believed that the Classic Period represents the successful overthrow of the immigrant Hohokam and the subsequent dominance of the local people, the Ootam.

These ideas are opposed by newer but not necessarily more accurate views. Some archaeologists do not believe any migration took place. Instead they view the Classic Period changes as a local phenomenon, the culmination of a long period of development and gradual change within Hohokam Culture.

Bioarchaeologist Christy Turner offers interesting evidence relevant to this issue. His analysis of the characteristics of teeth from pre-Classic and Classic Period people demonstrates two important things. First, the pre-Classic Hohokam were unlike any other prehistoric southwestern population that Turner has studied, supporting the notion of a Hohokam migration from Mexico. Second, the Classic Period people are much more similar to Mogollon populations than to any other group. A migration theory certainly is supported by Turner's data.

Most archaeologists agree that the Hohokam Culture collapsed at the end of the Sedentary Period and that the Classic Period represents a reorganization of culture and lifeways in the wake of this collapse. What caused the collapse remains an enigma. Environmental change, changes in trade and political alliance networks, and population intrusions have been suggested. The unexplained phenomena of the Classic Period underscore the pressing need for research before the evidence is buried or destroyed by modern development.

The Transition to History

Long before the Spanish *conquistadores* set foot in southern Arizona, the Hohokam Culture had vanished. We have yet to solve the puzzle surrounding the disappearance of the Hohokam. The numerous large villages of the Classic Period began to be abandoned in the late 1300s, and there is a distressing gap in the evidence between the latest Hohokam settlements and the first Spanish chronicles that documented the occupation of the desert by Piman peoples.

The abandonment of the Arizona deserts was part of the widespread changes that took place throughout the Southwest at this time. Population generally shifted and realigned in many areas during the late 1300s and early 1400s. The mountain zone of central Arizona was abandoned, and the villages of the Colorado Plateau were relocated as the population coalesced into what are now the modern towns of Hopi and Zuni. Such changes may have affected the Hohokam indirectly, forcing them to relocate in the face of demographic pressure from the north. The possibility of conflict as a result or cause of these widespread changes has been suggested by archaeologists, and there is some evidence to support this notion, such as the establishment of trincheras.

There also may have been conflict and turmoil within Hohokam society itself, whether as a product of regional social and demographic conflict or independent of such problems. At some sites archaeologists have found evidence indicating that the latest phase of occupation, called the Polvorón phase in the Phoenix area, represented a collapse of the platform mound system and a return to much simpler lifeways. Before the villages were completely abandoned, the people stopped erecting platform mounds and building adobe houses, and returned to simple pit houses. In addition, a much less complex economy and social organization than in previous times is indicated.

Climatic deterioration and drought have been suggested as causes of this change. The late archaeologist and dendroclimatologist Donald Graybill reconstructed from the tree-ring evidence clear support for disastrous floods in the early A.D. 1380s. Hohokam villages and irrigation systems may have been destroyed, and it simply may have been too difficult for the Hohokam to regroup and prosper after such a disaster.

Another possible cause for abandonment is the salinization of agricultural fields from centuries of irrigation with the mineral-laden desert water. The presence of a salt-tolerant wild barley in some late Hohokam sites suggests that this may indeed have happened. At present there is no evidence to suggest that disease epidemics or natural catastrophes were responsible for the Hohokam disappearance, and it may be possible that archaeologists simply have not recognized the latest Hohokam settlements. Locating such sites is made most difficult because archaeological dating techniques do not work well for sites that were occupied between A.D. 1400 and the present.

Some archaeologists support the theory that the desert was not abandoned at all but that, instead, the modern Piman peoples actually are descendants of the Hohokam who adopted a simpler style of life following the collapse of their culture. There are some parallels between the economy and material culture of the modern and ancient desert dwellers. Their houses are similar in construction, and the modern people made red-on-buff and red-on-brown pottery with materials much like the Hohokam used and with the same manufacturing techniques. Like the Hohokam, the Pimans living near the rivers built irrigation canals to water their fields, and the desert-dwelling people relied on rainfall and floodwater farming. Village organization also may have been similar. The Native Americans now living in the desert do not, however, construct ballcourts or platform mounds, nor do they have elaborate arts and crafts like the Hohokam.

To what degree the similarities between prehistoric and historical cultures are the product of a shared ancestry or represent a common adaptation to the Sonoran Desert by unrelated peoples has yet to be demonstrated. As with the question of abandonment, we cannot say with certainty that there is a relationship between the modern Native Americans of southern Arizona and the Hohokam, because of the lack of archaeological evidence. Arguing against the theory that the Piman peoples are the descendants of the Hohokam is the fact that all upper Pimans, whether living in Mexico or Arizona, speak dialects of the same language that all can understand to some degree. If the Pima are descended from the Hohokam, we might expect that more distinct language dialects would have developed through time. The linguistic evidence suggests that the Pima arrived rather late and spread out to fill what was virtually uninhabited territory. Christy Turner's research on the physical characteristics of teeth indicates that the Hohokam were not similar to the Pimans.

Whatever its cause, the time after 1400 was filled with unrest, population movement, and possible turmoil. This period ended with the discovery of the New World. The accounts of the earliest Spanish explorers do little to clarify the fate of the Hohokam. When Francisco Vásquez de Coronado arrived in northern New Spain in 1540, he found the river valleys of Sonora populated heavily by industrious agricultural people. Farther north, Coronado's army encountered a poorer people who lived on wild desert products such as agave and cactus fruits. At the edge of the populated area they found a nomadic people who lived by hunting and in impermanent *rancherías*. Here the Spanish soldiers of fortune camped at sites already lying in ruin. Finally, they crossed a *despoblado,* or depopulated area, before reaching Zuni.

The Native Americans Coronado met in Arizona may have been Upper Piman people. The Jesuit padres in the late 1600s and 1700s described the people living along the San Pedro, Gila, and Santa Cruz Rivers as industrious and skilled farmers who readily adopted Spanish wheat, cattle, and horses. The skills of the nineteenth-century Piman farmers were legendary. Pima wheat and produce fed the U.S. military and their horses, the Butterfield Overland Stage horses and drivers, and the forty-niners on their way to the California goldfields. Not long after, the Salt River would be dammed and the water diverted to Anglo fields in Phoenix, leaving Pima corn to wither.

We leave the solving of these puzzles and the answering of these questions to other archaeologists, who join with Native Americans as they develop their own archaeological programs in forging an understanding of their past. We have come a long way indeed from our sketchy understanding of the forgotten people when their story first began to unfold. Harold Gladwin and Emil Haury no longer are with us, and Gila Pueblo now houses a community college. New voices are heard, and new tales will continue to be told. Some stories, it seems, are simply too good to end.

5 THE PATAYAN

From Gila Bend and Ajo westward to California and from Yuma northeast to the Grand Canyon lies a vast region that was the home of the Patayan people. Much of this land is sere and forbidding desert, and a tiny fraction is a rich country, a linear oasis and a delta where crops sow themselves. And a river runs through it all, the great Colorado.

The Patayan Culture is, archaeologically speaking, one of the most poorly known prehistoric cultures of the Southwest. There are many reasons why this is so, not the least of which is the harsh and hostile nature of the desert itself. No intensive archaeological research has been carried out, and there has been little excavation of Patayan sites. As a result, we look to the historical Yuman peoples who occupied the land and who are the probable descendants of the Patayan for models to understand how the prehistoric people adapted to their environment, wrested a living from the desert, and transformed the desert surface into a living representation of their cosmology and beliefs.

Land and People

Patayan country consists of two distinct regions linked by the river that flows through them. The lowland region borders the lower Colorado River and the surrounding desert. From the Gila River's juncture with the Colorado near Yuma, Arizona, the desert along the Gila eastward to Gila Bend also was Patayan territory. Today this country is the home of the River and Delta Yumans. The upland region consists of the canyon-cut plateaus of the upper Colorado River, occupied in historical times by the Upland Yumans.

The river is the lifeblood of this land. The Colorado River originates in the Rocky Mountains far from the Arizona desert and flows some 1,700 miles before reaching the Gulf of California. This was not a placid, peaceful river. Before it was tamed by dam construction, the Colorado was notorious for raging floods, peaking in the spring from snowmelt hundreds of miles away.

A vigorous "Arizona Fleet" once navigated the Colorado River. Beginning in 1852, steamboats plied the river to bring supplies to the army troops stationed at Fort Yuma and Fort Mojave, and to miners in the goldfields of California and Arizona. Steamboats such as the *Cocopah* and the *Uncle Sam* burned huge quantities of wood to overcome the stiff river current. The fleet continued as the main supply network until the coming of the railroad in 1877.

The area called the lowland country is just that. The Colorado River delta dips to a low point of less than a hundred feet above sea level at the present international border. At this large delta at the mouth of the "Nile of Arizona," the river disintegrates into a maze of shallow braided channels hidden by dense vegetation. The floodplain of the Gila and Colorado Rivers and the Colorado delta are rich and green with dense vegetation. Honey mesquite, ironwood, and cottonwoods grow thickly; bulrush, arrow-weed, and cattail line the marshy pools. The river once teemed with fish, most of which were big enough to take with hook and line.

Away from the river, the desert landscape is lunar and surreal. Stark mountain ranges separate basins forming sandy plains, and sand dunes stretch seemingly endlessly. The unique volcanic fields of the Sierra Pinacate lie between the Gulf of California and the Arizona border, and these forbidding mountains are isolated by a ring of barren dunes. Julian Hayden wrote of this land that "in complete silence and isolation, it was like what walking on the moon must be."

Much of this desert land is covered with a layer of pebbles, called "desert pavement." The pavement is coated with "desert varnish," a dark deposit of microbial origin that develops under desert conditions of highly alkaline soils, little rainfall, and dust storms. Supposedly taking thousands of years to form, desert varnish is a controversial factor in dating prehistoric sites in the desert, as noted in the discussion of the Malpais people in chapter 2.

The lowland Colorado region is the hottest and driest part of the Sonoran desertscrub landscape. Water is scarce, and even the sparse and stunted plants must compete for it. The desert pavement is almost devoid of perennial plant life, supporting only a wispy growth of annuals. Big galleta grass is the main stabilizer of desert sand dunes, upon which little else grows. Elsewhere, plants may arrange themselves along small runnels and washes where water can be found, forming lines of green mesquite and ironwood in the otherwise brown desert landscape. Thousands of acres are covered only with creosote, bursage, and saltbush. Creosote, known scientifically as *Larrea tridentata,* has an incredible ability to reproduce itself from shoots and roots, often forming an enormous clump that genetically is a single plant. Gary Nabhan reports that one of the largest of these, near Old Woman Springs in California, is seventy-two feet in diameter and is older than the most ancient bristlecone pine.

The desert's denizens manage to thrive—reptiles are adapted uniquely to sand, and the desert bighorn sheep and Sonoran pronghorn have accommodated to the rugged mountains and sandy plains. The Yuman peoples sang hunting songs for the sheep and named constellations of stars after them, and piles of mountain sheep horns and bones in the desert attest to the rituals that were involved in hunting. Today the desert foothills have been colonized by burros that impact desert vegetation and landscape, and can disturb fragile archaeological sites.

The upland portions of the Patayan homeland are more diverse than the lowlands. This broad area includes several different ecological zones, and plants and wildlife are varied. The grasslands dotted with yucca and cactus give way to pinyon and juniper in the higher ranges that crosscut the area. The Colorado River and its tributaries have cut steep-walled canyons into the plateau country, which rises to elevations of more than 8,000 feet. The lower-elevation areas support chaparral and grasslands. Thick mesquite stands thrive in the desert washes. Game is abundant in all of these zones, and the plateaus in particular teem with deer, antelope, and mountain sheep.

The people who lived in this region in historical times are known to anthropologists as Yumans. There are several language subgroups that correspond to major cultural units. Three of these groups—the River, Delta, and Upland Yumans—lived in Arizona. The Delta Yumans, which include the Cocopah, are the southernmost of the groups. The River Yumans include the Quechan (also simply called Yuman), the Mohave, and the Maricopa of the middle Gila River. The language, culture, and lifestyles of the River and Delta Yumans are similar and form one large group, the Lowland Yumans, who can be contrasted with the Upland Yumans, or Pai speakers. The latter are the Hualapai, Havasupai, and Yavapai of central and northwestern Arizona. The two broad Yuman groups parallel the lowland and upland environmental divisions.

The Lowland Yumans are an amalgam of agricultural peoples who focused their lives on the lower Colorado and Gila Rivers. Their history is difficult to understand, for these tribes perpetually warred, forming alliances and shifting their homes in the wake of conflict. By the middle of the nineteenth century, the numerous lowland tribes had been reduced to three, the Quechan, Mohave, and Cocopah. The Maricopa once dwelled along the lower Colorado River, but some time after 1700 they allied themselves with Akimel O'odham living on the middle Gila River. By the mid-1800s, remnants of several other groups had fled the hostilities of the lower Colorado to join the Maricopa. Even there, among new allies, the battles did not cease. In 1857 a group of Quechan and Mohave Indians trekked more than 160 miles across the desert to the Gila River. There, aided by Yavapai and Western Apaches, the Yumans attacked the Maricopas and Pimas living near Pima Butte. The Yuman warriors were all but annihilated in the fight. Anthropologists Clifton Kroeber and Bernard Fontana refer to this massacre as the last major battle between Native Americans.

The Lowland Yumans were united by their dependence on the Colorado River. Although there were occasional crop failures, the rich, silt-laden fields that emerged when the floodwaters receded each year produced a predictable and substantial supply of food. Corn, wheat, squash, beans, and panicgrass were sown in the delta mudflat fields. After spring floods, native fish such as the Colorado squawfish and the Gila chub would become trapped in pools cut off from the main river and were easy to catch with nets, traps, and scoops. Waterfowl also were abundant along the river. Mesquite and cattails were staple foods, especially in the colder months. In their adopted country the Maricopa based their livelihood on the same riverine agriculture as their allies the Akimel O'odham, harvesting abundant crops of corn and wheat.

Three groups of Upland Yumans occupied the high, arid plateau south of the Colorado River. The Havasupai inhabit a wonderful isolated world in their reservation in Cataract Canyon, a lush but inaccessible side canyon of the Grand Canyon. The Hualapai and Yavapai once ranged over a huge tract of land to the southwest and southeast of the river. Although all speak a similar language, the Hualapai and Havasupai were always on friendly terms and allied together against their common enemy, the Yavapai. The Upland Yumans did some farming, but their highly mobile lifestyle was not conducive to it. They followed the seasons, camping to gather and roast agave during the spring, collect cactus fruit in the summer, and reap pinyon nuts in the fall. Their winter encampments were larger and more permanent than their summer camps, which consisted of easily built, dome-shaped brush shelters. They also occupied rockshelters wherever they occurred.

Upland and Lowland Yumans alike practiced a fluid and exceedingly adaptable lifestyle, living in dispersed rancherías and moving as needed to supply their families with food and shelter. They are still renowned for their basketry, although as one would expect because of their lifestyle, the Yumans did not excel at making pottery. The Maricopa were an exception. Their lustrous, highly polished black-on-red pottery is prized by Native Americans and Anglo Americans alike.

Today the Yuman tribes occupy a fraction of their former home territory. The Havasupai are permanently entitled to use 95,000 acres of Grand Canyon National Park set aside for this purpose in addition to their canyon reservation. The Hualapai, once unhappily interned on the Colorado River Indian Reservation, now live on a tract of land around the town of Peach Springs. The Yavapai live in four reservation communities, those of Middle Verde, Clarkdale, and Fort McDowell along the Verde River, and the Prescott reservation. The Mohave occupy two reservations, one near Needles, California (Fort Mohave), and the other—the Colorado River Indian Reservation—near La Paz. Maricopa communities were chartered as separate districts of the Gila River and Salt River Reservations near Phoenix. The Quechan occupy the Fort Yuma Reservation along the All-American Canal, and the Cocopah live on two small plots of land south of Yuma.

Discovering the Patayan

In many ways the desert is responsible for our poor understanding of Patayan history and lifeways. Most of Patayan country is a stark and barren desert that is a most unattractive region for archaeological study and that demands incredible stamina of those few who choose to work there. Much of the research carried out here was conducted many years ago when travel was time-consuming and difficult, and vehicles were less dependable than today. Archaeologists faced hardships of heat, thirst, and exhaustion. Moreover, the region is as hard on archaeological sites as it is on archaeologists. The riverine sites are subject to frequent and disastrous flooding. Most sites are confined to the surface and lack the deep deposits of trash, houses, and other features that are common below the surface in Hohokam sites. This lack of depth and features makes it difficult to date sites and to determine the purposes for which they were used in the past. Further, the desert itself is fragile, easily damaged by vehicular, animal, and human travel. As Julian Hayden writes, once the archaeological pattern has been broken, it is impossible to reconstitute it.

These facts of Patayan archaeology make the accomplishments of two archaeologists, to whom we owe virtually all of our understanding of this culture, seem even more remarkable. These are Malcolm Rogers and Julian Hayden, who possessed the intense interest, dedication, and physical endurance to conduct pioneering archaeological studies in the bleak and uncompromising desert. Their discoveries are all the more remarkable because, unlike many archaeological pioneers, both lacked the financial backing and resources of private archaeological foundations. They were independent scholars, working unaided.

Malcolm Rogers, Patayan Pioneer

The Patayan Culture was explored and defined initially by Malcolm Rogers. Rogers was educated in mining chemistry and geology, not archaeology. Although he had been interested in archaeology as a boy, it was not until he returned to San Diego after World War I to raise avocados on a ranch with his father that Rogers began to study archaeology. While exploring the nearby mesas and terraces, he came across numerous scatters of stone tools, spurring him to further investigations.

The abundance of scraping tools among the stone artifacts of the San Diego area led Rogers to define what he called a "scraper-maker culture" there. This in turn led him to expand his studies into the Coastal Range of southern California and the Patayan country of southwestern Arizona, locating trails, shrines, and rockshelters, and eventually covering large tracts of land. Hayden writes of him: "With what now seems almost incredible stamina and endurance, Rogers walked literally hundreds of miles of prehistoric trails and logged hundreds of sites in his field book and site maps, at all seasons of the year." Because the sites lacked vertical stratigraphy, Rogers developed what he called "trail stratigraphy," a method that was both ingenious and simple. Consider a prehistoric trail along which travelers dropped and broke pottery vessels, resulting in a mixture of sherds of pottery types A and B. If mixed together, it is not possible to determine whether type A or B is the older. If, however, one segment of the trail is intersected by an arroyo, it may be possible to make such a determination. Imagine that a new trail branches from the original segment cut by the arroyo and on it is found only type B pottery. The trail segment abandoned because of the arroyo cut bears only type A. Type A must therefore be the older of the two pottery types. Using trail stratigraphy and the much rarer stratified cave and site deposits, Rogers worked out a sequence of change in pottery vessel shapes, designs, and temper materials that resulted in a three-part cultural sequence: Yuman I, II, and III.

Rogers published his first papers in the late 1920s. He was associated briefly with the Arizona Museum and then joined the Museum of Man in San Diego in 1928. While there, he continued his investigations of the desert Patayan into the 1940s.

In 1939 Rogers published the report of his survey work in California and Arizona, which focused on the early stone tool cultures that preceded the ceramic-producing people. He proposed the first Patayan chronology in 1945, basing it primarily on ceramic traits. Rogers' classification distinguished between the upland and lowland cultures of the Colorado River region. A later report contained the first professional discussion of the great rock figures of the Colorado desert, the intaglios. These are enormous human and animal figures created by scraping away the desert pavement.

Rogers left the San Diego Museum of Man in 1945, ending his fieldwork in the western deserts. He went on to explore the early stone tool cultures of the Tucson area, however, and began to synthesize his research.

According to Hayden, by the beginning of World War II Rogers had written his synthesis of the early stone-tool-making cultures of the desert and also his final report on Yuman ceramics. Both reports were destroyed during the war after Rogers had retired to his ranch, and no second copies existed. Rogers' untimely death in a car accident in 1960 precluded any possibility that his work could be reconstructed. We can only speculate how different the record of Patayan prehistory would be if Rogers had been able to publish his syntheses.

When Rogers died, Hayden carried his ashes into the Sierra Pinacate and scattered them on the desert land that meant so much to both of them. Later, when another explorer, the geographer Ronald Ives, passed away, Hayden strewed his ashes in the same location. "I wanted them to be together so they could argue with each other," he said.

Julian Hayden in the Sierra Pinacate

We typically picture archaeologists as erudite, pipe-smoking scholars. Julian Hayden is not such an archaeologist. His education came from experience, and there are few who can match its breadth. Hayden has consistently refused to accept the mainstream opinion, and his renegade theories are expressed as definite opinions by a man who obviously is unafraid to speak his mind. He is also a dedicated researcher whose tireless study of the Sierra Pinacate reflects his love of this land.

Hayden's father, Irwin, worked in many different fields despite holding a master's degree in archaeology from Harvard. After World War I, the family moved to Riverside, California. In 1929 the Haydens became involved in an archaeological dig in Nevada, and the rest, as they say, is history. Hayden recalls, "I thought digging things up with a trowel and a whisk broom was sissy work. Then I found my first arrowhead, and I was whipped." Soon Hayden was traveling from excavation to excavation, learning archaeology "on the job."

Hayden's list of excavation experiences reads like an archaeologist's dream résumé: the cliff dwelling called Kiet Siel on the Navajo Reservation in northeastern Arizona, the Hohokam Grewe site near Casa Grande, Ventana Cave, Pueblo Grande in Phoenix, and Snaketown. Like his father, Hayden worked at several trades. Between archaeological jobs, he "did what had to be done." At Snaketown Hayden met his wife, Helen, and the family moved to Tucson after World War II. Using adobe bricks that they made on the property, they began building a home that was never actually finished. He became a contractor while never abandoning his love of archaeology.

Hayden met Malcolm Rogers in 1930, and they excavated a site north of San Diego together in 1938. They became close friends, and Rogers later came to live with the Haydens in Tucson. Hayden first explored the Sierra Pinacate in 1958, and he soon became convinced that Rogers' framework for desert archaeology fit the area perfectly.

Hayden proposed some theories that plunged his colleagues into consternation. He believed that the desert cultures were far older than most people believed, arguing, as we saw in chapter 2, that humans occupied the Sierra Pinacate as early as 70,000 years ago. He also sketched the long and continuous evolution of a culture he called the Amargosan from its beginnings up into historical times. Pointing to the fact that the historical inhabitants of the Sierra Pinacate spoke a Piman language, he suggests that today's Piman peoples are descendants of the ancient Amargosans. Hayden easily dismisses the skepticism of his fellow archaeologists. Someone once remarked to him that "differences of opinion result in increased knowledge, and that is good." Hayden agrees: "It all becomes clear in time. Time usually reveals the truth."

Conceptualizing the Patayan

Three different labels have been applied to the Patayan Culture—Yuman, Patayan, and Hakataya. We review them briefly here as an introduction to the discussion of Patayan lifeways that follows. In the mid-1930s, the Gladwins of Gila Pueblo first labeled the archaeological sites lying to the west of the Hohokam area as Yuman. Later, Lyndon Hargrave of the Museum of Northern Arizona proposed that the culture be called Patayan. As the story goes, a Hualapai interpreter told Hargrave that this Yuman word meant "old people." In 1938, Harold S. Colton, also of the Museum of Northern Arizona and about whom we will learn more in chapter 8, suggested that *Patayan* be used instead of *Yuman* to avoid connecting the prehistoric cultures with the living peoples of the region.

Rogers' 1945 classification differentiated between the archaeological cultures of the Flagstaff and Prescott regions, which Colton had labeled *Patayan,* and the culture of the lower Colorado River region, which Rogers labeled *Yuman.*

The third label was devised by Albert H. Schroeder. Schroeder encompassed western Arizona under what he called the Hakataya Culture, after the Hualapai and Havasupai name for the Colorado River. Schroeder suggested that the Hakataya developed from the local Archaic cultural base and were ancestral to the historical Yuman speakers of the area. Schroeder viewed the Patayan as "rock-oriented" people, building rock-outlined jacal houses (mud and brush huts), dry-laid masonry houses, trail shrines, and ground figures, in contrast to the "dirt-oriented" Hohokam, with their pit houses and earthen ballcourts.

Schroeder's Hakataya concept incorporates archaeological cultures as diverse as the Pioneer Period Hohokam, the lowland Patayan of the Colorado River, prehistoric cultures of the Prescott and Flagstaff regions, and even the Salado and Sinagua Cultures. Although at one time archaeologists decided to use the Hakataya concept and discussions of the Hakataya Culture can be found in some scholarly books, most archaeologists believe the label mistakenly groups together a number of prehistoric peoples who differed greatly in their lifeways.

The problem in classifying the Patayan Culture was exacerbated by the loss of Rogers' field notes and draft reports, and the scrambling of his pottery collections. After 1945, when the San Diego Museum of Man was converting from its wartime status as a naval hospital to its usual peacetime pursuits, Rogers' files and field notes were disarranged, and the cabinets of type sherds were disordered and their contents mingled. Lacking the report, types could not be re-identified. Unfortunately, other archaeologists apparently attempted to use these collections and notes for comparison, being unaware of their essentially useless condition.

Rogers divided the Patayan into upland and lowland groups based on where they lived and the people with whom they had close contacts. Their ceramics also differed. The lowland folk made buff-colored pottery from fine-textured riverine clays, whereas the upland Patayan produced a coarser brown pottery. Present evidence suggests that this is an essentially good way of viewing the Patayan and that upland and lowland groups are a culturally similar group of people united by a particular way of life. In the following discussion we consider the Patayan Culture in this way.

Patayan Culture History

The origins of the Patayan Culture are obscure. We know that, as elsewhere in Arizona, the Patayan region was occupied by Archaic people long before the appearance of pottery. The initial occupation of the lower Colorado area by stone-tool-making people is termed San Dieguito. Hayden believes its earliest stage, the Malpais, may extend back to pre-Clovis times. A hot and dry climatic interval marked the appearance of the Amargosan Culture around 8,000 years ago. This pre-pottery, stone-tool-making variant of Archaic Culture was well adapted to the rigors of the desert along the Colorado.

Most archaeologists agree that the Amargosan Culture represents the indigenous people of the Colorado desert, but they disagree on the subsequent history of these people. Rogers suggested that the Amargosan lifestyle was replaced by a new pattern that required only the addition of pottery to transform it into the culture recognized as Patayan. Ceramics appear around A.D. 700. Who brought pottery to the desert? Rogers suggested that it was either Yuman-speaking people from southern California or non-Yuman speakers from the Papaguería or Sonora. He vigorously denied the possibility that the Hohokam were the ultimate authors of Patayan pottery, although Patayan pottery, like Hohokam, is made by the paddle and anvil technique.

We know even less about the origins of the upland Patayan. Based on present evidence, the most likely theory is that Yuman migrants moved into the upland areas that had been vacated by Basketmaker III people (see chapter 7), who left the region for better farmlands to the north and east.

The first ceramic period in the lowland region, Patayan I (Yuman I), dates between A.D. 700 and 1000. Rogers defined the period on the basis of two ceramic traits, the appearance of red ware pottery and a distinctive type of shoulder on jars. Some archaeologists have taken exception to the dating of these traits, believing that they were derived from the Hohokam Culture.

Early lowland Patayan pottery was made from a fine-textured, buff-colored riverine clay. Jars were of unique forms, often with extremely narrow necks and a shoulder that resembles a jar set inside a bowl. Sometimes appliqué or incised decorations were applied to the pottery, and occasionally it was coated with a red slip and burnished.

During this time, people lived primarily in the region south of present-day Parker. They made their homes along the Colorado River, the Sierra Pinacate, and the shoreline of Lake Cahuilla. Freshwater Lake Cahuilla was a prehistoric lake created by the periodic natural diversion of the Colorado River from its delta northward into the Salton Basin of California. Infilling alternated with drying cycles, when the river receded, drawing the lake waters with it. When the lake dried up, people would leave its shores for other areas.

In the upland Patayan region, the earliest period of ceramic-making culture history is called the Desert Period by Robert Euler. The dating of this period is roughly the same as Patayan I, beginning around A.D. 700 and lasting until about 1150. Little is known of upland Patayan lifeways during this time. It seems likely that the pattern of exchange between upland and lowland Patayan people that characterized their later history began during the Desert Period.

Rogers suggested that the Patayan I Period ended some time before 1150, and its close marked the only break that Rogers saw in Patayan cultural development, perhaps created by another wave of immigration. New ceramic traits defined Patayan II (Yuman II), including recurved rims and a whole array of new vessel forms. A unique type of finish, called "stucco," appeared. This is a mixture of clay and coarse sand applied thickly to the base and sides of a pot. This rough-textured surface was used for cooking vessels and may have helped to insulate the pots or simply to insure a better grip as the cook lifted dinner from the fire.

Rogers believed Patayan II, dated between 1000 and about 1500, was a period of expansion. It is true that Patayan pottery was distributed more widely at this time, being found in the Mojave Desert, northward along the Colorado River, and eastward to the Gila River. Fortified hills and trincheras sites in the western deserts were thought to represent defenses against marauding Patayan, perhaps Yavapai, as suggested by Rogers and Hayden. In western Arizona, Patayan II pottery is found along trails and at Hohokam sites, indicating an increase in interaction between Patayan and Hohokam. People continued to live along the Colorado River, the lower Gila River, and around Lake Cahuilla. A colony of Patayan people apparently occupied a barrio in the large Hohokam village of Las Colinas in Phoenix. As Hayden reminds us, there probably was as much variability among prehistoric Patayan as there is among historical Yuman peoples. Some groups fought against each other, and some groups were friends and traders. Hohokam and Patayan evidently were friendly, as were the Maricopa and the Akimel O'odham in historical times.

The upland Patayan at this time lived in rockshelters and jacal houses. Their villages were small, consisting of about ten houses. Euler labels this period the Territorial Expansion Period, and it lasted some 150 years between 1150 and 1300. Euler believes that during this time the upland Patayan expanded their territory onto the Coconino Plateau of northern Arizona, where they replaced the resident population. Euler terms the latter portion of the period, corresponding to lowland Patayan II, the period of maximum geographic expansion and stability and dates it between 1300 and 1850. He notes that in food collecting and farming practices, architecture, and village layout, the culture of this time corresponds to that of the historical Hualapai.

The Patayan III (Yuman III) Period of the lowland region begins around 1500 and continues into historical times. It also is defined by ceramic traits, but Patayan III ceramics are only subtly different from those of preceding times. Vessel shapes changed little, and the ceramic art as a whole became more refined.

The beginning of this period is marked by widespread population shifts caused by the gradual desiccation of Lake Cahuilla. Bands of Patayan people from the eastern shoreline of the lake came to reside along the lower Colorado River valley south to the delta. Those fleeing the western shores of drying Lake Cahuilla probably moved into the foothills and mountains of western California and Baja California, especially the San Bernardino Mountains and the Anza-Borrego Park area. Rogers believed that the ancestors of the Pai, or Upland Yumans, migrated into western Arizona at this time. In support of this notion is the replacement after 1300 of the original gray pottery made in this region with brown pottery thought to have been made by upland Patayan.

Food, Farming, and Settlements

Patayan people traveled regularly throughout riverine, upland, and lowland zones in search of various kinds of resources for trade and probably for ritual purposes. From the Papaguería to the Sierra Pinacate, from the Colorado to the Gila, and from Yuma to Wickenburg and Kingman, the pervasive appearance of their pottery marks the seasonal movement of the Patayan across the desert landscape.

The Patayan used a number of different resource areas as they followed the seasons. The length of time that people stayed in an area depended on their needs and what they were harvesting or collecting. The Colorado and Gila Rivers provided fish, waterfowl, and mesquite in abundance, as well as the land and water necessary to grow corn and other crops. Summer camps along the rivers were used for relatively long periods and were devoted to planting, tending, and harvesting crops. Archaeologists believe that the largest Patayan villages are now gone, buried under Colorado River silt or washed away during its periodic floods.

The uplands provided other important resources, such as game, pinyon nuts, and agave. The intervening desert areas supplied the rich food resources also prized by the Hohokam, particularly mesquite and cactus. These areas also were sources of raw materials, such as good stone for making flaked stone tools. A hill of stone near Yuma boasts evidence of hundreds, perhaps thousands, of years of use. Antelope Hill was a ground stone quarry site where the Patayan roughed out the blanks of stone pestles, metates, and other tools. Complete workshop areas occur on the hill, along with the debris from the manufacture of many tools. The dozens of petroglyphs pecked onto the rocks of Antelope Hill may have served to identify the ownership of the resource, recall myths and legends, or simply note who passed that way and when.

The Patayan moved among these areas seasonally, following game and camping among plant resources as they flowered and ripened. These short-term encampments were devoted to specific collecting and processing activities, such as gathering mesquite beans and preparing flour and bread from them. Most of these camps are of a size to suggest that they were occupied by individual families. Rockshelters were used as temporary camps for resource collection and by people who were traveling the trade and ceremonial trails. Base camps were larger, housing several families, and were typically located in the upland areas. These camps were occupied primarily during the fall and winter months when game was plentiful but other resources were temporarily in short supply.

Particular areas may have been occupied during times of hardship. When the river flooded, washing away the cornfields, or failed, drying them up, the Patayan would shift their homes to the desert foothill washes where rainfall farming was possible and where wild plant resources were abundant. Lake Cahuilla served as a refuge during its infilling periods. The lake provided cattail, tule, shellfish, freshwater fish, reeds, ducks, geese, and other waterfowl in abundance, drawing Patayan peoples from the western desert as well as people living west of the Colorado River. When it receded, the lakeshore residents also would have been forced to move into the deserts and uplands.

When archaeologists look at individual Patayan sites, therefore, they are viewing only small parts of a vast interconnected system for exploiting desert resources. Where the population stayed in place for a considerable period of time, such as along the shores of Lake Cahuilla, a picture emerges of what Patayan village structure must have been like. There was no single "village" there even where historical records indicate that a named village stood. Instead, there were numerous clusters of villages, temporary campsites, and specialized camps for procuring resources. The composition of these clusters shifted according to the seasons, political conditions, and environmental dynamics. Camps were distributed around a large settlement, thought to represent the home of the highest-ranking lineage leader. Each cluster relied on a permanent water source, particularly a spring, and had its own cremation area, associated ceremonial structures, and residence of the lineage leader.

Trails, Trade, and Travel

The Patayan traveled across the trackless desert not only in search of food and resources but also to trade. The historical Yuman peoples pursued trade relationships vigorously, which took them across great expanses of desert and created a network of trails. The Mohave, for example, traveled as far east as Zuni Pueblo and westward to the California coast. One well-worn trail across the desert linked the Mohave with coastal California Indians, such as the Serrano and Chumash, who provided shell and acorns to trade with the Colorado River Yumans. Cotton cloth and woven blankets provided by the Hopi were exchanged for shell from the coast.

The Upland and Lowland Yumans typically exchanged cultivated foods and manufactured goods for raw materials and collected foodstuffs. The Mohave offered corn, mesquite, dried pumpkin, pottery, shell, and beads to the Hualapai and Havasupai, who reciprocated with wild game, animal skins, eagle feathers, agave, and mineral pigments. Perhaps to cement this trading process, extensive tribal alliances were developed that promoted visiting, sharing of food surpluses, intermarriage, and cooperation in warfare.

The prehistoric Patayan evidently maintained similar relationships with the Hohokam. The co-occurrence of Patayan and Hohokam materials over a broad expanse of territory suggests a long history of trade and interaction, and even coresidence, as at the site of Las Colinas in Phoenix.

Yuman myths tell of widespread migrations created by food shortages when various resources failed, and conflicts over land-use rights along the Colorado River. Modern Quechan recall quarrels between the Quechan and Maricopa over the metate quarry at Antelope Hill, and the Quechan fought the Cocopah over access to Colorado River lands. In the dual settlement-subsistence system we have discussed, in which riverine people periodically shifted to the desert, it may have been necessary to mark tribal or band territories in some way to prevent additional conflicts over resources. The widespread occurrence of trails and features interpreted to be trail markers may connect and identify such territories. Natural landmarks, such as Antelope Hill, also could serve as territorial markers.

The western desert is crisscrossed with an enormous interconnected system of trails. Some trails no doubt were simply for travel, to move from place to place in search of food, during war, or to trade. Other trails had deeper significance, however. They may reflect pilgrimages to the sacred mountain Avikwaame and may link ceremonial grounds. Trails are often marked by cairns and shrines that may hold diverse offerings from food to pennies and nickels. There are campsites along the trails and among the ceremonial grounds, where people often camped for several days.

Desert Art and Ritual

The desert floor was the canvas on which the Patayan created gigantic art that probably reflects ritual beliefs, legends, and activities. The western desert is alive with geometric figures and figures of humans, animals, and stars excavated into the desert pavement. These intaglios—along with numerous stone constructions such as cleared circles, cairns, and rock-piles—were all linked by a system of prehistoric trails. Some of the most impressive intaglios occur near Blythe, California, and in the western desert near Yuma.

What were these giant figures in the earth, and who made them? Such questions are not answered easily. We suspect that most of the rock figures were made relatively late in time by Patayan peoples who literally drew their myths and legends in stone, who enacted their most sacred rituals on this rocky stage, and who trekked the well-worn trails along pilgrimages—the trail to Avikwaame.

The desert may be a map of the sacred world and the ways in which the Yuman people connected with that world. An important theme in Yuman religion centers on the creation of the Yuman world. The Yuman peoples and their homeland were created at the sacred mountain, Avikwaame. Today's Yuman peoples hold a four-day ceremony involving a sacred pilgrimage to Avikwaame that celebrates the original creation events. Many of the ground figures are thought to have been used for parts of this ritual, which is called the *keruk*. The ceremonies involved several dance patterns, and the cleared stone circles of the desert may be grounds where keruk dances were held. Other figures may represent symbolic journeys to the sacred mountain or places where dreamers created an entryway to the spirit world. The giant human and animal figures may represent heroes and gods, such as the creator twins and the hero Hipahipa, who saved the people by carrying them across the Colorado River on his outstretched arms and shoulders.

Prehistory Becomes History

Many archaeologists believe that the prehistoric Patayan were the ancestors of the modern Yuman peoples. The upland Patayan may be ancestral

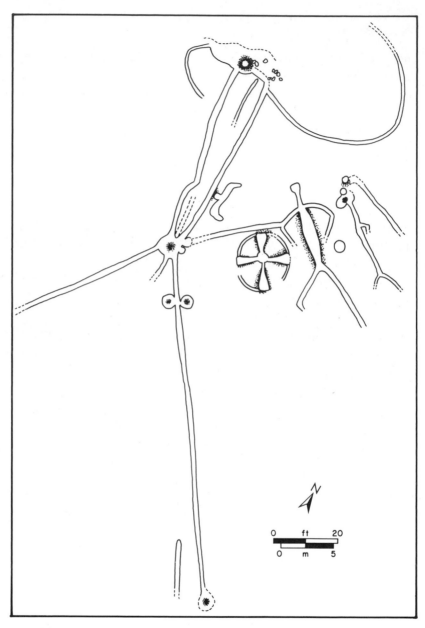

Intaglios, or geoglyphs, at the Ripley Geoglyph Complex near Yuma, Arizona.

Intaglios damaged by off-road vehicles.

to the Havasupai and Hualapai, and the Quechan, the Mojave, and others may have descended from lowland Patayan. Identifying such a continuum is made more difficult by the nature of Yuman material culture. As we have seen, the lifeways of the Yuman peoples involved a substantial degree of movement across a vast territory on a yearly basis. Such a lifestyle necessitates the use of lightweight, easily transportable artifacts. Unfortunately for the archaeologist, such items—baskets, nets, gourd containers, and brush shelters—invariably are perishable. The result is that historical Yuman sites are nearly invisible even when historical artifacts are present. Imagine then how ephemeral prehistoric Patayan sites must have been.

The Patayan Culture richly illustrates the flexibility and adaptability of the human spirit. Although, like the Hohokam, they lived in a harsh and unforgiving desert, the Patayan could not be more different from the sedentary, farming-focused Hohokam. Where the Hohokam responded to the vagaries of their environment by building more canals, expanding their reliance on collected foods, and enhancing their spiritual bulwark against times of stress, the Patayan responded by moving away, shifting their food sources, and expanding their trade networks. Even their belief system was focused on movement, if the trail network across the desert and the giant earth figures can be linked to Patayan rituals. The Hohokam felt stress and responded by digging in and becoming more entrenched; the Patayan took flight. Although the two lifestyles and responses to environmental stress were different, they were equally successful.

As always, more research is needed, but we are optimistic that archaeologists will continue to pore over the western desert, locating and excavating Patayan sites. Will the picture we have painted of Patayan lifeways change as new information is gathered? Probably, but in this we agree with Julian Hayden. His longtime friend and colleague Emil Haury once told Hayden, "The trouble with you, Julian, is that you change your mind too often." Hayden replied, "You're damned right, Emil. And if I find new evidence, I'll change it again tomorrow."

6 THE MOGOLLON

Many of our readers will not have heard of the Mogollon, for although you can visit the timeless homes in the cliffs where the Anasazi dwelled and the great adobe house of Casa Grande where once the Hohokam studied the night sky, there are few public sites for viewing the Mogollon's past. Their story is known only to archaeologists, and we do not know it well. For years after their discovery, the Mogollon were at the center of a heated controversy among the Southwest's most prominent scholars. We cannot even be certain if we have met any of their descendants, for the fate of the Mogollon is more elusive than that of any of the prehistoric peoples we have met already. Yet the Mogollon, for many personal reasons, are special to the authors of this book. The Mogollon pueblo of Grasshopper on the White Mountain Apache Reservation was our summer home for over twenty years as we studied the Mogollon who once lived there and as we taught a generation of students to understand the techniques and enjoy the excitement of archaeological fieldwork. Our daughter accompanied us, growing up listening to the echoes of the Mogollon who once dwelled there and the voices of the Cibecue Apache who live there today. The ancient Mogollon, their mountain homeland, and the historical Apache who followed in their footsteps are part of our lives and our hearts. We hope to share this unique perspective with our readers.

Who were the Mogollon? A simple answer is that they were a rugged mountain people who hunted deer and turkey, gathered wild plants, and cultivated small garden plots of corn, beans, and squash. Although accurate, this answer does not begin to define the essence of these most hardy and, to us, most fascinating people. We like to think of the Mogollon as developing the Southwest's most basic and unencumbered lifestyle, one that continued for thousands of years almost unchanged. Yet the Mogollon also were highly adaptable, freely borrowing ideas, techniques, and materials from other folk as necessary and sharing their lands and homes with others.

In the early centuries of the Christian era, when they began making pottery, small family groups of Mogollon roamed freely through the mountains and deserts of Arizona, New Mexico, and northern Mexico, much like the Western Apache who occupied this land historically. As their Hohokam neighbors settled the major river valleys of southern Arizona and the Anasazi laid claim to the scarce water resources of the Colorado Plateau, the Mogollon came to rely on the mountains, where limited farmland and an abundance of mineral resources and wild game and plants continued to foster a way of life based on hunting and gathering. But this freedom to live in small groups and to move with the seasons changed dramatically in Arizona in the A.D. 1200s, when farmers from the northern plateaus and the southern deserts migrated into the mountains to escape the harsh conditions of the Great Drought. By the end of the 1300s, after almost a century of living together in large pueblo communities, the last of the Mogollon joined with their more agriculturally sophisticated neighbors in leaving the mountains to become the pueblo farmers encountered by Coronado in the summer of 1540. The mountains of central Arizona no longer housed the Mogollon, but they continued to figure prominently in the lives of the pueblo farmers as the scene of hunting trips and excursions to collect steatite, argillite, hematite, and turquoise, and perhaps they were still central to their ceremonies and lay at the heart of their legends.

Land and People

The essence of Mogollon Culture lies in the mountains. Just as the Hohokam are identified with the Sonoran Desert, and the Colorado Plateau is synonymous with the Anasazi, mountains defined the Mogollon. Mountains even provided the name we know them by today. Emil Haury, discoverer and definer of the Mogollon Culture, took it from the Mogollon Mountains in southwestern New Mexico, which bear the name of their discoverer, Juan Ignacio Flores Mogollón, the Spanish governor of New Mexico from 1712 to 1715. Mogollon, New Mexico, the mining ghost town seventy-five miles northwest of Silver City, is reported to have been one of the wildest towns of the Old West, a fitting historical conclusion to its ancient predecessors.

Easterners conditioned to view Arizona as a land of desert, cactus, sunset-colored mesas, and deep canyons are astonished at the loftiness of its peaks and the extent of its high-altitude spruce and pine forests. As a quick comparison, consider Asheville, North Carolina, at the edge of the Appalachian Mountains. Nicknamed Sky City, Asheville, at an elevation of 1,985 feet, is *lower* than Tucson's 2,390 feet. Mount Mitchell, also in North Carolina, is the highest point east of the Mississippi at an elevation of 6,684 feet but is only 242 feet higher than the Arizona town of Show Low, located near the Mogollon Rim on the southern edge of the Colorado Plateau.

It is from the summit of Mount Baldy—sacred to the White Mountain Apache and prohibited to unescorted non-Apaches—that the Arizona domain of the Mogollon can be viewed in its full splendor. At noon on a summer day in early July when we climbed to the top (11,403 feet above sea level, well above the tree line), fields of snow hid in the shadows and the freezing wind howled relentlessly. To the north, the Colorado Plateau stretched to the horizon, colored by the sandy hues captured so well by the Navajo weavers of Wide Ruins. The Little Colorado River valley, the northern limit of Mogollon movement, is clearly visible in the middle ground. The eastern vista stops at the Gila Mountains of New Mexico, well into the eastern range of the Mogollon. The viewer is overwhelmed by the incredible undulation of mountain peaks, ridges, canyons, and basins to the south and west. On the day we ascended Mount Baldy the wind was fierce and cold, there was much haze in the air, and we could not claim to recognize the Catalina Mountains lying just to the northeast of Tucson some 120 miles away. But Andrew Kane, an Apache, assured us that the mountains are easily visible on clearer days. Not even his keen eyes could identify the land marking the southern extent of the Mogollon territory in the northern Mexican states of Sonora and Chihuahua. Andrew did locate Mount Graham, the Pinals, the Sierra Anchas, and behind them the Mazatzals at the western edge of Mogollon country. Then he pointed to the northwest, where the San Francisco Peaks, 12,633 feet above sea level, rise a mile above Flagstaff and beckoned prehistoric peoples throughout northern Arizona. It is not known to what extent the Mogollon may have incorporated the special character of mountains into their cosmology, yet if contemporary Indian views mirror the past, the mountains of the Mogollon were places of supernatural power at the junction of earth and sky where mountain spirits dwelled.

The Mogollon Rim forms the northern boundary of a zone of mountains running diagonally between the basin-and-range deserts on the south and the Colorado Plateau on the north. Geological faulting and volcanic activity in this zone have resulted in a heavily dissected terrain of high elevations, steep canyons, and narrow valleys. Above 6,000 feet, vegetation is dominated by western yellow pine. At intermediate elevations, evergreen woodlands of pinyon, juniper, and oak mix with brushy chaparral, while desert shrubs and cactus dominate below 3,500 feet. This diverse environment still possesses an abundance of native animals, plants, and minerals in a zone marginal to agriculture. The distribution and seasonal abundance of plants and animals throughout the mountains are dependent on water, most of it coming as snow and rain. Because precipitation in any one spot is highly variable, there is considerable uncertainty in predicting the availability of specific foods from year to year. The Western Apache who are the present-day inhabitants of the mountain zone mastered this uncertainty by means of flexibility and mobility. A dependence on hunting and gathering kept populations small, and the unpredictability of the Apaches' food sources made them ready to move their camp when conditions dictated and even to join temporarily with others during times of plenty. We do not know exactly how the Mogollon made a living for themselves in the mountains, but no doubt it was similar to the Western Apache way.

Three different regions—Forestdale, Point of Pines, and Grasshopper—give a fairly complete picture of the range of present-day Arizona environments in which the Mogollon lived. We know a great deal about Mogollon life in these three regions because of the results of almost fifty years of archaeological field school research by the University of Arizona.

Forestdale is a narrow mountain valley nestled just below the Mogollon Rim at an elevation of 6,500 feet. Farmland and water are abundant

Forestdale Valley, typical of the mountain valleys that were home to people of the Mogollon Culture. In the foreground is the Tla Kii Ruin, a small pueblo occupied during the early 1100s.

in this secluded, indescribably beautiful valley. Forestdale Creek, probably a perennial stream prehistorically, is augmented by numerous springs along the margin of the valley. A growing season estimated at 140 days and annual rainfall of twenty inches make this an excellent spot for many small family farmsteads. Ample game in the surrounding pine forest and in the pinyon-juniper woodland of the nearby plateau country would have contributed substantially to the people's diet.

Point of Pines, located on the San Carlos Apache Reservation, also is high in elevation (around 6,000 feet), but is a different landscape, more open and marked by a large grassland surrounded by pine forests and mixed evergreen woodlands. Throughout prehistory, the high water table was tapped easily with shallow hand-dug wells. Eighteen to nineteen inches of precipitation each year and a growing season of 165 to 170 days made Point of Pines an ideal mountain island for dry farming by people who also lived by hunting and gathering.

Grasshopper, on the White Mountain Apache Reservation, is located on a mountain plateau bounded by canyons to the east and west, the Mogollon Rim to the north, and the Salt River to the south. Elevations range from 3,000 feet at the Salt River to over 7,000 feet at the rim. Although there are ample pine woods in the northern part of the plateau, most of the area inhabited prehistorically is evergreen woodland and thick chaparral with patches of grassland. Salt River Draw, a small intermittent stream, is the major drainage for this plateau, which would have made it necessary for the Mogollon to capture water for household use at springs, seeps, and places where a high water table could be reached with shallow wells. Although precipitation was abundant (about twenty inches a year), it was unpredictable and fell unevenly across the land. The proximity and abundance of desert plants and animals made farming a less productive endeavor than hunting and gathering.

Discovering the Mogollon

No single discovery created a greater furor in southwestern archaeology than that of the Mogollon Culture. The story of that discovery is a tale of original insight followed by diligent research. It illustrates well an important point: Significant archaeological discoveries are not simply made; they also must be documented and accepted by the highly critical scientific community.

The Mogollon were discovered by the energetic group of scholars of the Gila Pueblo Archaeological Foundation. According to Harold and Winifred Gladwin, it was a 1931 survey into eastern Arizona and western New Mexico by Emil Haury and Russell Hastings that yielded the first clues that the Mogollon existed. Haury later excavated the first Mogollon sites: Mogollon Village in 1933 and the Harris Village the following summer. His 1936 report on these excavations defined and described the Mogollon Culture.

In retrospect, Haury's book *The Mogollon Culture of Southwestern New Mexico* (reprinted in Reid and Doyel 1986) must be seen as one of the most provocative publications in the history of southwestern archaeology because it created an intellectual schism that lasted for more than twenty years. Haury did this by posing three striking new ideas: (1) that the Mogollon should be recognized as a third culture distinct from Hohokam and Anasazi; (2) that the Mogollon Culture was at least as old as the Anasazi and that, indeed, the Mogollon produced pottery earlier; and (3) that late in Mogollon's development the Mogollon and Anasazi Cultures merged.

In the year following Haury's academic bombshell, Paul S. Martin (who later became a major contributor to our understanding of Mogollon prehistory and who is different from the archaeologist of the same name we met in chapter 2) reviewed *The Mogollon Culture* and described it as "so astonishing, so far-reaching, and so unorthodox that the worth of this report and of the new data contained therein probably will not be understood or esteemed for some years." Prophetically, Martin anticipated that "the hypothesis set forth in this excellent report will doubtless be scoffed at by many competent people." Events proved Martin correct, and his own research placed him beside Haury and firmly in the midst of the mounting controversy.

The anti-Mogollon point of view was articulated by A. V. Kidder, then considered the outstanding scholar of southwestern archaeology. He saw the Mogollon as the result of the mixing of Anasazi and Hohokam people and lifeways. To him the Mogollon were "receptive rather than radiating," meaning that they lacked individuality and borrowed many ideas from other cultures. For Kidder, the only distinctive thing about the Mogollon Culture was its early pottery, and Kidder dispensed even with this by seeing it as originating in Mexico. "If this be true," wrote Kidder, "Mogollon loses its sole significant claim to individuality."

Two questions lay at the heart of the Mogollon debate. First, were these mountain people sufficiently distinct from the Anasazi and Hohokam to warrant separate and equivalent status as one of the primary southwestern cultures? Second, putting the issue of distinctiveness aside, who made the earliest pottery—the Anasazi or the Mogollon? Elements of opinion and faith far removed from an objective evaluation of the evidence began to creep into the discussion of these legitimate research questions, as we will see.

Among the first such articles of faith was a reluctance to modify the notion that the Anasazi were the dominant culture in the Southwest. The personality and authority of the venerable Kidder are linked to this conservative stance. Earl Morris, a premier Anasazi archaeologist in his own right, explained this point of view when he said that archaeologists "under the grip of the northern bias" were content to accept the Anasazi as basic and probably parental to the relatively late cultures in regions south of the San Juan River center.

By 1939 it was obvious that, if the Mogollon Culture concept was to be accepted by such eminent scholars as Kidder, additional archaeological research was required. Accordingly, Haury, who by this time had left Gila Pueblo to become the head of anthropology at the University of Arizona and director of the Arizona State Museum, initiated his field school program in the Forestdale Valley, and Paul Martin established a field research station in the Pine Lawn–Reserve region of western New Mexico.

That year in the Forestdale Valley, Haury defined at the Bear Village a pit house occupation dated between A.D. 600 and 800, contemporary with Mogollon and Harris Villages. Although he thought that the Mogollon living in the valley at this time displayed a number of Anasazi influences, Haury also made a substantial case for the distinctiveness of these people, in terms of both the artifacts found there and the geographic extension of these traits into the mountains of east central Arizona. Joining the Bear Village evidence in support of the Mogollon was the first of three reports on the excavations at the SU site in New Mexico by Paul Martin and John Rinaldo, who estimated the occupation of this pit house village to have been prior to A.D. 500, earlier than any Mogollon site excavated at that time. The strongest evidence for Mogollon antiquity was uncovered by Haury in 1944. Completing excavation at Bluff Village in the Forestdale Valley, Haury recovered tree-ring dates that demonstrated that the Mogollon lived there in A.D. 300.

Into a postwar atmosphere of accumulating evidence and growing consensus came J. O. Brew's report on Alkali Ridge in southeastern Utah, in which he presented a case against Mogollon integrity and antiquity. After devoting considerable attention to the lack of distinctiveness in architecture, stone artifacts, and pottery, Brew concluded that the concept of Mogollon Culture was far from being established as equal to Hohokam and Anasazi. Clearly, still more fieldwork and analysis were needed.

In 1946, Haury began fifteen years of field school research at Point of Pines to probe the Mogollon question with more intensity than was possible at Forestdale. In the following year, J. O. Brew initiated the Harvard Peabody Museum's Upper Gila Expedition in west central New Mexico— an area geographically intermediate between the Anasazi and the Mogo-

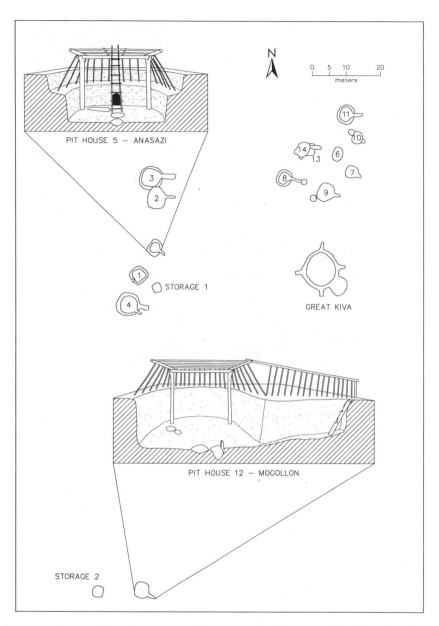

Bear Village, with enlargements of an Anasazi pit house and a Mogollon pit house.

A University of Arizona Archaeological Field School student cleaning an Anasazi black-on-white jar from Point of Pines.

llon—to investigate for himself what E. B. (Ned) Danson and he called the "enigmatic Mogollon culture."

After this came a virtual flood of significant excavations and reports that provided evidence supporting the Mogollon concept. Much of this flowed from Paul Martin's research team working in New Mexico and from Haury and his students at Point of Pines. It is no accident, therefore, that out of Point of Pines would come Joe Ben Wheat's doctoral dissertation, a full report on excavations at a pit house village and a compendium of Mogollon archaeology. Wheat's exhaustive catalog of evidence fully documented claims for the distinctiveness and antiquity of the Mogollon Culture.

Signaling the changes brought about by Wheat's synthesis was the first major publication of the Peabody Museum's Upper Gila Expedition, in which E. B. Danson supported the Mogollon concept and suggested an environmental basis for differences between Mogollon and Anasazi.

By the end of the 1950s the Mogollon controversy, which had occupied so much scholarly attention and had influenced so many fieldwork decisions, was barely audible. By the middle sixties the Mogollon debate had been largely forgotten or had been shelved along with other relics of a bygone era by the many young people entering archaeology. For the next twenty years they would call for rigorous procedures of scientific investigation and for the examination of questions relevant to general anthropology and contemporary society. Since 1982 the biennial Mogollon Conference has combined the insights of Haury, Martin, Rinaldo, Reed, and Wheat with contemporary research to expand and clarify the concept of a Mogollon Culture and a Mogollon people.

Mogollon Origins and Development

Archaeologists agree that the Mogollon developed from the Cochise Culture. At the Cienega Creek site in the Point of Pines region, Emil Haury uncovered remains, particularly stone tools, that provided evidence for continuity between Cochise people and the pottery-making Mogollon. Other evidence found in southeastern Arizona, the Tucson Basin, and western New Mexico indicates that the earliest Mogollon lifeway was little changed from that of the prepottery Archaic Period. Some archaeologists now think that the earliest Mogollon Culture represents a sort of basal culture pattern that eventually gave rise to other cultures. Many aspects of the Mogollon lifeway resemble the Archaic pattern. The Mogollon people were mobile, used a broad range of resources, and relied on generalized farming rather than the specialized techniques of the Hohokam and Anasazi. In this sense, the Mogollon lifeway was perhaps the most basic and readily adaptable of all southwestern lifestyles.

Mogollon development is most conveniently divided into three periods: Early Pit House, Late Pit House, and Mogollon Pueblo. The Early Pit House Period began around A.D. 200 with the addition of pottery to a Late Archaic tool kit and ended in the A.D. 600s at about the time red-on-brown decorated pottery appeared. The following Late Pit House Period ended with the construction of masonry pueblos, which in Arizona began in the 1100s, a hundred years later than in western New Mexico. The Mogollon Pueblo Period in Arizona extended from the middle 1100s to 1400, when the central mountains were abandoned.

The Early Pit House Period (A.D. 200 to 600)

Around A.D. 200, the Mogollon lifeway was transformed from that of the Late Archaic Period by the appearance of pottery. The earliest pottery was brown plain ware, and although well made, it was produced in a limited range of shapes and with poor control of the firing conditions. Pots were not plentiful and did not replace baskets, for we think that the Mogollon moved around considerably in the quest for food, and baskets remained the most useful containers. Small pit house villages located on hilltops and ridges suggest a concern for defense at this time. Round pit houses dug deep into the ground, often with a ground-level entry, were typical. From the beginning, Mogollon houses were distinctive as "true" pit houses, with the house walls formed by the side of the pit. Some sites, such as Bluff Village, also had a large pit house or communal structure, which indicates that these were the central settlements within a dispersed community. Such structures probably were used for group ceremonial activities, drawing residents from nearby camps. The populations of the early villages were small, and their resources were scattered across the landscape. To exploit resources effectively, people moved their residence frequently. The products of hunting and gathering dominated the diet, with some contribution from gardening. The Mogollon were much less committed to cultivation at this time than their Anasazi and Hohokam neighbors.

Bluff Village in the Forestdale Valley, which is the earliest well-dated Mogollon site, provides a view into Mogollon lifeways of this period. Excavating this site was another of the lucky accidents that punctuated Haury's career. Haury initially assessed the site, which is situated on the end of a high ridge overlooking the valley and which requires a difficult climb, as representing a protohistoric Apache site because of the brown plain ware pottery found on the surface. Much to everyone's surprise, the site not only proved to be an early Mogollon village, it also produced the earliest tree-ring dates for Mogollon pottery—well worth that daily climb to work!

On the ridge top are pit houses dug three to four feet deep into the fractured bedrock and roofed with logs and earth. Families spent most of their indoor time in large houses with cooking hearths. Smaller structures lacking hearths and with plant-grinding equipment on the floor were used for storage and food processing. The Mogollon were an outdoor people, however, and many of their everyday activities—such as food preparation, cooking, and tool manufacture—were conducted outdoors. A large pit house served community social and ritual functions involving the inhabitants of Bluff Village as well as those from similar small villages and homesteads scattered throughout the Forestdale Valley. Communal buildings such as this one developed in later periods into the religious structures called great kivas.

The diet of the people who lived at Bluff Village is only suggested by the scant food remains found in the excavation. The presence of knives, arrowheads, and grinding equipment, however, indicates a mixed food strategy of hunting and gathering. Proximity to good garden plots and the presence of developed grinding stones led Haury to infer the cultivation of corn.

The Mogollon living at Bluff Village built substantial dwellings that they could return to year after year. Living on top of a steep ridge, they were secure from casual raids and could defend themselves against an assault. The women and children would have been safe when the men had to leave for many days of hunting or for trips to other camps to barter for goods. And though the bluff top would have been windy in the winter, the deep pit houses avoided the cold air settling on the valley floor and would have been warm and cozy. Winter also would have been a time when storytelling and ritual in the community pit house dominated the life of the people as the snow built up outside.

The Late Pit House Period (A.D. 600 to 1150)

This period in the Arizona mountains was characterized by pit house villages contemporaneous with the Mogollon and Harris Villages. It was a time of population expansion and regional differentiation. The tendency at this time was for pit house villages to be located on the valley floor adjacent to land suited to cultivation, not on easily defended locations, as in the preceding period. This suggests not only the growing significance of gardening but probably also the relaxation of previous economic and social uncertainties. Pit houses generally were rectangular, with a ramped entrance on one of the long sides. At this time, the formal great kiva concept was developed, and great kivas were present at the larger villages. The presence of great kivas indicates a continuation of central settlements within a community of scattered homesteads. Although more corn was grown and eaten than during previous times, subsistence was little changed, with dietary needs still met primarily through hunting and gathering. Gardening with domesticated plants contributed to the diet in proportion to highly localized growing conditions; in fertile areas, more corn would be grown. Residential mobility still characterized the Mogollon throughout most of the area in which they ranged except where localized resources were plentiful and more stable settlements could develop. People of different cultures resided alongside the Mogollon and used the mountains, indicating an increase in communication with the Anasazi and Hohokam.

The Bear Village in the Forestdale Valley reflects the behaviors typical of this period of Mogollon development. This pit house village is on the valley floor near Forestdale Creek, where pit houses could be dug deep into the alluvial clay. Haury excavated seventeen houses, about half of the total present, in the early 1940s. Although three rectangular houses were excavated, the majority were round, and all of the houses exhibited mixed architectural features characteristic of the Mogollon and the Anasazi. Inside the pit houses were cooking hearths, food-processing equipment, and storage pits dug into the floor. Two excavated houses served as structures for food storage.

Animal remains indicate an emphasis on hunting deer, whereas milling equipment attests to the processing of plant foods. Although only one charred corn cob was recovered, it is almost certain that corn was a major component of the diet.

The great kiva at Bear Village was an unusual structure in the form of a four-legged animal whose odd-shaped head served as the entrance. Four huge support posts held up a massive roof of timbers and earth to create an almost soundproof artificial cavern for secret religious rites.

Prehistoric southwesterners typically secured their babies to wooden or woven cradleboards. The soft skulls of the babies were gradually deformed by the pressure of the cradleboards, and adult skulls retained the artificial shape. Different methods of binding resulted in different skull shapes, and mothers of different cultural traditions used distinct types of cradleboards and binding. At the Bear Village, Haury observed this type of variability in head deformation. Although Haury's field appraisal of the poorly preserved crania led him to estimate that the majority of the people buried at Bear Village had the type of head deformation associated with the Mogollon, skulls showing the type of deformation typical of the Anasazi and one undeformed skull also were present.

Evidence from the Bear Village suggests that not all the people dwelling in the Forestdale Valley were Mogollon. In addition to the fact that people were buried at Bear Village whose mothers used different types of infant cradleboards, the varied house types and houses with mixed architectural features suggest that people of diverse house-building traditions cooperated in construction. These cultural differences also were expressed in the pottery and in a mixture of mortuary practices common to the Mogollon and Anasazi. We think that the chief purpose of the great kiva was to bring together people of different cultural traditions, as well as those living in the scattered homesteads throughout the valley, in an unthreatening communal setting for social and religious events. No doubt the people of mixed cultures cooperated in many other aspects of life as well.

The coming together of different people, in particular Mogollon and Anasazi, was one consequence of population movement throughout the Southwest during this period. It resulted in a shift in village locations down from defensible locations and in the construction of great kivas as community ceremonial structures. The coresidence of Mogollon and Anasazi glimpsed at Bear Village foreshadows events we see much more clearly 600 years later at the large pueblos of Grasshopper and Point of Pines. A long-term result of coresidence was the exchange of technology and ideas that produced the similarities in archaeological remains between the Mogollon and Anasazi after A.D. 1000.

The Mogollon Pueblo Period: Reorganization (A.D. 1150 to 1300)

The century and a half after 1150 was a time of adjustment for the Mogollon brought about by contact with the Anasazi and by the experimentation required to adapt subsistence and social organization to diverse

Painted corrugated and plain pottery of the Mogollon Culture.

mountain environments. The most apparent change is the appearance of surface architecture and larger settlements. Large masonry pueblos appeared around 1000 in the Mimbres Valley in New Mexico and around the mid-1200s at Point of Pines but did not appear until 1300 in the Grasshopper region. The accelerated development of the Mimbres people was the result of interaction with other cultures to the north and south.

In Arizona the small pueblos dotting the landscape suggest favorable environmental conditions for early agriculturalists experimenting with plant varieties and the technology of dry farming. As long as the population remained small, hunting and gathering were productive. Gardening may even have served as part of the hunting strategy to lure deer to within range of the bow and arrow.

Mogollon life at this time is glimpsed at Tla Kii Ruin in the Forestdale Valley, excavated by Haury in the 1940s. Tree-ring dates place the occupation of this small pueblo of twenty-one rooms and a circular great kiva between 1100 and 1150. Tla Kii was a small agricultural community with fields on the valley floor. Contact and exchange between groups of Mogollon and Anasazi continued, indicated by architecture, ceramics, and mortuary practices like those at the Bear Village. Ceramics continued in the tradition of Mogollon brown pottery. Some pots were made with a smoothed surface, and others were corrugated, providing a pleasing, textured exterior surface. Some vessels were red-slipped, with polished exteriors and glossy, blackened interiors. Decorated black-on-white pottery brought into Tla Kii from the Colorado Plateau along with masonry architecture confirms a strong Anasazi connection. The circular great kiva, similar to others on the Colorado Plateau, was linked to a religious system encompassing more than the scattered population of the Forestdale Valley. It is evident that people of different cultures lived side-by-side in the fertile Forestdale Valley. No doubt there was a great deal of overlap among these cultures, as people drew spouses from groups other than their own.

During the 1200s much larger pueblos than Tla Kii sprang up in the Point of Pines region. The 335-room Turkey Creek Pueblo, estimated to have been founded around 1240, was the first large pueblo community there. This pueblo was divided into northern and southern halves, united by a rectangular great kiva in the center of the pueblo. During the last quarter of the thirteenth century, Point of Pines Pueblo attracted a group of Anasazi emigrants from north of the Little Colorado River. Their distinctive polychrome pottery and other artifacts, as well as their styles of architectural construction, distinguish them from the local Mogollon. A D-shaped kiva probably was used by this Anasazi population. Although they apparently lived peacefully among the Mogollon for a while, this did not last. Many of the seventy rooms identified as belonging to the Kayenta immigrants were burned intentionally, and the burned rooms were cleaned out, remodeled, and reoccupied by the local people. This disastrous event, which although undated is thought to have occurred before 1300, clearly indicates a renewal of social tensions in the mountains during the late 1200s. We think that unrest developed when the mountain region began to fill with newcomers as Anasazi on the Colorado Plateau fled the devastating effects of the Great Drought.

For a closer look at Mogollon life during the final decades of this period and for examples of how archaeological investigation reveals the past,

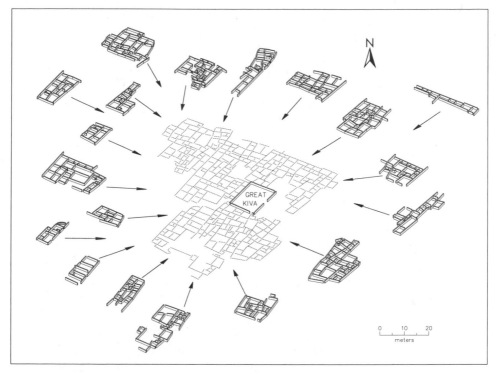

Turkey Creek Pueblo, showing how an aggregated pueblo is formed from sets of rooms.

we now turn to Chodistaas Pueblo in the Grasshopper Region. Chodistaas provides abundant and unparalleled evidence for the processes of population movement that took place at this time and the results of these events.

Chodistaas Pueblo

Chodistaas Pueblo (Chodistaas means "scorpion" in the Western Apache language) is located on a bluff overlooking the largest expanse of agricultural soil in the region, one mile north of Grasshopper Pueblo. It is an eighteen-room pueblo constructed of low, dressed stone walls arranged into two room blocks separated by a walled plaza. Tree-ring dates tell us that construction of rooms in the northern room block began in A.D. 1263 and continued through the 1270s. The southern room block was built between 1280 and 1285, during the height of the Great Drought that swept the Southwest between 1276 and 1299. The pueblo probably was occupied seasonally until four storage rooms were built in the middle 1280s to support a year-round occupation.

Chodistaas Pueblo is more than this simple description implies. It was, literally, a buried treasure whose value was in data rather than dollars. Chodistaas was burned, and this event created an unparalleled opportunity for archaeologists. The residents of the village left all of their everyday equipment on the floors of the houses that were burned, whether by design or because they were caught by accident in a burning pueblo from which they had to flee. Pottery vessels, metates, stone tools, and other items on the floors of these houses are a rich source of information for reconstructing the lifeways of those who once lived at Chodistaas. Another important result was the preservation of charred roof timbers that hundreds of years later could be sampled by archaeologists and dated by the tree-ring laboratory. The burning of Chodistaas thus gave us precise dates and a great wealth of information. The importance of this unusual situation becomes clear when we compare Chodistaas with one portion of the Hohokam West Branch site in the Tucson Basin. The entire collection of pottery vessels from West Branch, collected from about the same number of structures as at Chodistaas, was less than the average collection from *one room* at Chodistaas.

Chodistaas Pueblo gives us a glimpse of household organization during the time when villages were small and were made up of people related through blood ties and marriage. Each room block had eight dwelling rooms and one ceremonial room, suggesting the presence of two social groups. We imagine that the four or five households that lived in the southern room block were related to one another. The distribution of artifacts on the floors of rooms in the southern room block and the construction of rooms suggests that although two households shared a habitation room, a storage and manufacturing room, and a kiva or ritual room, each household also had its own food storage room. By the time Chodistaas was destroyed by fire, the pattern of two households sharing rooms had changed to one in which each household had its own dwelling, storage, and other rooms. The pattern of households at Chodistaas suggests the importance of kinship ties as well as the independence of kin-based groups.

The Chodistaas ceramics illustrate the critical role of pottery in understanding the past and the importance of modern physical and chemical analysis in this investigation. This unusual ceramic collection consists of 296 whole vessels, most from room floors, and thousands of potsherds from trash areas. Using state-of-the-art techniques of neutron activation analysis, María Nieves Zedeño was able to verify with ceramics the notion that had been suggested by other evidence: that there was population movement between plateau and mountains and, later, that the Anasazi came to settle in the mountains. She demonstrated that the black-on-white pots used during the early years of occupation at Chodistaas had been made on the Colorado Plateau and had been brought into the pueblo. Later the black-and-white pots were made from local clays. A similar pattern of nonlocal manufacture preceding local production of decorated pottery held for bowls of black-on-red and polychrome pottery. This indicated that people from the Colorado Plateau had settled Chodistaas Pueblo, bringing with them their pottery, but with the passage of time and the breakage of pots, they began to make their own pottery with local materials.

Another astounding discovery was made by Barbara Montgomery. In studying household ceramics, she determined the circumstances surrounding the abandonment of Chodistaas Pueblo. Analyzing the broken pieces of pottery in the trash and dirt fill of rooms, she determined that the pueblo had been ritually buried. The fill of dirt, potsherds, and other refuse within the rooms was deposited so quickly that it smothered the still-burning timbers. The density of sherds in this intentional fill is high, and the important point Montgomery made was that, because the pueblo was abandoned, there was no one living there to generate trash that might have filled the rooms through natural depositional processes. She inferred that after the pueblo was burned, it was filled in and covered over deliberately. It is as though the pueblo home literally "died," was cremated, and then was buried with dirt and broken pottery from the surrounding trash on the surface. Some of the Chodistaas people may have then founded a new home at Grasshopper Pueblo, which began its rapid growth after Chodistaas burned.

We think that, as the population grew, the competition for resources increased, especially that for scarce agricultural land. The broad territory that the Mogollon had exploited and moved through in previous times shrank under the pressure of competition with outsiders. We see clearly the effects of the population influx at Chodistaas Pueblo. One result was that people moved their residences less frequently and shifted their traditional patterns of earning a living. The packing of people in the mountains restricted the annual movements and access to resources of the Mogollon occupants. They, in turn, began to stay full-time at sites previously occupied only temporarily. We see this at Chodistaas when in the 1280s, the driest decade of the Great Drought, rooms were built to expand storage space. The mixed subsistence strategy based on hunting, gathering, and gardening that had served the Mogollon well for many hundreds of years was well suited to a mobile people who moved annually between the mountains and adjacent desert lowlands. This strategy was forced to evolve quickly into one completely dependent on the cultivation of corn and beans using sophisticated dry-farming techniques introduced by the newcomers from the north. Another result of the atmosphere of social and economic uncertainty may have been conflict. Not only Chodistaas but all the excavated sites dating to this period were burned, perhaps intentionally.

The Mogollon Pueblo Period: Aggregation (A.D. 1300 to 1400)

The 1300s mark a unique moment in Mogollon prehistory when the majority of the population lived in pueblo communities of a hundred to a thousand rooms. The Great Drought, which contributed to agricultural shortages on the Colorado Plateau, caused Anasazi to move into the central mountains in large numbers, to live with the Mogollon and in many cases to establish separate Anasazi communities. These demographic shifts created sudden population increases and aggregation, and also contributed to the consolidation of the Southwest pueblo farming pattern. By the mid-1300s, however, it had become clear that corn agriculture could no longer feed a growing population, and exhausted wild plant and animal resources were inadequate to compensate for the shortfall. The Mogollon, now fully committed village farmers, had abandoned the central mountains of Arizona by 1400 for farmland elsewhere.

The final and most dramatic prehistoric occupation of Arizona's mountains can be seen at the large pueblos of Tundastusa, Kinishba, Point of Pines, and Q Ranch, and at the cliff dwellings of the Sierra Ancha. Throughout the mountains, pueblos increased in size and population coalesced as people living in small, vulnerable communities responded to demographic shifts and economic uncertainty. This period is documented best at Grasshopper Pueblo and the surrounding region, where thirty years of archaeological investigation have provided a view of prehistoric life unparalleled for its detail and accuracy.

Grasshopper Pueblo

A continued influx of people into the mountains and competition for resources created a situation where small communities, such as Chodistaas, could not protect themselves from marauders seeking food and perhaps captives. These and other factors caused the people of Chodistaas to abandon their village and band together with others from similar villages at Grasshopper Pueblo. A sister community to Chodistaas at Grasshopper Spring Pueblo also was abandoned at this time, suggesting that these people, too, moved to Grasshopper. It is intriguing that initially three groups of rooms were built at Grasshopper Pueblo, and they differed in size and layout, suggesting a founding population of three different groups. This tripartite division continued throughout its subsequent growth and remodeling.

Grasshopper Pueblo was the largest community in the region and was located in the middle of the largest continuous expanse of agricultural land. The 500-room pueblo was organized into three distinct blocks of rooms with three plazas, one of which was later roofed and converted into a great kiva. Unlike Chodistaas, which was built of low-walled masonry rooms, Grasshopper consisted of full-standing, masonry-walled rooms one to two stories in height. A roofed corridor leading into the pueblo from the south was the only entrance into the village and opened into the largest plaza. Rooms clustered around the plazas, with ladders leading to roof hatchways. Great care was taken with dressing the stone used for walls that would face public areas. Because the inner walls of rooms were plastered, however, these could be built of more roughly shaped stone.

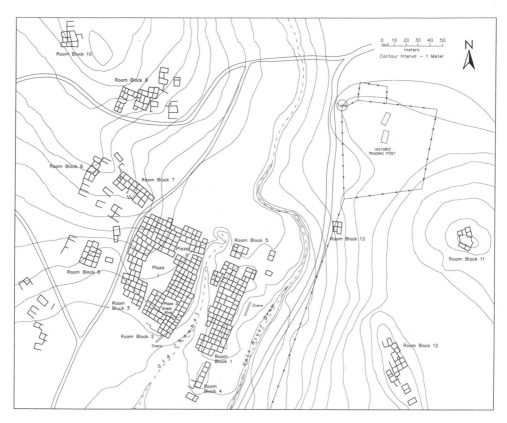

Grasshopper Pueblo, one of the large mountain pueblos where the Mogollon people came together to cooperate in farming and mutual defense in the 1300s.

The pueblo was divided in half by Salt River Draw, which at that time ran through the village. Trash areas surrounded the pueblo, and some of the dead were buried there. The villagers dammed Salt River Draw to create a pond north of the settlement. Surrounding knolls were topped with smaller groups of rooms, usually of the same type of low-walled masonry seen at Chodistaas. For some three decades a generation of archaeology students excavated at Grasshopper Pueblo, learning not only a great deal about how to become professional archaeologists but also a great deal about the past. The fact that the Grasshopper story can now be told is largely due to their diligent efforts.

Field school students excavating the floor of a storage room at Grasshopper Pueblo.

Subsistence and Settlement. The process of adopting food production, discussed in chapter 3, is illustrated well at Grasshopper Pueblo in the early 1300s, long after it had occurred in most of the rest of the Southwest. As we have seen, the inhabitants of Chodistaas Pueblo relied on a mixed strategy that included hunting, plant gathering, and growing corn and beans. At this time there even were technological innovations that increased hunting efficiency and the contribution of wild game to the diet. An analysis of projectile points by Leon Lorentzen, for example, demonstrates that the Grasshopper Spring people gave up using the atlatl and dart to adopt the bow and arrow. One effect of this technological change would have been to increase hunting effectiveness, especially in regard to the mule deer.

The population explosion at Grasshopper Pueblo began around 1300 and lasted for twenty-five years during a time of abnormally high precipitation. During the early decades of the 1300s, the Mogollon living at Grasshopper continued to supplement hunting and gathering with gardening. At the same time, the Anasazi, having perfected dry-farming techniques on the Colorado Plateau, brought their agricultural expertise to Grasshopper Pueblo. In time, as the population increased and the animals and wild plants decreased in abundance, the Mogollon learned how to be successful dry farmers and increasingly came to depend on agriculture for food. At the same time, a dependence on nutritionally poor maize fostered dietary stress that was exacerbated by the depletion of collected foods.

A twenty-year drought beginning in the middle 1330s, when the regional population was at its highest, produced the final impetus for the transition to total dependence on agriculture. Almost immediately, satellite communities were established to bring additional, but more marginal, land under cultivation in an attempt to maintain crop production at predrought levels. In a little over a generation, according to John Welch's analysis, the Mogollon of Grasshopper Pueblo had made the transition from hunting, gathering, and gardening to being totally dependent on agriculture.

Over the next thirty to forty years, they tried to adjust agricultural productivity to the demands of a growing regional population but were unsuccessful. Agriculture could not sustain such large pueblo communities, so the Grasshopper region and the central mountains of Arizona were abandoned except for excursions to collect scarce resources such as salt, turquoise, and hematite.

The Grasshopper case illustrates two important points introduced in chapter 3. The first is that climatic change, technological change, residential stability, population movement, and competition for scarce resources all interacted in causing people to accept food production. Second, a knowledge of food production is necessary but not sufficient for change. The Mogollon had a knowledge of cultivation and had practiced gardening for centuries, but they committed wholeheartedly to agriculture only when wild resources had been depleted through population increase and overexploitation. Once they made the change, they stuck to it, preferring to leave the mountains to pursue an agricultural way of life in areas where it could be sustained for many generations. They relinquished their mountain homeland and their mobile existence to the Western Apache, who maintained this way of life until nearly the present day.

The earlier settlement system, based largely on residential moves and illustrated at Chodistaas Pueblo, had come to an abrupt end by 1300 with population aggregation and the rapid growth of Grasshopper Pueblo. Before 1300 there was a total of little more than 200 rooms in the small, scattered pueblos of the Grasshopper region; by the early part of the next century, there were 2,000 rooms, distributed mostly among eleven pueblos. At least for a generation or two, people spent most of the year in a reasonably large pueblo community living close by their neighbors day and night. Such an aggregation of the population required the development of social structures to organize people and solve disputes.

Social Organization. Our reconstruction of social organization is based on two sets of evidence: mortuary information and artifacts from room floors. With this evidence, archaeologists recreate the broad patterns of organization that affected the individual and the important social groups to which each person belonged.

The basic social unit at Grasshopper was the household. Building upon earlier studies by Richard Ciolek-Torrello, we can identify two broad categories of households at Grasshopper: large households that occupied two or more rooms, and small households that had only one room. These differences reflected distinctions between larger, older, and in some cases more prosperous families and families that were younger, had fewer children, and accumulated fewer goods. Households were linked through kinship ties and through the sharing of ceremonial rooms and kivas. Households probably functioned in matters of social control and discipline as well as in domestic concerns.

The importance of kinship groups in the organization of the pueblo is indicated by several lines of evidence. The tripartite architectural division of the pueblo was sustained rigidly throughout its occupation and was accompanied by distinctions in diet, the use of fuelwood, and other differences that indicate that each group maintained particular ways of doing things. Joseph Ezzo conducted bone chemistry analysis and found that the residents of the three room blocks had somewhat different diets. Residents of Room Block 3 ate more maize, for example, which can be interpreted as indicating that they held more extensive or more productive agricultural land. This suggests that kinship groups controlled land tenure.

The health and social position of individuals is reconstructed best from their skeletal remains and from their mortuary treatment. We think that, in addition to kinship ties, the position of individuals at Grasshopper Pueblo was based on their age, their gender, their participation in religious life, and their ethnic group or cultural affiliation.

Everyday life was clouded by the sadness of a high mortality rate for children—56 percent died before reaching the age of twelve. We believe that rather simple illnesses that today are little cause for alarm claimed the lives of many babies. Intestinal and respiratory illnesses probably were widespread and were among the primary causes of death. Examination of these children by Madeleine Hinkes, a biological anthropologist, also reveals abnormalities in the bones that indicate physical stress, including repeated episodes of food shortage and anemia.

A person who survived childhood had a good chance of living another couple of decades, however. In a group of 173 adults over the age of fifteen, 21 percent died in their twenties, 28 percent in their thirties, 26 percent in their forties, and 15 percent lived to be over fifty. Walter Birkby, who is also a biological anthropologist, estimates that women in their twenties and thirties died at twice the rate of men, confirming the heavy toll exacted by childbirth in a preindustrial agricultural society. The fact that the people of Grasshopper were not as healthy as those in some pueblo communities on the Colorado Plateau and had one of the highest levels of dental pathology recorded in the Southwest is balanced partly by the lack of much evidence of violence. The picture we see at Grasshopper is one of a people with chronic aches and pains subsisting on a diet poor in nutrients and punctuated by severe periodic shortages.

Some time between the age of nine and fifteen, adult status was conferred on a child. At this time the burial accompaniments changed from those typical of children—ornaments and little else—to the pattern characteristic of adults, in which ceramic vessels, tools, and ceremonial paraphernalia also accompanied the deceased. We think that this shift indicates that young people were considered to be fully participating members of the Grasshopper social and ceremonial community when they reached this age.

Adult men apparently were accorded greater prestige than women, if the number of burial accompaniments is an indicator of prestige. We believe men held this higher position largely because they were the ones who participated most intensively in religious life and who were the skilled craftspeople and specialists in the community. Artifacts suggesting a special skill or role, especially ritual artifacts, were found only with the burials of men. Several men were buried with leather or skin bags of such ritual items as quartz crystals, concretions, and oddly shaped stone tools. In addition, there were real economic benefits to be gained from being a man. Analyzing bone chemistry, Joseph Ezzo found that adult men apparently enjoyed better diets than women and children. The presumed religious leaders, however, did not have better diets or better health than other men.

The elderly were accorded great respect, to judge from the increase in burial accompaniments, particularly the number of ceramic vessels. Around age forty, women as well as men became revered elders of the community, if we can infer this from a considerable increase in the number of burial goods.

Another dimension of group identification was along cultural lines. Two and possibly three different groups resided at Grasshopper, each identified by the distinctive form of cranial deformation found earlier at the Bear Village—one type associated with the Mogollon, another associated with the Anasazi, and undeformed skulls that on the basis of present evidence are not associated with a particular group. The group with the largest population was the Mogollon, as was the pueblo leader discussed below. An Anasazi enclave is represented by twenty-eight people, most of whom were women. Unlike Point of Pines Pueblo, where Emil Haury identified an Anasazi occupation that was burned out, there is no evidence at Grasshopper to suggest that the people's stay was threatened. Anasazi men joined the same ceremonial societies as Mogollon men, although none are present in the arrow society. The Anasazi buried at Grasshopper most likely were women who had married into local families.

Religion. We have no way of knowing for certain, but we think it is highly likely that religion and ritual played a central role in the life of the Grasshopper people. Although some religious artifacts accompanied the mortuary ritual and suggest the presence of religious specialists, the best evidence for these activities comes from architecture. Religious activities were held in ceremonial rooms, kivas, plazas, and great kivas. Each of these structures was used by different groups of people within the community.

Ceremonial rooms were built much like typical habitation rooms except for the presence of circular stone hearths and stone-lined ash boxes, which probably were used for placing prayer sticks. Storage containers and manufacturing equipment are often found on the floors of ceremonial rooms, suggesting that secular activities, such as stone tool manufacture, took place when ritual activities were not being conducted there. There is no evidence for food storage or preparation, however, and no indication that people lived in these rooms. Three or four households cooperatively used each ceremonial room.

Unlike ceremonial rooms, kivas have special architectural indicators of their religious use. Kivas are marked by a masonry bench along one wall, through which opened a ventilator to bring in fresh air. These are absent in all other types of rooms. Like ceremonial rooms, kivas also have a circular stone-lined hearth, usually located near the bench. Artifacts, food-processing facilities, and other features indicating domestic life are rarely found on the floors of kivas, indicating that they were used only for ritual purposes. Some kivas have been found with holes in the floor for setting the support posts of weaving looms. Weaving evidently was done by the men at certain times in some of the kivas. Ritually buried macaws are sometimes found behind the bench just below the kiva floors. The importance of birds, particularly macaws, in ceremonial life is common among the modern Western Pueblo people (see chapter 7), and their presence in Grasshopper kivas may indicate a belief in the Katsinam (see chapters 7 and 8). Kivas were used by a larger group of people than ceremonial rooms and may have been used primarily by a single ceremonial society. Among modern Western Pueblo peoples, kinship groups called clans own kivas and the ceremonials performed in them.

The mortuary data indicate that about half of the adult men belonged to ceremonial societies that may have used the kivas. We draw our interpretations of these groups from living Pueblo peoples. Ceremonial societies probably were devoted to bringing rain and abundant crops, healing the sick, and generally helping the community remain healthy and prosperous. We have identified four societies at Grasshopper Pueblo. Three are identified by stylized ornaments, presumably worn as part of the ceremonial costume in which a man was buried. These societies are represented by glycymeris shell pendants, conus shell tinklers, and bone hair-pins, and were mutually exclusive—a man belonged to only one. A fourth society was represented by clusters of arrows and apparently was dedicated to war or hunting or both. A man belonging to this group was buried with his personal quiver of arrows, typically placed upside down at the left shoulder, as well as with other goods. This society drew its membership from men affiliated with each of the other three. There are two other possible societies, one identified by glycymeris shell bracelets worn on the arm by women as well as men.

Pueblo leadership and authority apparently were vested in the leadership of societies. A Mogollon man of forty to forty-five years of age probably was the most prominent man in the community at one time because of his leadership of the societies represented by arrows and bone hairpins, and his membership in the one signified by glycymeris shell bracelets. His leadership of these groups, we believe, was signaled by the carved decorations and the turquoise and shell mosaic decorations of the hairpins that he wore, which are unique; no other hairpins were so decorated. Other indications of leadership and prestige are the presence of symbolic items, such as a carved wand made from a grizzly bear thigh bone, and the treatment he was accorded. During the burial ritual, men who probably were members of the arrow society contributed clusters of two to twenty arrows as offerings, sprinkling the arrows with powdered specular hematite. The leader's personal quiver was placed at his shoulder, and it is possible that he was left-handed, as his quiver is the only one to have been placed at the right shoulder instead of the left.

Grasshopper has three plazas associated with the three room blocks of the main pueblo. Although some food preparation, tool manufacture, and other activities took place in the plazas, we think that their primary function was ceremonial. The village layout, which focuses on internal plazas, is a recurrent pattern of Mogollon pueblo communities of the Arizona mountains and appears to represent a particular form of outdoor public religious performance. Katsina dances that we have been privileged to view at Hopi help us picture the spectacle presented by a ceremonial dance at Grasshopper Pueblo. Imagine the entire community, young and old alike, lining the plaza, standing on the rooftops, and swinging their legs over the roofs as they watched. Masked, costumed dancers that were the earthly representations of the spirits swept through the corridor to appear suddenly in the big plaza, where they danced for rain, health, and peace. Laughter erupted as clown Katsinam made bawdy jokes between dances, and fearsome Katsinam standing at the edge of the crowd kept order and ensured proper respect. The celebration concluded with an exciting free-for-all as the Katsinam distributed roasted ears of corn, bread, and other favorite foods to the spectators.

The Great Kiva was built by fully enclosing the walls and roofing over the open space of Plaza III, which was located in the central room block. This event represents the addition to the Grasshopper ceremonial organization of a type of group ritual that in earlier times always was more common in the Arizona mountains to the east of Grasshopper. The construction date of the Great Kiva around A.D. 1330 coincides with a period of decreased precipitation and a dispersal of the population to satellite communities throughout the Grasshopper Plateau. It is not too far-fetched to believe that the Great Kiva was used as the scene for public appeals to the spirits for rain and healthy crops. The Great Kiva was, as the name suggests, large in size, about 82 feet long. The roof was supported by nine massive juniper posts. There was no bench or ventilator. A metate set into the ground was used for grinding white clay, and there was a large firepit near the center. Most striking was a foot drum, a masonry-lined hollow trough into which were set wooden logs or planks that would create a thundering rumble when struck by the feet of dancers. Numerous ritual macaw burials were found just below the floor of the kiva. No doubt the entire community participated in rituals carried out in the Great Kiva, and it probably served to integrate a diverse community composed of different kinship, residence, and cultural groups.

The ritual architecture of Grasshopper Pueblo underscores the critical importance of religion in community life, especially under conditions of population aggregation and coresidence of people belonging to different ethnic or cultural groups. An important role of religion was to facilitate decision making by people who did not know one another well during a time of rapid, wrenching change in their way of life.

Mogollon Abandonment of the Mountains

Because many different regions throughout the central mountains of Arizona—the communities at Forestdale, Point of Pines, and Grasshopper—

Kinishba Pueblo after reconstruction by Byron Cummings. A sister site to Grasshopper Pueblo, it was abandoned along with all the other Mogollon communities of the mountains by 1400.

were abandoned at the same time, the conditions and events that characterize Grasshopper may represent the general pattern of abandonment
in the mountains. At its peak in the mid-1300s, the population in the
Grasshopper region would have been near the maximum for their agricultural technology, and there is no evidence to indicate attempts at agricultural intensification except by bringing more marginal land under cultivation. At this time there was an expansion in settlement to include cliff
dwellings and networks of small, butte-top pueblos. The choice of defensible locations for several major pueblos and the siting of small pueblos
atop buttes, as well as the extensive use of cliff shelters as areas for secure
food storage, all suggest an increase in economic and social tensions.

The correlation between the expansion of this settlement pattern and
changes in precipitation is suggestive. The most recent evidence analyzed
by Donald Graybill indicates that after a period of ample rainfall from
1300 to the mid-1330s, the Grasshopper region experienced about twenty
years of below-average precipitation. Construction of the satellite cliff-
dwelling community of Canyon Creek in the late 1320s, which was preceded by an apparent stockpiling of construction timbers, points to an
anticipation of recurrent environmental changes and a short response
time for adjustments to agricultural shortfalls. The combined effects of
increased population, reduced soil fertility, depleted resources, and poor
climate created nutritional deficiencies. Joseph Ezzo found that differences between men's and women's diets decreased during the late period
of occupation at Grasshopper Pueblo, as everyone consumed fewer wild
foodstuffs. At the same time, increased physiological stress among children, seen in bone growth abnormalities and anemia, indicates periodic
food shortages consistent with failing agriculture.

As we have seen, the Anasazi immigrants who moved into the mountains beginning in the 1280s, during the height of the Great Drought, introduced more efficient dry-farming techniques to the mountains as well
as organizational features of large-pueblo life and probably also a number
of religious practices. If our interpretation of differences in the lifestyles
at the Chodistaas and Grasshopper Pueblos is correct, then around 1300
the local Mogollon underwent a radical alteration in lifestyle that brought
them closer to living like the Anasazi in terms of subsistence, social organization, and religion.

By 1400, when the last mountain pueblo had been abandoned, the Mogollon had swapped their traditional emphasis on mobile hunting, gathering, and gardening for the life of the pueblo village farmer, where-upon they became indistinguishable in the archaeological record from the Anasazi. At this point in prehistory, archaeologists lose track of the Mogollon, at least as currently understood. The mountain Mogollon adjusted, changed, and disappeared from the archaeological record of the Arizona mountains.

It is for this reason that the Mogollon cannot be tracked into the historical period, as can the Anasazi. We know that their descendants must live on among today's Pueblo peoples, just as we know that the Mogollon lifestyle was the core from which other, more divergent lifestyles were elaborated. The mountains of central Arizona were completely abandoned when Francisco Vásquez de Coronado marched his vanguard through them in the early summer of 1540, forming a great *despoblado* that was perilous for man and beast. We cannot say where the Mogollon went when they left the mountains forever. We can, however, say that their mark upon the past was indelible, and the clues they left behind in their mountain stronghold will no doubt one day allow archaeologists and other interested people to unravel the mystery of their disappearance.

7 THE ANASAZI

When the typical American thinks of the prehistoric people of the Southwest, the Anasazi Culture is the image that comes to mind. Pueblo ruins atop sandstone mesas and cliff dwellings tucked into shadowy canyon ledges combine with pictures of contemporary Pueblo people at Hopi, Zuni, Acoma, or Taos to form the popular conception of the Southwest American Indian. So deeply etched is this image that even the 1993 movie on the life of Geronimo was filmed in the plateau country of canyons, buttes, and mesas—which he probably never even saw—rather than in Geronimo's real but less spectacular homeland in southeastern Arizona and northern Mexico.

There is no doubt that the Anasazi are the most highly visible people of the past. Their stunning multistoried pueblos occupy some of the most scenic country in the nation and have been made into public parks visited by millions of American and foreign tourists. American archaeology also began with the Anasazi. The first explorers and later the earliest scientists focused on the incredibly rich archaeology of the Colorado Plateau. The classification of prehistoric cultures in time and space stemmed from work among the Anasazi. And indeed the Anasazi are fascinating, for they wrought wondrous feats in an unforgiving environment. The Anasazi were master farmers of the Colorado Plateau, a harsh and hostile, although photogenic, land. Far more than farmers, they were architects, artisans, artists, and astronomers. They embraced a religious worldview that survives to this day and that competes favorably with the world's major religions in depth of spirituality and longevity of tradition.

The Anasazi occupied a vast territory across the Four Corners country, and their culture was complex, with many different branches that may have been akin to tribal or linguistic groups. Anasazi, which is an English approximation of a Navajo word often translated as "ancient enemies" or "enemy ancestors," refers collectively to all the prehistoric pueblo peoples throughout the Colorado Plateau. The broadest division of the Anasazi is between the Eastern and Western Anasazi. This archaeological division conforms to distinctions anthropologists have made among Eastern and Western Pueblo peoples of today. The Eastern Anasazi lived in what is today New Mexico along its northern border with Colorado. It was the Eastern Anasazi who created, between A.D. 850 and 1150, the phenomenon that was Chaco, perhaps the most complicated culture of the prehistoric Southwest. The planned, formal pueblos with huge great kivas linked by a system of roads can be seen today at the Chaco Culture National Historic Park, south of Farmington, New Mexico.

The Western Anasazi lived in what is today Arizona and southeastern Utah. Some of the more spectacular Western Anasazi sites are in Navajo National Monument and Canyon de Chelly National Monument in northeastern Arizona.

The Eastern and Western Anasazi are divided into a number of different branches. We are concerned here primarily with the Kayenta Branch Anasazi, who occupied northeastern Arizona. We use the Hopi word *Hisatsinom*—meaning "our ancestors"—to label these Western Anasazi in Arizona. The Hisatsinom maintained a rather isolated independence that can also be said to characterize their present-day Hopi descendants.

The first Anasazi are called Basketmakers, for they lacked pottery. Although there are differences of opinion concerning the origins of the Basketmaker people of northern Arizona, the lifeways of these first Hisatsinom are well understood. They were mobile hunters and gatherers who depended heavily on corn agriculture, living in rockshelters as well as open sites. Subsequent Basketmaker lifeways were characterized by pit house villages, an expansion of farming, and the introduction of pottery. During the following Pueblo Period, the Hisatsinom continued to live in pit houses several centuries after the Eastern Anasazi had begun to build masonry pueblos. In fact, Chaco Culture, with its monumental buildings, was well established by the time small pueblo communities began to appear on the Arizona landscape. The widespread occupation of northern Arizona culminated in the pueblos of Canyon de Chelly and the cliff

Second Mesa, one of the three Hopi Mesas on the southern edge of Black Mesa, is typical of the the Colorado Plateau landscape mastered by the Anasazi.

houses of Kiet Siel and Betatakin, which were built, occupied, and abandoned within the short span of fifty years between A.D. 1250 and 1300. By 1300 much of northern Arizona had been abandoned, along with the vast territory of the San Juan River drainage.

The widespread abandonment of the Four Corners region—once the great mystery of Southwest prehistory—is understood now as a natural response of Pueblo people to their changing plateau environment. The

1300s were a time when people moved hundreds of miles to establish new villages or to join other Anasazi and Mogollon communities. It was a time for learning new ways, rearranging and teaching old ways to other people, and incorporating new ideas and practices into a coherent philosophy of life. A belief in the Katsinam, so prominent in contemporary Hopi religion, is thought by some archaeologists to have developed at this time. By the 1400s Hisatsinom settlements in the mountains of central Arizona had been abandoned for communities located increasingly closer to the modern-day Hopi Mesas. By the summer of 1540, when Anasazi prehistory ended, the Hisatsinom had coalesced along the southern fringes of Black Mesa into the ancient villages of the Hopi.

Land and People

The Colorado Plateau

As the Anasazi make up the popular image of native southwesterners, so too does their land define a photogenic landscape memorialized in pictures, postcards, and the epic westerns of movie director John Ford. The Colorado Plateau is a landscape of water-deposited sediments, sand dunes, and the shells of ancient seas, all of which have been cemented into rock, buckled by shifts in the earth's crust and volcanic pressure from below, and eroded into spires, buttes, and canyons by the relentless abrasion of wind and water. It is a vast panorama of geological time and process, where—given enough time, heat, and pressure—layers of rock can be lightly folded into a marbled earth, sliced, and displayed to all who would drive the roads, hike the trails, or float the rivers. Geological time has little meaning when discussed as millions of years of change, yet it takes on an unimagined reality when one is close enough to touch it.

Although the highways of northern Arizona are a quick and safe approach to this country and its scenic vistas, it is from the rivers and trails that one confronts most intimately the awesome forces of nature and the immensity of time. On the Four Corners Seminar that Jeffrey Dean and Jefferson Reid once led for the Crow Canyon Archaeological Center, we would spend a day rafting the San Juan River between Bluff and Mexican Hat, Utah, a twenty-six-mile journey through millions of years of geological deposition, rearrangement, and erosion. Competent young river guides would steer huge rubber rafts casually around the sand bars and through the rapids while explaining the rock formations as though we were on a tour bus in Rome. Few of the easterners and midwesterners who take part in this seminar climb out of the raft at day's end without a profound sense of the overwhelming power and majesty of the Arizona canyon country.

The Grand Canyon certainly is the most popular and most familiar place to encounter nature on the Colorado Plateau. The sensation from the rim of the canyon is visual—a vast sculpture of colors and shapes that has inspired so many. But to understand the canyon as the story of geological processes operating over eons of time requires a different place to stand and stare. Such an opportunity arose for Erin and Jefferson Reid when they hiked down Hermit's Trail into the canyon heartland, where respect for nature and the Anasazi is multiplied a hundredfold. Down near the bottom, we stood on the open Tonto Plateau surrounded by cliff walls roofed with a starry sky. Humility shaded into feelings of awe that were disturbingly indistinguishable from the first sensations of abject fear. Little wonder that the Hopi view the Grand Canyon as the place of their emergence and the residence of departed ancestors and the Katsinam.

The visual and spiritual character of the Colorado Plateau is better experienced than described. Its geographical dimensions provide the basis for understanding the significance of this landscape to its ancient and modern inhabitants. The Colorado Plateau comprises the northern drainage of the Colorado River, including all but the Gila River drainage of southern Arizona. The southern boundary of the plateau is the Mogollon Rim, the eastern limit is defined by the Rocky Mountains, and a northern extension runs up Utah's Green River into Wyoming. It is the southern portion of this great region that was home to the Anasazi, an area roughly bounded by the Mogollon Rim on the south, the San Juan River on the north, the Colorado River on the west, and the Rio Grande on the east.

Elevations on the Colorado Plateau average around 5,000 feet above sea level (making it the highest plateau in North America) and climb to 12,655 feet atop Mount Humphrey, the tallest of the San Francisco Peaks. The plateau is marked by mountains—distinctive landmarks rising above the surrounding country. Many of these are sacred to Native Americans, such as the four sacred mountains that bound the Navajo world. A prominent topographic feature and the center of Arizona's piece of the Colorado Plateau is Black Mesa, which took its name from the dense pinyon-juniper cover that darkens the mesa against the surrounding landscape. Today the northern portion of Black Mesa is being strip-mined to fuel generating plants at Page and Bullhead City. Prehistorically, coal was mined by the Hisatsinom, who used it to fire their famous yellow-ware pottery.

High above Chinle Wash, the White House cliff dwelling in Canyon de Chelly overlooks a great house of the Chaco Culture.

Black Mesa represents an upland environment, one of three major environments—upland, river valley, and canyon—mastered by the Hisatsinom farmers. Uplands are typified by pinyon-juniper woodland and scarce surface water, requiring farming techniques dependent on precipitation and rainfall runoff. Farming in the river valleys was constrained by the steep canyons through which so many rivers flow and the devastating force of summer thunderstorms.

The plateau is cut by a series of rugged canyons, the third environment that was home to the Anasazi farmers. Canyon bottoms provided a limited amount of farmland, but even that was vulnerable to flash-flood erosion and variability in the water table, the primary source of water for growing crops. Caves and overhanging rockshelters, often high above the canyon floor, protected the multistoried Anasazi houses. The most spectacular in northeastern Arizona are Tsegi Canyon and Canyon de Chelly. Navajo National Monument protects the cliff dwellings of Betatakin and Kiet Siel in Tsegi Canyon. Canyon de Chelly literally sneaks up; unless coming upon it from the air, one would never know it lies ahead. It opens innocently on the outskirts of Chinle, deepening rapidly inside steep, red sandstone walls marking Canyons de Chelly and del Muerto. Vast islands of stone eroded by time and nature dwarf the Navajo hogans and sheep in the canyon bottom.

In 1932 Harold Colton and Frank Baxter published as bulletin number 2 of the Northern Arizona Society of Science and Art a small guidebook to the wonders of northern Arizona that outlined a number of trips for the adventurous motorist. One wonders how many visitors to northern Arizona ever availed themselves of Colton's guide, for the "cautions" they present for the motorist certainly are intimidating. We quote these cautions to capture the wildness and rough terrain of the plateau country:

(1) A car should be equipped with (a) chains, (b) a good jack, (c) a good pump, (d) a shovel, (e) a small axe or hatchet, (f) a stout tow line, (g) cans of gas, oil and water.

(2) If stuck in heavy dry sand, as in some dry washes, do not try to drive the car through with jerks, as a broken axle or ring gear may result. If the rear tires are partially deflated, or blocks of wood placed on the rear axle to lift the car off the rear springs so as to prevent jumping, the car can usually pull through.

(3) When a sandy wash in the Hopi Reservation is running, use particular caution. (a) If possible, get local advice and aid before attempting to cross; it may save your car. The nearest Indian trader can be relied upon. It is sometimes a wise precaution to employ Indians with a team to tow the car across, so as to prevent stalling. (b) If local advice is unobtainable, wade across, testing for holes and quicksand. (c) Do not attempt to cross if the water is over the hubs of the car. (d) If the banks are quakey but the bottom hard, cut brush may make the banks passable. (e) If the water is over six inches deep, cover the radiator with a piece of canvas and tie a bag loosely over the air intake of the carburetor. (f) In crossing use low or intermediate gears and do not stop the car. If a car stops in running water on a sandy bottom, it begins to sink at once. The authors have known cars to sink out of sight.

(4) If stuck in a muddy chuck hole or small arroyo, do not try to get out by filling the hole with rocks and sticks and jerking the motor. On the other hand, (a) if possible, dig a trench draining the hole, (b) jack up the car using the floor boards if a foundation is necessary, (c) put on chains, (d) now if material is available, fill in the hole with rocks or brush, before letting down the car. It is better to spend twenty minutes in preparatory work than to wait several days for a new part.

The Colorado Plateau demands respect for the value of water and the extent of nature's power. It also teaches ingenuity, and in earlier times it encouraged the Anasazi to develop and master dry-farming techniques and to build a culture that harkened back to before the beginning of the Christian era.

A Pueblo People Today

From the first encounter with the members of the Coronado Expedition (1540–1542), the Pueblo people of the northern Southwest fascinated early explorers, scholars, and travelers. Popular images and narratives tend to portray a unified, homogeneous culture, when in fact Pueblo peoples are different in many ways. Superficial resemblances in housing and the material culture of everyday life, along with similar lifestyles as village farmers, serve to disguise dramatic differences in language and philosophy.

Although the peoples' languages differ, anthropologists group the Hopi, Zuni, Acoma, and Laguna into the Western Pueblos on the basis of broad cultural similarities and the fact that they are culturally distinct from the Eastern Pueblo villages along the Rio Grande and its tributaries in New Mexico. This division between Eastern and Western Pueblos mirrors in a general way a similar distinction that existed in prehistory between the Eastern and Western Anasazi.

The Hopi are the only Pueblo people in Arizona today and are considered by archaeologists and Hopi themselves to be descendants of the Hisatsinom Anasazi. Hopi communities center on three mesas that are the southern fingers of Black Mesa. First Mesa villages include Walpi, Sichomovi, and Hano on top and Polacca at the base. Second Mesa, ten miles farther west, includes the villages of Shungopavi, Shipaulovi, and Mishongnovi. Between Second and Third Mesa is Kykotsmovi, where the Hopi tribal offices are located. On Third Mesa is Oraibi (founded in A.D. 1100), Hotevilla, and Bacavi. Finally, Moenkopi is located on the western edge of Hopi country near the Navajo town of Tuba City.

The Hopi remain the master dry farmers of the Colorado Plateau. Today along the edges of mesas, in sand dunes, in small canyons, around springs, and on the alluvial fans of small washes they grow corn, beans, squash, melons, and other crops. They have developed special techniques for retaining topsoil and moisture in a dry, windswept environment. Most farmers have fields in different locations as a hedge against erratic rainfall and killing frosts.

Like other village farmers of the Southwest, the Hopi organize themselves into kinship groups reckoned through mothers and sisters, the most socially significant of which is the clan. Clans have their own rituals, and clan members are responsible for performing them for the benefit of the community. Clan rituals and their performance are the public expression of a Hopi religion that teaches peace, goodwill, and harmony. Many ritual dances are intended to bring good health, rain for crops, and a happy life to the Hopi. The Katsinam perform the public ceremonies as embodiments of the spirit beings so sacred to the Hopi people. Each village has its own open area or plaza where public ceremonies are held and several subterranean ceremonial rooms or kivas where important secret rituals take place.

Discovering the Anasazi

The Anasazi remain the best known of the Southwest's prehistoric cultures because of their unique characteristics of culture and climate. They dwelled in compact masonry pueblos that have withstood time and remain as highly visible ruins. The climate fosters the preservation of perishable materials, especially in the dry caves where so many Anasazi sites are located but also in surface sites. Tree-ring dating and tree-ring-based climatic reconstructions can be applied because of the Anasazi's use of datable conifers. There has been extensive archaeological research, encouraged by the moderate summer climate and large cultural resource management projects. The historical connection with contemporary Pueblo Indians aids the interpretation of prehistoric sites and offers hypotheses that can be tested scientifically. Not to be excluded are the efforts of energetic explorers and scholars, exemplified best by the work of Richard Wetherill, A. V. Kidder, A. E. Douglass, and Jeffrey S. Dean.

Richard Wetherill: Cowboy and Explorer

The most famous, even notorious, and certainly the most picturesque of the pioneer explorers was Richard Wetherill—rancher, cowboy, and the oldest of five sons and one daughter born to Quakers Benjamin and Marion Wetherill. In 1880 the senior Wetherill and his family established the Alamo Ranch along the Mancos River on the eastern flank of Mesa Verde, Colorado. As he cowboyed among the canyons and mesas on the ranch, Richard found numerous prehistoric sites to whet his interest in lost civilizations. It was not until a cold December day in 1888, however, that Richard Wetherill's life reached its junction with archaeological exploration. With his brother-in-law Charlie Mason, he was searching for stray cattle on Chapin Mesa in present-day Mesa Verde National Park. When he looked across the canyon, he discovered Cliff Palace, the largest cliff dwelling in the Southwest. That afternoon, after Charlie and he split up to search side canyons for ruins, he discovered Spruce Tree House, and the next morning they found Square Tower House.

The combination of Wetherill's responsibilities in running the Alamo Ranch and his growing interest in archaeology presented a dilemma, which

Wetherill resolved by devoting his winters to exploring ancient ruins and the spring through fall months to ranching. Even with this hectic pace he rather quickly established a reputation as a guide to the ancient wonders of the Four Corners region.

In the summer of 1891, Wetherill guided the Swedish baron Gustaf Nordenskiold and assisted in his excavations of Mesa Verde. Then, after exhausting the exploration of Mesa Verde, he turned to the Grand Gulch area of southern Utah and the Marsh Pass–Tsegi Canyon region of northern Arizona. In 1895 he became the first Anglo to see Kiet Siel, the largest cliff dwelling in Arizona, and in the fall of that fateful year he took his first trip to Chaco Canyon with the Palmers, a family of musicians whose eighteen-year-old daughter, Marietta, would become his wife. Although they had known each other for most of a year, it was not until the harrowing crossing of the flooded San Juan River that Richard got the nerve to propose. As Wetherill's biographer, Frank McNitt, recalls the tale,

Before she knew it the river was up to the wagon bed, the current had swung the tailboard sharply downstream and the two mules were plunging forward, now swimming, now scrabbling for a footing when they touched bottom. They made headway but it was slow, and Marietta could see they were being carried on the muddy tide. Near midstream Richard swung toward her and yelled: "Are you afraid?"

"Sure I am—I'm scared to death!" Marietta shouted back. But she was smiling and her brown eyes were sparkling with excitement.

"Hold tight," he ordered, "the worst is coming." And a moment later: "If the wagon begins to tip or the current really takes it, I'm going to cut the team loose. If I do, you jump for it. Grab the nearest mule by the tail—understand? He'll get you to shore."

Marietta nodded that she heard.

For a minute or two, in the swiftest channel of the river, wagon and mules were swept helplessly downstream. Then, with redoubled fury in response to Richard's roaring encouragement, the mules swam diagonally against the current and began to narrow the distance to the north bank. As the animals at last gained a sure footing Richard climbed out on the wagon tongue clutching a coil of rope, and leaped into water up to his waist. He staggered ashore, wheeled, and roped the smaller of the mules around the neck. Then he dug his heels into the steep bank and tugged. Mules and wagon, Marietta swaying on top, came dripping onto dry sand. . . .

"Is there anything you are afraid of?" asked Richard.

"Oh, I guess not." She didn't quite know what to answer.

"Tell me, what do you do with your fear?"

"Well, Mr. Wetherill, I don't know. I suppose I just swallow it."

There was a pause. Then: "Will you marry me?"

In 1896 the newly married Richard set out to dig Pueblo Bonito in Chaco Canyon—perhaps the most famous prehistoric ruin in North America—for Talbot and Frederick Hyde, two New York millionaires. He would dig nearly 200 of Bonito's 900 rooms before the emerging professional archaeological community, led by Edgar Lee Hewitt, forced him to cease all digging. Meanwhile, he and Marietta had established a trading post in the shadow of Pueblo Bonito and had sought to include the ruin in their homestead claim.

The professional evaluation of Wetherill's contributions to southwestern prehistory has shifted several times, but some points are clear. Most of his explorations and diggings would be illegal today, though this indictment also applies to much of the early archaeological work. Richard Wetherill recognized the critical stratigraphic relation between the Basket Makers and the later Cliff Dwellers, and with training, who knows what a man of his intelligence and energy would have contributed to our understanding of the past.

By 1910, the year Wetherill was shot and killed by a Navajo in Chaco Canyon not far from his home at Pueblo Bonito, southwestern archaeology had changed irrevocably. This new direction is best exemplified by Alfred Vincent Kidder, often called the father of southwestern archaeology, who joined energy and exploration with the methods of history and science.

Alfred Vincent Kidder: Archaeologist as Anthropologist

By his own admission, A. V. Kidder got into archaeology quite by accident. As a Harvard undergraduate seeking to avoid early morning and Saturday classes, he registered for a course in the archaeology and ethnology of the

American Indian, and like so many others of us, immediately became hooked. His fate was sealed when he volunteered to do survey work for Edgar Lee Hewitt in southwestern Colorado. At the beginning of the summer of 1907, along with two other Harvard undergraduates, he was given a shotgun, flour, beans, canned goods, mules, and instructions to survey a canyon for archaeological sites. Hewitt would return in three weeks to pick up the fledgling archaeologists. This first venture into fieldwork, which might have been intimidating to some, did not deter Kidder; by the time he returned to Harvard he was a committed archaeologist. He completed his bachelor's degree in 1908 and his doctorate in 1914.

Like Wetherill, Kidder was in his element in the field, seeking the past in dusty deposits in rockshelters and caves. In Marsh Pass, Kidder and Samuel Guernsey found a wealth of evidence to embellish the picture of the earliest Basketmaker people whom Richard Wetherill had discovered in Grand Gulch. In 1915 Kidder was ready to take on a big pueblo project. After much consideration he selected Pecos Pueblo in northwestern New Mexico because of the potential for its lengthy occupation to reveal details of late prehistory and early history. From this research station Kidder synthesized the prehistory of the Colorado Plateau and developed the methods of prehistoric archaeology that would inspire and direct the next two generations of southwestern archaeologists.

The first major contribution to emerge from Kidder's Pecos work came in 1924 with the publication of *An Introduction to the Study of Southwestern Archaeology*. This remarkable book synthesized all that was known at the time about southwestern prehistory. Three years later Kidder convened a conference of archaeologists and anthropologists interested in the Southwest. The crowning achievement of this first Pecos Conference, now an annual gathering, was to formalize the classification system that is still in use today—Basketmaker II, Basketmaker III, Pueblo I, Pueblo II, Pueblo III, Pueblo IV, and Pueblo V. Each of these cultural units was characterized by artifacts and other material culture traits, especially architecture and pottery. The relative chronological sequence was well attested by the stratigraphic position of houses and pottery at sites throughout the Colorado Plateau, but the absolute chronology was uncertain. Soon, however, in the summer of 1929—the same year Kidder concluded work at Pecos and turned to research in Middle America—tree-ring dating would be perfected by A. E. Douglass. Anasazi archaeologists would have absolute dates in the Christian calendar that are still the envy of prehistoric archaeologists elsewhere in the world.

Although Kidder ceased active fieldwork in the Southwest, he continued to report on his Pecos work, and in 1936 he proposed the term *Anasazi* to replace *Basketmaker-Pueblo* as the label for the prehistoric culture and people of the Colorado Plateau. He was widely consulted by the new leaders of southwestern archaeology, such as Emil Haury and J. O. Brew, and probably was the most influential scholar in developing the culture history approach in American archaeology.

Andrew Ellicott Douglass: Astronomer and Discoverer of Tree-Ring Dating

Anasazi research and tree-ring dating are inseparable, yet only the barest outline of the amazing story of the discovery of tree-ring dating can be told here. It begins with A. E. Douglass, an astronomer and scientist of immense genius. In searching for a method of studying the effects of sunspot activity on the earth's climate, Douglass discovered that annual growth rings in pine trees around Flagstaff mirrored certain features of past climate, most notably rainfall. Wide rings indicate years of high rainfall, whereas the narrowest rings were grown during years of drought. Important to archaeologists was the fact that recurrent patterns of ring width variability could be used to build something like a tree-ring calendar that could be extended back in time from the present. This special feature of Douglass's research prompted the National Geographic Society to sponsor the Beam Expeditions to collect prehistoric wood from which Douglass could build a master tree-ring chronology.

By the summer of 1929, Douglass had pieced together two tree-ring chronologies. One extended from 1929 back to shortly before A.D. 1300. A second chronology, based on archaeological specimens from prehistoric ruins, floated unattached to the first chronology. In a brilliant piece of deductive science, the Third Beam Expedition selected several sites located near pine forests and yielding pottery that indicated occupation around A.D. 1300, the critical point when the dated chronology ended. At the Show Low Ruin, on the Plateau side of the Mogollon Rim, Emil Haury, then a young man of twenty-five, and Lyndon Hargrave unearthed a burned roof beam recorded as HH-39. That evening in their hotel room in

A. E. Douglass, the father of tree-ring dating, at Forestdale Valley around 1940.

Show Low, in what Haury describes as the single most exciting moment of his long professional career, A. E. Douglass announced that the gap between the two chronologies had been bridged, and he proceeded to assign calendar dates for the first time ever to the major Anasazi ruins of the northern Southwest. In retrospect, Douglass realized there had been no gap at all but an overlap of only a few years obscured by the extremely narrow rings formed during the Great Drought of A.D. 1276 to 1299. Finding evidence for the Great Drought was the second great discovery of that singular moment in Show Low, the "town named by the turn of a card." For many years a Circle K convenience store stood atop the historic Show Low ruin, but in time it gave way to an auto glass shop and a car wash.

Jeffrey S. Dean: Archaeologist as Scientist

In 1962, only thirty-three years after the discovery at Show Low and twice that long since the discovery of Kiet Siel by Richard Wetherill, the National

Park Service initiated a tree-ring study of the Anasazi ruin of Betatakin. They contacted the only organization capable of such a study—the Laboratory of Tree-Ring Research at the University of Arizona. Jeffrey S. Dean, a graduate student in anthropology and dendrochronology, was assigned the study as a doctoral research project. So successful was Dean's work at Betatakin that it was expanded to Kiet Siel the following year.

Dean's doctoral dissertation, later published as *Chronological Analysis of Tsegi Phase Sites in Northeastern Arizona,* made revolutionary contributions to archaeological method and theory, and the techniques by which prehistory is reconstructed. Dean demonstrated the rapidity with which prehistoric peoples could shift traditional cultural practices and the extent to which people at contemporary villages—Betatakin and Kiet Siel—could behave so differently. Perhaps most important, he conducted a thoroughly documented analysis of the environmental causes for the abandonment of Tsegi Canyon by A.D. 1300, one episode in the region-wide abandonment of the Four Corners region. Dean also developed procedures for investigating the household as the basic social unit within these cliff-dwelling communities and advanced the methods of tree-ring analysis to encompass a wide array of past human behaviors as well as diversity in past environments. The results of his research appear often in the discussion that follows.

The activities of Richard Wetherill in his explorations throughout the Four Corners, Kidder at Pecos, Douglass at Show Low, and Dean at Kiet Siel and Betatakin stand as major landmarks in the development of prehistory in northern Arizona. A complete history of Anasazi discovery in Arizona would have to include Jesse Walter Fewkes, Victor and Cosmos Mindeleff, Byron Cummings, Harold and Mary-Russell Ferrell Colton, J. O. Brew, Al Lancaster, Earl Morris and his daughter Elizabeth, Watson Smith, Robert Euler, George Gumerman, Alexander Lindsay, and Douglas Schwartz. These and many others conducted the archaeological investigations essential to our current understanding of the Anasazi past.

Basketmaker to Pueblo: The Hisatsinom

We have unraveled the tale of Hisatsinom discovery by Richard Wetherill, who named the "Basket Makers" and first recognized that they were earlier than the "Cliff Dwellers." Later, A. V. Kidder and Sam Guernsey explored Basketmaker caves of northern Arizona, uncovering in dry caves and rockshelters the well-preserved baskets, bags, sandals, and wooden tools of daily existence lost to most excavators. Kidder went on to codify Hisatsinom culture history and provide scientific validation, and Douglass gave the fabric of Anasazi life calendrical dates. Today archaeologists like Dean and many others build on the foundation of a century of archaeological discovery to weave a tapestry of Hisatsinom life. We direct our attention to the story of the Hisatsinom from Basketmaker to Pueblo.

The Basketmaker II Period (500 B.C. to A.D. 600)

A. V. Kidder and the original framers of the Anasazi cultural sequence in 1927 envisioned the existence of Archaic ancestors, so they left the "Basketmaker I" time and people open for subsequent definition. Basketmaker II now is regarded as equivalent to the Late Archaic Period in central and southern Arizona, in that the Basketmakers practiced corn agriculture but lacked pottery. There is no Basketmaker I.

Although many archaeologists subscribe to the notion that Basketmakers descended from local Archaic people, R. G. Matson's recent research on Cedar Mesa in southern Utah and reevaluation of the Late Archaic Period throughout the Southwest leads him to a different interpretation. Matson proposes that Basketmaker II people appeared on the Colorado Plateau as a result of a migration of San Pedro Cochise people from southern Arizona, bringing corn agriculture with them. Matson envisions corn cultivation developing in three stages in the Southwest. First there was floodwater farming in the low-elevation deserts of the Southwest, then floodwater farming was adopted on the Colorado Plateau, and finally rainfall dry farming was developed on the upland and wetter areas of the Plateau. Matson interprets Basketmaker II subsistence as largely dependent on corn.

Shelter was provided conveniently by the overhang of caves, the housing of choice throughout Archaic times because it provided a safe, comfortable base camp to which hunters, plant collectors, and part-time farmers could return regularly. But caves are not distributed evenly across the landscape, and they are definitely not portable. These features presented few problems to sparse populations of hunters and gatherers, who had to be mobile in their food quest, but eventually they would constrain the corn farmer's need to secure fertile new farmland and to be close enough to the farm plots to tend them regularly. The Basketmakers' dependence on corn agriculture required them to establish sites in the uplands of Black Mesa and elsewhere. The expansion of temporary farmsteads and the development of stable communities in areas of abundant farmland made possible, even encouraged, population increase.

A source of disappointment for southwestern archaeologists, who can live by ceramic analysis alone, is the absence of pottery during this time. Corn agriculture and pottery did not arrive together, and a dependence on corn as a major dietary staple was apparently not contingent on having cooking pots. The rapidity with which the Basketmakers took up corn farming illustrates how quickly agriculture can be adopted by a local people and adapted to new regions by people moving into an area, as well as the obvious importance of corn to prehistoric southwesterners.

The Basketmakers are renowned for the skill and beauty of the baskets, textiles, netting, and other objects of fiber that they created for containers, clothing, ornament, and tools. Cone-shaped carrying baskets often were decorated with red and black geometric figures. Coated heavily with pinyon gum, they served as water baskets. Coiled basketry, sometimes containing meal and other food offerings, invariably accompanied the dead. Cloth bags were woven and decorated. Twined fur robes provided warmth in cold weather, served as sleeping blankets, and wrapped the dead before burial. Human hair was used widely as cordage and netting. Tied bunches of human hair were stored carefully as raw material for future use. Apparently the hair came from the heads of women, for their hair was worn short, no more than two inches long. Men, by contrast, wore their hair long, often elaborately parted, braided, or tied in a club.

Our notions of Basketmaker lifestyles began to emerge with the explorations of Kidder and Guernsey. Beginning in 1914 and continuing through 1923, Kidder and Guernsey ranged out of Kayenta to explore the Marsh Pass region at the northern edge of Black Mesa not many miles south of Wetherill's Grand Gulch. Here they found numerous dry caves with pits dug into the floor and filled with well-preserved textiles and wooden artifacts.

White Dog Cave, discovered by Kidder and Guernsey in 1916 and the most famous of these Basketmaker sites, provides a glimpse into the daily life of the earliest Hisatsinom Anasazi. The cave is hidden from the valley below and is reached "after a stiff climb of 100 feet up a steep talus" slope. The spacious shelter is approximately 70 feet deep and 120 feet across at the opening, with a floor that rises gradually from front to back. Through-out the excavated portion of the cave are storage pits to seal corn, pine nuts, and other foods against the insects and small creatures that can rob or ruin a pantry. Much care and attention was given to the construction of facilities for storing food, especially for keeping the seed needed for the following year's planting. It was only in these storage pits, some reused as burial chambers, that Kidder and Guernsey found the tools of the Basketmakers.

Along with corn, the Basketmakers cultivated squash, collected wild seeds, and depended heavily on pinyon nuts. They continued to hunt with the atlatl and dart. The scarcity of animal bones suggests that hunting did not contribute greatly to the diet, but the abundance of deerskin, mountain sheep hides, sinew, and deer bone tools verifies that these animals were killed routinely for essential raw materials as well as food. Perhaps the missing animal bones became part of the diet of the local dogs, who kept the cave a little more sanitary than it would have been without them and who also functioned to warn of the approach of strangers. Their presence probably was much appreciated on cold winter nights as well. Two different types of dogs, well preserved as mummies, were found at White Dog Cave. One, for which the cave was named, was a nearly white, long-haired dog about the size of a small collie, with erect ears and a long, bushy tail. The other was a much smaller black-and-white dog about the size of a terrier. It had a shorter coat, erect ears, and a long, full tail. Its muzzle was short and stubby compared with the long, slender muzzle of the other dog.

Unusual, even bizarre, features have been unearthed in Basketmaker caves, such as the removal of human skulls and limb bones from burials, the burning of human bones, and the taking of trophies. In a Marsh Pass burial, Kidder found the skin of a human head stripped from the bone in sections and sewn back together to form a macabre mask. One wonders if this apparent violence, much of it postmortem, was a product of the disruption of traditional ways of life and of population increase, bringing about a rise in the incidence of witchcraft accusations and raiding. If so, the Basketmakers were challenged to develop new organizational and ideological strategies to promote social harmony and agricultural productivity. The appearance of the kiva much later in time represents the architectural expression of a pervasive religious philosophy that may have had its roots in this early time.

The human burials dating to this period were accompanied by a greater quantity and higher quality of turquoise and shell ornaments than during any subsequent period of Anasazi development. Even with such "personal wealth" accompanying the deceased, there is no evidence to suggest a social arrangement more complicated than that of a large family in which parental authority prevails, grandparents are respected for their accumulated wisdom, talented individuals are praised, and daily tasks are divided according to age and gender. Could the accumulation of "personal wealth" be an attempt to resolve mounting social organizational problems by consolidating power and authority in the hands of individual leaders? If it was, then this early experiment failed and was replaced in time by a kin-based system of shared authority and decision making.

That life was hard for these Basketmakers is borne out by the many burials found in White Dog Cave. Infant mortality was high. A glimpse of the loss of life so early and the great care afforded the dead is seen in the burials of tiny infants, placed tenderly in the grave in their cradleboards, wrapped in blankets and with their fiber diapers and umbilical pads still in place as in life.

The Basketmaker III Period (A.D. 600 to 800)

Kidder recognized and labeled the Basketmaker III stage of development the "Slab-house Culture" for the pit houses the Basketmakers dug into the ground, lined partially with stone slabs, and roofed with logs and earth. An important item of material culture to appear at this time was pottery, and domesticated beans were added to the menu.

Although rockshelters continued in use, they were replaced for the most part by pit house villages located in the lowlands along the margins of alluvial floodplains suitable for farming. Whether this location near fields reflects an increasing concern for land ownership is uncertain, but the requirements of farming are evident in settlement locations and in the increased permanence of villages.

Villages were composed of anywhere from several to many pit houses built to standard forms and furnished in similar ways. Circular, slab-lined storage pits set into the ground behind the pit house were common. Individual households occupied a pit house, and related households were grouped together into what archaeologists recognize as villages, many of which appear larger upon excavation because of the succession of building and rebuilding over a long period of time. Richard Ahlstrom's research indicating that pit houses lasted little more than ten to twenty years provides a caution to archaeologists tempted to infer a large number of contemporaneous houses in a single village.

The presence of a great kiva—a communal ceremonial building—at the Juniper Cove Village near Marsh Pass, one of the few known for the Western Anasazi, suggests continuing experimentation in religion and social organization. In this instance, religious practices may have been borrowed from the mountain Mogollon Culture, where great kivas appeared early and were distributed widely. As it did for the Mogollon in the Forestdale Valley, the Juniper Cove great kiva may have served a dispersed community made up of nearby farmsteads. The fact that this single experiment was short-lived—the great kiva system presumably failed among the Hisatsinom—supports the notion that another religious organization, one not focused on great kivas, was present by the end of Basketmaker III times if not earlier. The Basketmakers' failure to adopt the great kiva system is one of several cultural features that separate the Hisatsinom from their Anasazi cousins to the east. For reasons we do not understand at present, the great Chaco cultural system that swept up so much of the Four Corners region in its religious and organizational embrace left the Hisatsinom essentially untouched.

The presence, at last, of the ceramic pot, so important to the archaeologist and so essential to reconstructing southwestern prehistory, may well have been an event of little significance to the people themselves. In studying Basketmaker III containers from caves in the Prayer Rock District, Kelley Ann Hays-Gilpin notes the continued importance of baskets over the newly introduced ceramic containers. Recent research suggests

Black-on-white painted pottery of the Anasazi Culture.

that ceramics functioned initially to protect valuable seeds from insects and mold. Without seeds, a farmer becomes either a hunter-gatherer or a raider, sometimes both, to avert starvation. Eventually, ceramic pots became as important as other containers, as home and hearth became permanent at most of the Basketmaker III villages.

The earliest Anasazi pottery was plain ware, gray in color and made by the coil-and-scrape technique. Like other early pottery, it was made in a limited variety of shapes primarily designed for storage purposes. Soon, experimenting with the new technology, the Anasazi would produce painted ware with black designs on a gray ground and eventually the black-on-white pottery for which they are so well known.

Developmental Pueblo: The Pueblo I Period (A.D. 800 to 1000) and the Pueblo II Period (A.D. 1000 to 1150)

The Pueblo I Period was marked by the appearance and widespread distribution of decorated black-on-white pottery, which, together with the above-ground masonry pueblo, is the hallmark of Anasazi Culture. To the Eastern Anasazi, this time was the beginning of their most exuberant era—the development of Chaco Culture.

Nevertheless, among the Hisatsinom of Arizona there is little to distinguish the lifeways of this period from previous patterns established in Basketmaker III times. An increase in the size of pit house villages indicates either a substantial growth in population or the localization of people in one area, but we do not know for certain because few sites dating to this time have been excavated. Pit houses similar to those of Basketmaker III are the principal means of shelter in contrast to the Eastern Anasazi, who in Chaco Canyon were building Pueblo Bonito, a 900-room, four-story masonry pueblo.

The new millennium ushered in the Pueblo II Period, a time of change for many throughout the Colorado Plateau but muted in Arizona by the conservatism of the Hisatsinom Anasazi. Whereas the Eastern Anasazi continued to be dominated by an expansionist Chaco Culture, their Arizona kinfolk remained seemingly unaffected by Chaco material culture, preferring to adopt at long last some of the construction techniques and house plans that had become commonplace elsewhere. In this the Hisatsinom were much like the Hopi, who many centuries later were highly selective in what they adopted from Spanish culture.

So much of what we know of Pueblo II lifeways in Arizona has come from the research of the Black Mesa Archaeological Project. Because the company was planning to strip-mine coal on northern Black Mesa, federal regulations mandated that the Peabody Coal Company support archaeological research in advance of site destruction. Seventeen years of fieldwork and analysis under the direction of George Gumerman and Robert Euler have produced an unparalleled body of information on the prehistoric culture and climate of northern Black Mesa.

Paleoclimatic research by the Black Mesa Archaeological Project indicates that the environments of the Colorado Plateau were ideal for agriculture at this time. Alluvial areas were stable or building, water tables were high, and adequate precipitation occurred.

On northern Black Mesa, according to George Gumerman, the typical small village consisted of a row of contiguous, above-ground masonry storage rooms joined at both ends by jacal habitation rooms to form a

U-shaped pattern. In the opening of this arc of surface rooms was a sub-surface kiva and often another subsurface room for grinding corn. House-hold trash, discarded in a midden beyond the kiva, completed the com-mon linear arrangement of storerooms, habitation rooms, ceremonial room, and midden labeled the "unit pueblo." These small pueblo villages were located throughout lowland and upland areas wherever crops could be grown during this period of favorable farming conditions.

To see for yourself the transition from pit house living to life in pueb-los, stop at the roadside exhibits along Ruins Road in Mesa Verde National Park. Actual structures, excavated and stabilized, illustrate architectural changes from Basketmaker III to the end of Pueblo III. Although built by Anasazi of the Mesa Verde Branch, these pit houses represent the general sequence of architectural development.

Village architecture and the arrangement of domestic space suggest important features of society and religion. The size and durable construc-tion of storerooms, and the presence of rooms devoted to mealing activi-ties, attest to the significance of corn in the life of the villagers. Abundant land, favorable farming environments, and a presumed relaxation of so-cial tensions favored an emphasis on household production and perhaps also the institutionalization of the household as the basic unit of agricul-tural production and consumption. Construction of a kiva in these small villages of no more than several households strongly suggests a religion and worldview anchored in kinship.

Great Pueblo: The Pueblo III Period (A.D. 1150 to 1300)

The beginning of the Great Pueblo Period was marked by the collapse of the Chaco Culture in Chaco Canyon and its reorganization on the Colo-rado Plateau, a succession of events attributed to a decrease in rainfall and a return to dry conditions. The effects of these processes on the Hisatsi-nom are difficult to assess because so few sites from the first hundred years of this period have been excavated. Several trends mark the time from 1150 to 1250 as one of continuing transition and change.

The uplands of Black Mesa and elsewhere were abandoned for settle-ment, and the once-dispersed population was localized in lowland areas of resource advantage separated from other population concentrations by uninhabited land. The small unit-pueblos of the preceding period were replaced by two different settlement types, one of scattered pit houses associated with masonry-lined kivas and the other with a masonry room block facing an open plaza space containing one or more kivas.

A good example of a masonry room block village is the Tusayan Ruin, a U-shaped pueblo of four or five habitation rooms, associated storerooms, and two circular kivas on the South Rim of the Grand Canyon. The Tusayan Ruin has been preserved, and a small museum has been built there. In 1930 this little ruin was excavated by Emil Haury as his first archaeological project for Gila Pueblo.

Between 1150 and 1175, the Hisatsinom adjusted to twenty-five years of harsher farming conditions than had existed previously by contracting the area of occupation and building rather small settlements. The Eastern Anasazi responded to a similar situation by aggregating into large pueblo communities. Both adjustments reveal the Anasazi readiness to move when conditions warranted and the flexibility to organize themselves either in small groups or in large communities. Anasazi throughout the Colorado Plateau had adapted dry farming to a variety of hostile environments and had formalized the social rules and procedures for getting along with one another in densely packed communities.

In contrast to the first hundred years of this period, the last fifty years are the best known in Hisatsinom prehistory because of the high visibility of the architecture and the years of early exploration and modern scientific research that have been devoted to studying it. This period was the brief shining moment of the "Cliff Dwellers" uncovered by Richard Wetherill at Cliff Palace, by Earl Morris and Don Morris at Antelope House in Canyon de Chelly, and by Jeffrey Dean at Betatakin and Kiet Siel. It was the prelude to the massive reshuffling of population that resulted in the Anasazi abandonment of the Four Corners region forever.

Antelope House, located in the Canyon del Muerto branch of Canyon de Chelly National Monument, was built against the sandstone cliff on the canyon floor and has been exposed to flooding in recent years. Increasing threats of damage to this priceless ruin prompted the National Park Service to preserve it through excavation and stabilization. Under the supervision of Don P. Morris (no relation to Earl Morris, who worked there decades before), the excavation and analysis of Antelope House has

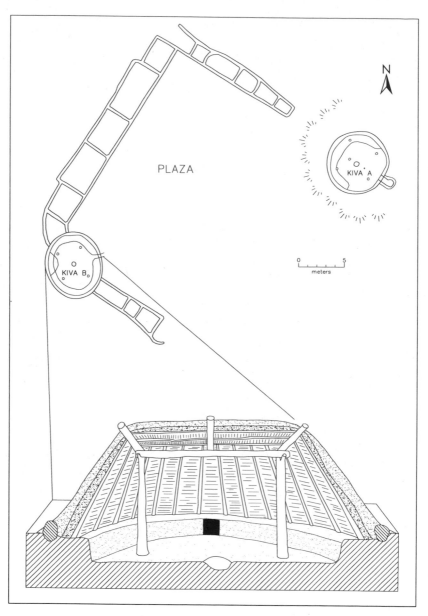

Tusayan Village at the Grand Canyon, one of the Anasazi masonry room-block villages. The enlargement shows how an Anasazi kiva was constructed.

provided a close look at the economic life of a pueblo community in the late 1200s.

The analysis of fossil pollen helps to define the function of various rooms. The storage rooms contained large amounts of economically important food plants, such as corn, beeweed, and cattail. Living rooms contained little pollen, and kivas yielded high concentrations of pine, juniper, and cattail pollen. These plants were used in ceremonies and also may have been stored in the kivas.

Plant remains, so rare in most open sites but abundant at Antelope House, indicate a monotonous diet dominated by corn supplemented with cactus, squash, pine nuts, cotton seeds, and a few beans. Stews made of ground ingredients—basically a mush or gruel—were the primary food. Hunting contributed the occasional mule deer, antelope, and bighorn sheep, and rabbits apparently were taken by everyone working in the fields. The importance of corn is revealed by the discovery of "sacred" ears of corn. These perfect specimens, straight and missing not a single kernel, were found wrapped in deerskin pouches sewn with cotton thread and adorned with bits of turquoise, macaw feathers, and polished hematite.

Coprolites reveal that the vegetarian diet was supplemented by virtually every edible nut, seed, and berry growing near the canyon: grape, purslane, wild rye, dropseed, yucca, panic grass, sunflower, beeweed, Indian rice grass, amaranth, squawbush, wild onion, ground cherry, and goosefoot. As Morris writes, the diet at Antelope House can be characterized as corn plus "whatever was handy." Charcoal, bits of grit and debris, insect parts, feathers, hair, and even string found in the coprolites attest to food preparation practices and a general inattention to kitchen cleanliness. Two cooking pots found in the ruin with scraps of meals still adhering to their inside surfaces conjure an image of a stew simmering over a low fire awaiting sporadic contributions from hunting, gathering, and farming and constantly replenished as it was consumed.

Raising turkeys may have provided an additional source of food. More likely, however, was their use for making turkey feather blankets, which, along with cotton textiles, were the principal items of exchange outside the canyon. Turkey mummies found in the cave suggest a rather moth-eaten flock of birds, indicating that their feathers were allowed to grow just to usable size before being plucked.

The inadequacies of the diet are revealed in the skeletal remains, which display a high rate of bone abnormalities caused by anemia. A diet high in corn provides little iron and calcium. The unfortunate inhabitants also were infected with parasites, including an epidemic infection of pinworms. Some parasites apparently were conveyed through host grain beetles, which inadvertently were ground and ingested along with the corn. We can only guess at the hardships the people must have endured.

The people of Antelope House were corn and cotton farmers skilled in farming the bottomlands and in using the wild plant and animal resources of the canyon's diverse microenvironments. In this regard, the Antelope House Anasazi were much like the Navajo who live on the canyon floor and farm these same lands today.

The cliff dwellings of Tsegi Canyon provide information on community organization and the adaptive flexibility of plateau farmers. From the visitor center at Navajo National Monument one can walk down a half mile of caprock trail to a point overlooking a side canyon. Across the canyon a giant alcove opens to a height of nearly 500 feet, big enough to swallow the Washington Monument. Nestled near the bottom of the alcove is the ancient cliff dwelling of Betatakin, or "ledge house" in Navajo. As early as 1250, a few people lived in the alcove while farming nearby bottomland. In the late 1260s, according to Jeffrey Dean's tree-ring analysis, they began to cut and stockpile building timbers for the relocation of the whole community from another location. That move took place in 1275. Construction lasted for a mere eleven years, then ceased abruptly. The "house on the ledge" was abandoned, and again the entire community moved away to build another village elsewhere.

Betatakin's sister site of Kiet Siel—meaning "broken pieces of pottery" in Navajo—ultimately experienced the same fate as Betatakin, though as a result of the movement of individual households rather than the whole community. Established a number of years before Betatakin, Kiet Siel also experienced a growth boom in the 1270s as the result of separate households moving in to build "room clusters"—living rooms, storerooms, and granaries around an open courtyard. Room Cluster 2, on the eastern edge of the village, held two living rooms, eight storage chambers, two or three courtyards, and an associated grinding room. Each of the eight kivas in the village was shared by a number of households.

The Betatakin cliff dwelling at Navajo National Monument.

Why did the Hisatsinom build villages high in the cliffs? A frequent answer, and one given by Jonathan Haas and a number of other archaeologists, is for defense against enemies. Clearly, a cliff dwelling perched fifty feet above the canyon floor and difficult or impossible to reach when the ladders were drawn up, provides an added measure of security for people and provisions during times when populations were moving more frequently and when residents, in traveling farther to some of their fields, might be away from home for longer periods. Jeffrey Dean, who has spent a lifetime studying these ruins and others like them, believes cliff dwellings were built less for protection than to be near springs and to avoid using scarce bottomland for nonagricultural purposes.

Many cliff dwellings, Betatakin and Kiet Siel included, face in a southeasterly direction, which maximizes winter sunlight and heat. This location also avoids both the cold air along the canyon floor and the brutal northwesterly winds that punish inhabitants of the mesa tops. With these advantages in mind, the mystery of why cliff dwellers lived in cliffs dissolves.

We have seen that since the times of White Dog Cave the Hisatsinom enjoyed the use of rockshelters, caves, and cliffs for habitation. Perhaps they only reluctantly took up residence elsewhere, when the local geology prohibited the formation of stable natural shelters.

Like Betatakin, room construction and presumably growth at Kiet Siel ceased in the mid-1280s, but unlike at Betatakin the Kiet Siel inhabitants left as they had come—household by household—rather than together as a community. That the inhabitants of each village left as they had arrived points away from catastrophe or sudden disaster as the cause and toward the habitual option of packing up and moving as the economy declined.

Jeffrey Dean's analysis of social organization combined with a reconstruction of the effect of environmental changes on agricultural productivity reveals the most reasonable environmental causes for the abandonment of Betatakin and Kiet Siel. The quarter-century prior to the abandonment in 1300 was characterized by the Great Drought of 1276 to 1299, which was discovered by A. E. Douglass in 1929. To the Tsegi Canyon farmers it was not so much the reduced rainfall as the lowered water table in the canyon that brought about the erosion of farmland. The detrimental effects of erosion are not sudden; they accumulate year by year through the upstream progression of erosion. The farmer has some advance warning, knowing that this year or next a field will disappear into the arroyo and be washed away.

The rapid and deleterious consequences of severe erosion are revealed dramatically in a Hopi example. In historical times, the best farmland at the village of Oraibi was on the alluvial fan of Oraibi Wash. Farmers holding fields in the floodplain were able to grow corn and cotton during all except the worst droughts. Evidence suggests that erosion in the early twentieth century destroyed arable acreage at Oraibi at a rapid rate. These were years of prolonged and severe drought, such that springs dried and little rain fell.

The rapidity with which farmland could be lost to erosion is demonstrated by studies of Oraibi made by anthropologists Maitland Bradfield and Mischa Titiev. In the 1930s when Titiev studied Oraibi, the floodplain of Oraibi Wash was being extensively cultivated. A scant thirty years later, Bradfield's research demonstrated that all 820 acres of arable floodplain land had been lost to erosion and were abandoned. The consequences of losing so much of the best farmland would have been as disastrous for Kiet Siel as it was for Oraibi.

This Hopi example also explains away the "mystery" of abandonment. During times of serious drought, families with poorly watered lands would seek farming sites at some distance from the village. During short-lived droughts, a family could sometimes survive by farming several distant fields, which reduces the chance of complete crop failure. When increasing distance to well-watered farmland made the establishment of new fields impractical, residential colonies were established. During the drought-ridden years at the turn of the century, farming colonies were founded at Bacavi and Moenkopi by the farmers of Oraibi who were the most land poor. This system of periodic group fissioning brought the relationship between population and land into a more balanced state. Sometimes it was a part of the village that was abandoned, but at times clearly the entire village packed up to move to better land.

So why is abandonment still considered by many to be a mystery? The answer is that, in Tsegi Canyon, where extensive contemporary scientific research has been carried out by Jeffrey Dean, there is no mystery. Unfortunately, equivalent research has not been conducted at other sites of the

Four Corners region that were abandoned at this time. Where modern archaeological research is done, mysteries and speculation vanish in the face of confirmed knowledge. Elsewhere, we view "mysteries" of the past as research questions framed in popular language. In this sense there always will be mysteries.

The Pueblo IV Period (A.D. 1300 to 1540)

This final period of Hisatsinom prehistory begins with the massive relocation of population and movement over vast stretches of the northern and central Southwest. The Four Corners–San Juan River drainage was abandoned for full-time residential use. Inhabitants of large pueblos and cliff dwellings founded new villages in the central mountains, along the Little Colorado River, and on the southern extensions of Black Mesa. In some cases they established separate communities among the mountain Mogollon, and in others, like Point of Pines and Grasshopper Pueblos, they joined with local people to become part of growing communities. This movement appears to have been accompanied by sufficient advanced information about the destination to permit migration over great distances. As Erik Reed commented years ago, "All prehistoric Southwestern communities probably were more or less in contact and acquainted with each other directly or indirectly."

Emil Haury identified a migration of Hisatsinom Anasazi from the Kayenta-Hopi area to Point of Pines Pueblo. During the 1280s, fifty to sixty families (we do not know exactly how many) walked nearly 200 miles to Point of Pines, where they built about seventy pueblo rooms and at least one D-shaped subterranean kiva. Other evidence of their move included Kayenta-type pottery and artifacts at the new location. The preservation of this evidence is due largely to their houses having been burned at harvest time when storerooms were filled with corn—twenty-five bushels of charred corn were recovered from one burned room alone. In another room a family was trapped and died. Most of the Anasazi escaped, fortunately, probably fleeing to the Safford Valley and the middle San Pedro River. After this catastrophe, which can only be interpreted as intentional burning, their rooms were remodeled and reoccupied, presumably by the Mogollon who had forced them out.

But not all cases of Anasazi living with Mogollon ended in conflict and death. In fact, we suspect that the Grasshopper Pueblo example was more the norm, where a small group of Anasazi—it is unclear whether they were related to Hisatsinom or to more easterly Anasazi—were incorporated into the Mogollon community. Daughters and sisters married local boys and remained to be buried at Grasshopper, and some of the men and boys were initiated into the all-male religious societies that we think were critical to community governance.

Ceramic analysis by Daniela Triadan indicates that these Anasazi brought with them techniques of ceramic production that they applied using local materials. At Grasshopper Pueblo we envision an Anasazi enclave incorporated into the community and continuing to pursue traditional crafts using local materials. It is not uncommon in many parts of the world for families without farmland to turn to craft production for a livelihood. There is no evidence that their life at Grasshopper Pueblo was anything other than harmonious.

What happened at Grasshopper Pueblo may have taken place over much of the mountain region, part of larger processes in the development of the historical Pueblo people. In Hopi legend, this time marked the emergence of the people into the Fourth World—the present one—and the beginning of the migrations that would take clans across long distances and through many abandoned pueblos to settle at last in the present-day Hopi homelands. Archaeologists studying Grasshopper believe that the resident Anasazi introduced improved dry-farming techniques to the mountain Mogollon so that by the time that the central mountains of Arizona were abandoned, the Mogollon and Anasazi no longer were distinguishable on the basis of their way of life. The Mogollon had joined the Anasazi in becoming fully committed pueblo farmers. It is unclear, however, what the Anasazi may have received from the Mogollon. Perhaps we will never know in this specific case, but the research of Charles Adams into the origin of the Katsinam sheds considerable light on the general question of Anasazi-Mogollon relations.

Homol'ovi—"the place of little hills" in the Hopi language—is a state park on the outskirts of Winslow, Arizona, and comprises four separate pueblo ruins on both sides of the Little Colorado River. The largest ruins, Homol'ovi I and II, were occupied during the A.D. 1300s and are the only ones presently accessible to visitors. Hopis believe that the smaller village of Homol'ovi I was home to the Water and Sand clan people and that the Tobacco, Rabbit, Sun, and several other clans lived in the larger Homol'ovi II. Homol'ovi III and IV, which were inhabited during the later part of the 1200s, reflect the movement of people from different regions to settle in the well-watered valley of the Little Colorado River. According to Adams's interpretation of the ceramics, the builders of Homol'ovi IV were Anasazi from the Hopi Mesas, whereas Homol'ovi III was settled by immigrants from the upper Little Colorado River drainage with strong Mogollon connections.

The largest ruin is Homol'ovi II, with approximately a thousand rooms, and it is here that Adams and his research team have uncovered information on the fourteenth-century world of the Anasazi. Homol'ovi II was a major center for the exchange of ceramics, shell, and obsidian within a network that reached from Flagstaff on the west to Zuni on the east and from the Hopi Mesas in the north to the Salt and Gila River valleys of the southern desert. Whereas some archaeologists think that the movement of these goods was managed by an elite group, Adams finds no evidence for this in the Homol'ovi data. Rather, he sees Homol'ovi II people exchanging goods with similar pueblos on the basis of reciprocity, as in gift-giving, and at the community level. There is strong evidence for the exchange of cotton grown at Homol'ovi II for pottery made at Awat'ovi, more than fifty miles to the north.

A Katsina face painted on a ceramic bowl indicates the presence of the Katsina cult at Homol'ovi. Katsinam are the physical and public manifestation of spiritual beings sacred to all Pueblo Indians. At Hopi they are personified in kachina "dolls"—portable figures carved from cottonwood root and painted to reflect ceremonial clothing—and in ceremonial dances and processions by masked beings. Charles Adams's research at the Homol'ovi Ruins, other ancestral Hopi villages, and the historic village of Walpi led him to conclude that the Katsina concept developed during the A.D. 1300s from Mexican-derived ideas and icons. It is the presence of masks on ceramic bowls and as rock art that Adams uses to mark the appearance of the Katsinam. Another interesting connection between the Mogollon and Hisatsinom Anasazi is that historic Hopi kivas are rectangular, like those of the Mogollon, rather than round like the kivas typical of the Anasazi. The role of the mountain Mogollon in the development and transmission of the Katsinam is an intriguing unsolved question, perhaps another mystery.

The picture we have from Homol'ovi II is limited yet sharp. The people were highly successful farmers who depended on growing corn for food and cotton as a valuable commodity for exchange. In their agriculturally rich but firewood-poor environment, it was economic to exchange cotton and perhaps other farm products for the coal-fired yellow pottery produced at Awat'ovi and other communities on the Hopi Mesas. Along with the importance of corn, cotton, and ceramics to Hisatsinom economics and the significance of community autonomy for political organization, we see rather clear evidence for the presence of the Katsinam in ceremonial life. Further consolidation of the Hopi way would necessitate abandonment of Homol'ovi II as well as other large pueblo communities in accord with divine prophecy embodied in the Hopi migration legends. From Homol'ovi, people of the Water, Sand, and other clans trekked northward, settling eventually on the mesas that they occupy still.

Pedro de Tovar and the Transition to History

We end the story of the Hisatsinom in the summer of 1540 at the Hopi village of Awat'ovi on Antelope Mesa overlooking the Jeddito Valley when the Spaniard Pedro de Tovar met the Hopi. By this time the village of Homol'ovi and the other villages of the Little Colorado River valley, as well as the pueblo towns farther south in the mountains, were abandoned in favor of towns in the Hopi country. Prehistory and the labels we use today for prehistoric peoples suddenly shifted into Spanish history in that year, when General Francisco Vásquez de Coronado's expedition encountered Pueblo Indians. One day it was prehistory; the next, it was history for all time to come.

In 1540 Coronado and his men forged a path from Compostela in today's Mexican state of Nayarit to the Pueblo of Zuni in New Mexico in search of gold and the fabled Seven Cities of Cibola. In July, Coronado's officer Pedro de Tovar led a small exploratory expedition from Zuni to present-day Hopi. The journal of Pedro de Castañeda, the chronicler who accompanied Coronado's expedition, records this initial encounter with the Hopi at Awat'ovi. That historic moment is worth recounting in full:

> General Francisco Vazquez [de Coronado] found out from the [Zuni] people of the provinces that lay around it. . . . [T]hey informed him about a province with seven villages of the same sort as theirs, although somewhat different. They had nothing to do with these people. This province is called Tusayan. It is twenty-five leagues from Cibola [Zuni]. The villages are high and the people are warlike.
>
> The general had sent Don Pedro de Tovar to these villages with seventeen horsemen and three or four foot soldiers. Juan de Padilla, Franciscan friar, who had been a fighting man in his youth, went with them. When they reached the region, they entered the country so quietly that nobody observed them, because there were no settlements or farms between one village and another and the people do not leave the villages except to go to their farms, especially at this time when they had heard that Cibola [Zuni] had been captured by very fierce people, who travelled on animals which ate people. This information was generally believed by those who had never seen horses, although it was so strange as to cause much wonder. Our men arrived after nightfall and were able to conceal themselves under the edge of the village, where they heard the natives talking in their houses. But in the morning they were discovered and drew up in regular order, while the natives came out to meet them, with bows, and shields, and wooden clubs, drawn up in lines without any confusion. The interpreter was given a chance to speak to them and give them due warning, for they were intelligent people, but nevertheless they drew lines and insisted that our men should not go across these lines toward their village.
>
> While they were talking, some men acted as if they would cross the lines, and one of the natives lost control of himself and struck a horse a blow on the cheek of the bridle with his club. Friar Juan, fretted by the time that was being wasted in talking with them, said to the captain: "To tell the truth, I do not know why we came here." When the men heard this, they gave the Santiago so suddenly that they ran down many Indians and the others fled to the town in confusion. Some indeed did not have a chance to do this, so quickly did the people in the village come out with presents, asking for peace. The captain ordered

his force to collect, and, as the natives did not do any more harm, he and those who were with him found a place to establish their headquarters near the village. They had dismounted here when the natives came peacefully, saying that they had come to give in the submission of the whole province and that they wanted him to be friends with them and to accept the presents which they gave him. This was some cotton cloth, although not much, because they do not make it in that district. They also gave him some dressed skins and corn meal, and pine nuts and corn and birds of the country. Afterward they presented some turquoises, but not many. The people of the whole district came together that day and submitted themselves, and they allowed him to enter their villages freely to visit, buy, sell, and barter with them.

It is governed like Cibola [Zuni], by an assembly of the oldest men. They have their governors and generals. This was where they obtained the information about a large river. . . .

As Don Pedro de Tovar was not commissioned to go farther, he returned from there and gave this information to the general, who dispatched Don Garcia Lopez de Cardenas with about twelve companions to go see this river [the Colorado running through the Grand Canyon].

The brief, violent history of Spanish colonialism among the Hopi is recorded in subsequent events at Awat'ovi. The Franciscan mission of San Bernardo de Aguatubi was established there in 1629 and abandoned in 1680, when Pueblo Indians of Arizona and New Mexico revolted and threw off the yoke of Spanish colonial domination. The entire village was abandoned in the winter of 1700 to crumble slowly into the archaeological record encountered by J. O. Brew, director of the Awatovi Expedition (1935–1939), sponsored by Harvard University's Peabody Museum. By the time Harvard reached Awat'ovi in the mid-1930s, the Anasazi throughout the Colorado Plateau—particularly the Hisatsinom Anasazi—were the best known of all the Southwest's prehistoric cultures. In fact, when the Harvard team began in 1935, the reports that would define the Mogollon and Hohokam had not yet been published.

Like Awat'ovi, many other Hopi villages would be abandoned in their own time and in their own way, a process that had been going on for a thousand years. Once occupying a vast territory stretching from the Grand Canyon to the Lukachukai Mountains and from the San Juan River

to the Mogollon Rim, the Hopi were fixed by prophecy and historical cir-
cumstance to the villages of the three mesas they occupy today, a small
reservation surrounded by the Navajo Nation. It is the Navajo, a Native
American people unrelated to the Hopi, and the Navajo Nation offices for
managing cultural resources who have assumed the stewardship of many
of the Hisatsinom's ancestral sites.

8 THE SINAGUA

The story of the Sinagua, like so many other stories of the Southwest, is one of people and places, past and present. It is the story of a man, the institution that he founded, and the archaeology of the place he knew so well—the country of the black sand. The story of the Sinagua also is a study in disaster, magic, and the human capacity to adapt and go on with life after calamity.

The Sinagua are one of Arizona's most enigmatic prehistoric peoples. Less archaeological attention has been focused on the Sinagua than on the Hohokam, Mogollon, or Anasazi. The reasons why this is so are even now not completely clear. Unlike the Patayan, who left only ephemeral traces of their presence, the Sinagua built visible and often stunning stone pueblos and cliff dwellings. Perhaps we can look for an explanation in the nature of their culture, which has been viewed from the beginning as an amalgam, borrowed from other people, and thus difficult to study and understand. Or possibly their neglect stems from the land in which the Sinagua lived—remote from modern population centers and unlikely to draw archaeologists and their students.

Archaeologists divide the Sinagua into two branches. The Northern Sinagua occupied the area around modern Flagstaff, and the Southern Sinagua lived along the middle stretches of the Verde River in the central part of the state. Although one man essentially discovered and defined both branches, their story diverges from that point. Our telling of their story also considers each apart from the other.

Discovering the Sinagua

The story begins with a honeymoon. In 1912 Harold Sellers Colton and his wife, Mary-Russell Ferrell Colton, visited Flagstaff during their honeymoon trip. Colton was a professor of zoology at the University of Pennsylvania, and his wife was a successful water-color artist in Philadelphia. On their trip they developed an instant fascination with the glorious Southwest. They returned in 1916 to establish Flagstaff as their vacation camp, exploring the surrounding countryside. The Coltons' interest in archaeology was sparked accidentally at a family picnic in the pines when their son Ferrell found a prehistoric potsherd. In seeking the story behind the sherd, the Coltons launched a new era in southwestern archaeology.

Having learned that Flagstaff was the locale for intensive prehistoric occupation, the Coltons began to study the small sites in the area enthusiastically. Each summer the Coltons surveyed the region around Flagstaff, collecting pottery and mapping the distribution of ruins. Their work resulted in a decision to make Arizona their permanent home, which they did in 1926.

Around this time a controversy erupted among the citizens of Flagstaff. The Sinagua site of Elden Pueblo just outside the town was being excavated by the notable figure Jesse W. Fewkes, who removed the artifacts he recovered to the Smithsonian Institution in Washington, D.C. Although, as we saw in chapter 1, this was a common practice at the time, the citizens of Flagstaff were nevertheless outraged. Public pressure mounted to build a local museum to prevent what they viewed as the pilfering of artifacts. As a result, in 1928 the Museum of Northern Arizona was founded and the Northern Arizona Society of Science and Art was formed to administer it. Harold Colton was named as president of the society and director of the museum, and Mary-Russell Colton was selected to act as the curator of art. The museum opened officially on September 6, 1928, with Byron Cummings as the guest speaker at this gala event.

The Museum of Northern Arizona became one of three landmark private institutions in Arizona that together would shape Arizona archaeology. Along with the Amerind Foundation and Gila Pueblo, the Museum of Northern Arizona would push the boundaries of our understanding, discovering new cultures and new concepts. The museum was not only an archaeological institution, however. The diverse range of topics considered at the museum under Colton's direction included geology, zoology, meteorology, and ethnology. The overarching theme of these studies was the relationship between people and the environment.

Colton was ideally suited for museum work. His background in zoology provided him with the patience and skill he needed to collect, system-
atize, and synthesize large bodies of data. Potsherds would become his
lifelong means of discovering the past. The first Pecos Conference in 1927
gave Colton a framework for classifying sites and defining styles of architecture, pottery, and other materials. Perhaps more important, in 1929 A.
E. Douglass was able to close the gap between the "floating" prehistoric
tree-ring chronology and the historical chronology, supplying the means
to determine secure dates for the trends of the past. Colton was, as Christian Downum writes, ready to discover "one grand history" in the ruins
and potsherds of northern Arizona.

Colton soon hired Lyndon L. Hargrave as the assistant director of the
new museum. Together Hargrave and Colton would create the system for
identifying pottery types that is still used today. In 1930 they began the
first full season in the field, beginning with ruins in Deadmans Flat. How
exciting that time must have been! Hargrave and Colton were the first archaeologists to study the ruins of the area more than cursorily; the slate of
its prehistory was clean. Colton described one museum expedition, giving
us a feeling for what the experience was like. He relates that although it
was sometimes possible to commute daily to the dig, most of the time a
camp was pitched among the pines or junipers in a spot sheltered from
the wind that so often blows in the northern country. Above the tents flew
the museum's white and blue flag. After a long day in the field, the excavators would gather to write up their notes, compare the day's results, or
"hold a bull session around the campfire under the stars." Colton also
noted what every field archaeologist knows: "A cook can make or break
the expedition."

A monumental discovery was made that first summer. The first clue
came by accident. A water-color artist from Australia named H. Neville-
Smith, who was exhibiting his work in the museum, wanted to paint Sunset Crater Volcano, the stark, brightly colored cinder cone some fifteen
miles northeast of Flagstaff. Lionel F. Brady, who was at that time the curator of geology at the museum, kindly drove him to the crater and helped
him set up his easel. While waiting for the painting to be finished, Brady
strolled casually around among the cinders that covered the ground. He
happened upon a cluster of black-on-white potsherds *on top of* the cinder

deposit. It was curious; how and why did they come to rest there?

Shortly thereafter, archaeologists who were excavating nearby discovered pit houses filled with a thick deposit of ash and cinders. The sherds found by Brady evidently had worked their way to the surface, through the action of tunneling rodents or pushing tree roots, from below the same volcanic debris that filled the abandoned houses. The Sunset Crater Volcano had erupted *while* the pit houses had been occupied. Because other sites were known to have been constructed on top of the cinder layer, the importance of this event was evident. Human occupation also continued *after* the eruption in what must have been a radically altered landscape.

This theme of human adaptation to a natural calamity would guide the archaeology carried out by the museum for many years. Attention turned first to determining when the eruption took place by applying tree-ring dating to burned houses lying under the layer of volcanic ash. It was clear that a dramatic change had taken place in prehistoric settlement after the eruption of the Sunset Crater Volcano, and the archaeologists wanted to learn why. In the following years they excavated a number of sites around Flagstaff that provided some pieces of the puzzle but that also created new questions. Large, elongated depressions of unknown function were discovered, and traces of Hohokam "influence" in the form of red-on-buff pottery and trash mounds had been found. What were Hohokam people doing so far away from their desert homes? Excavation soon demonstrated yet more Hohokam traits, such as ceramic vessels, cremations, and Hohokam-style pit houses.

In 1933 Colton turned his attention to Wupatki Pueblo, the largest Pueblo III Period ruin in the area and a national monument since 1924. Excavations at Wupatki in 1933 and 1934 were funded by the Civil Works Administration. A smaller pueblo, Nalakihu, also was excavated. When they failed to date definitively the eruption of Sunset Crater Volcano by 1935, archaeologists turned to defining the culture of the region more precisely. By this time the excavations at Snaketown had revealed that the mysterious elongated depressions or "bowls" in the Flagstaff area probably were ballcourts, and two were excavated, one of which is now restored at Wupatki National Monument. In 1938 and 1939, John C. McGregor, who was then a graduate student, excavated Winona Village and Ridge

Ruin, resulting in a great deal of new information. Much data had been collected; it was now time for synthesis.

At that time, one of the primary tasks of archaeology was to classify cultures. Arizona had been peopled by diverse cultures that had left behind a permanent record, much like the fossil record. By sorting through these material remains, winnowing and tabulating traits, and finally assigning prehistoric cultures to a category, Colton defined a framework for understanding the prehistory of the Flagstaff region in which migrations and cultural diversity figured prominently. Colton believed that the prehistoric people of the Flagstaff area were unlike any of the three major southwestern cultures. They appeared to display a mixture of cultural traits from the Anasazi, Mogollon, and Hohokam. For this reason, Colton concluded that it was necessary to define a new culture.

But what to name this mixed and fascinating culture? He took the name from history. In Spanish colonial times, Governor Oñate of New Mexico dispatched Captains Farfán and Quesada to search for gold and other precious metals in the Verde Valley. Leaving the Hopi town of Oraibi, they crossed the Little Colorado River and passed to the south of the San Francisco Peaks. They called these mountains the Sierra sin Agua, or "Mountains without Water." Colton chose the name Sinagua for the culture because "this practically waterless area" once was home to a thriving population.

Comparing traits between the cultures, Colton identified the Sinagua as a branch of the larger Mogollon Culture. Not surprisingly, ceramics were the chief trait that characterized the Sinagua—a red or brown plain ware known as Alameda Brown Ware. It bore the unmistakable signs of its origin: a temper of crushed volcanic rock, tuff, or cinders. Alameda Brown Ware was made with the paddle-and-anvil technique used by the prehistoric Patayan people, the Hohokam, and others. This was one of the traits that Colton considered to be of Hohokam origin. In addition to pottery, the Sinagua were identified by deep timber pit houses, alcove houses, and extended burials.

When Colton plotted the distribution of Alameda Brown Ware, he found that it came from two different areas: sites in the north around Flagstaff and sites in the south along the Verde and East Verde Rivers. In 1946 Colton defined these culture areas as the Northern Sinagua and

Wupatki Ruin, with
a great kiva in the
right foreground.

the Southern Sinagua. The Sinagua were no backwoods farmers. Colton viewed these people as a cosmopolitan and sophisticated amalgam of Hohokam, Hisatsinom (Kayenta) Anasazi, and other peoples who had been drawn to the Flagstaff area by the eruption of the Sunset Crater Volcano in A.D. 1064. We present the story of the Northern Sinagua first, and then turn to the Southern Sinagua.

Northern Sinagua

Flagstaff is a jewel set in the highlands of the Colorado Plateau. To the north, the San Francisco Peaks, clothed in conifers and capped with snow, rise to almost 13,000 feet. The mountains are sacred to the Hopis, who call them Nuva-tukia-ovi, "The Place of Snow on the Very Top" or "The Snow Mountains." Here dwell the Katsinam, the beneficent spirits who bring the rain to the Hopi cornfields. Beyond the mountains is the spectacular Grand Canyon of the Colorado River. Less grand but no less impressive are the smaller canyons cut by the Little Colorado River and Walnut Creek. Beyond the peaks, the country flattens, the pines disappear, and the vast stretch of the Colorado Plateau begins.

The land around Flagstaff has been scarred by fire—not forest fires but the primeval fire that explodes from the very earth itself. Volcanic cones rise blackly against the eastern sky, and the ground is covered with cinders. For this reason Colton called the Sinagua the "People of the Black Sand."

It is cold here, and the summers are short. Snows may begin in September and continue until April. The wind always blows, ceaseless and irritating. Wresting a living from the land is not easy. Why would this place attract Hohokam, Anasazi, and Mogollon peoples? We will see that Colton sought an answer in the sand that gave the land its name.

Life before the Eruption

The Sinagua story begins, as it does everywhere in the Southwest, with the time before pottery was invented. Only limited evidence of the earliest people has been found to date, including a Clovis point found at Wupatki National Monument. Clovis hunters no doubt ranged through this region, but there seems to have been little intensive occupation such as we see

The San Francisco Peaks from the Lomaki Ruin at Wupatki National Monument.

in southeastern Arizona. Archaic people living in the Grand Canyon area made animal figurines of split twigs and left them in caves in the Redwall Limestone formation. Associated with Archaic-style projectile points, the figurines may be as much as four thousand years old. The figurines probably were used in some kind of hunting magic, as they seem to represent deer and other animals.

The Cinder Park Phase (A.D. 600 to 825). The first settlements recognized as Sinagua—with pottery, well-built houses, and corn agriculture—appeared in the Flagstaff area around A.D. 600 during the Cinder Park phase. Sinagua houses were what archaeologists call "true" pit houses, in which the wall of the pit forms part of the wall of the house. The perimeter posts forming the sides of the house were set into the ground surface, and several posts, usually four in number, supported the roof. The pits excavated for the houses were as much as six feet deep, more like Mogollon architecture than contemporary Anasazi houses. The mixture of material traits that characterized the Sinagua Culture was apparent in this earliest phase: although the pottery seems to borrow from the Hohokam, in building their houses the Sinagua used a Mogollon style.

The first Sinagua settlements were built in the parklike areas of the region near the most fertile land and typically were small in size. The population was relatively sparse at this time. The Sinagua appear to have developed communal ceremonial practices and structures in which to conduct their rituals, as extremely large houses that probably served this purpose occasionally are found at Cinder Park phase sites. Similar large houses, although constructed differently, also occur among early Mogollon and Hohokam settlements around this time. The Sinagua's relationships with their neighbors seem to have been cordial, as the Sinagua obtained pottery from other groups living in the plateau country.

The Sunset Phase (A.D. 825 to 1000) and the Rio de Flag Phase (A.D. 1000 to 1070). The period from 825 to 1070 was a time of growth and diversification. There were minor changes in architecture, and settlements became larger, indicating that the population also was growing during this period. The Sinagua moved into new, diverse areas, adapting their farming techniques to the land on which they settled. They used check dams to control rainwater and channel it onto their fields, which were typically located along major washes. In these areas the Sinagua built field houses, which were single-room structures located near fields and built to house the farmer and family during the summer. Tending the crop closely was necessary to prevent animals and birds from stealing the harvest, and the use of field houses helped the farmers avoid daily travel to and from the home base. It must have been pleasant and peaceful at the farms in late summer, waiting for the harvest and feasts.

This peaceful, bucolic lifestyle was to change dramatically in the late fall of 1064. At that time the earth literally exploded beneath the feet of the Sinagua as the Sunset Crater Volcano erupted for the first time. A huge fissure ten miles long opened in the earth, and a lava flow five miles long spewed forth. Hot, black cinders blanketed the ground over an area of about fifteen square miles. It must have been an awesome and terrifying sight, a vision of fire and smoke accompanied by earthshaking tremors and a terrible roaring noise. The air was filled with poisonous gases, and volcanic bombs rained down from the sky. No doubt the trees caught fire, adding the fury of forest fire to the spectacle. The Sinagua must have thought the world was coming to an end. Terrifying as the eruption was, however, the Sinagua apparently had sufficient time to gather their possessions and flee; no human remains have yet been discovered buried in the ash, as happened at the famous Pompeii.

The eruption in 1064 was only the first of many. A second major eruption may have occurred sometime in 1066 or 1067, and over the next fifty years or so the cinder cone of Sunset Crater Volcano developed and belched black and red cinders into the air, which the prevailing winds carried as far away as Kansas. There were more flows of lava in 1150 and 1220. Finally, in 1250 the sequence of volcanism ended with a last deposit of red cinders on the rim of the cone. Since then, Sunset Crater Volcano has remained silent. Only its rosy-hued cinders, which moved Major John Wesley Powell to name it Sunset Crater in 1885, give evidence of its fiery past.

Aftermath: The Center of the Sacred World

Just as it altered the landscape irrevocably, the aftermath of the first eruption changed the Sinagua lifeway forever. Diverse people from different areas apparently moved into the region after the eruption, bringing with them new architectural and ceramic styles, burial practices, and ceremonial buildings. Why were people drawn to the Flagstaff region? Colton originally proposed that the land was the magnet. The volcanic cinders deposited over the region during the eruptions, he hypothesized, served as a mulch to hold moisture in the soil as well as to enrich it, making the farmland more fertile after the eruption than before. Farmers from distant areas were drawn to this newly fertile land. The Sinagua Culture was transformed through contact with these new people and new ideas into something strikingly different from what it had been before the eruption. Colton defined the Winona and Padre phases to describe the unique cultural differences of the posteruption period between 1070 and 1150. The following Elden phase represented the amalgamation of the newly arrived immigrant groups.

The Winona and Padre Phases (A.D. 1070 to 1150). One striking aspect of posteruption culture was a distinct Hohokam presence. Colton used the term *Winona phase* to refer to these Hohokam settlements. The Hohokam villages were distinguished by pit houses like those of the southern deserts, which were "houses in pits" rather than true pit houses. Hohokam ceramics also appeared, and a number of ballcourts were built around the time of the eruption or shortly afterward. The ballcourts also were much like those of the desert, being constructed of earth with openings at each end for entryways and having center and end markers (see chapter 4).

The Padre phase also represented features brought by new arrivals. It was distinguished by masonry pit houses, in which the house was dug into the ground and lined with stone, with a ventilator constructed to bring fresh air into the semisubterranean room. Colton suggested that the Padre phase houses represented a mixture of architectural styles from different cultures. The Anasazi contributed masonry, the ventilator was a Sinagua characteristic, and the roof construction was Hohokam. The Sinagua must have had house-building parties much like traditional American barn raisings to learn so many different building techniques and employ them effectively!

The Elden Phase (A.D. 1150 to 1220). Colton viewed the Elden phase as one of population growth and expansion, and he attributed this new cultural energy to the immigrants who flocked to the Flagstaff area after the Sunset Crater Volcano erupted, launching a new era in Sinagua Culture.

Was Colton's vision of the Sinagua before and after the eruption of Sunset Crater accurate? Not surprisingly, some archaeologists disagree with his interpretation. Peter Pilles, Jr., does not think that the eruption made Flagstaff area farmland more fertile. He points out that, although cinders may add nutrients to the soil, the process can take many hundreds of years and would have occurred long after the supposed migrations took place. He also notes that pine trees growing today in the cinder zone are stunted and deformed, indicating that they are growing under stressful rather than beneficial conditions.

Instead, Pilles believes that the evidence for migrations of different peoples into the Flagstaff area—in the form of nonlocal ceramics, architecture, and other traits—can better be attributed to an increase in trading between the Sinagua and their neighbors. This may well be true, but Pilles's theory does not explain why this increase in trading took place or why nonmovable facilities such as ballcourts were present.

If the lure of better farmland or better trading did not draw Hohokam, Anasazi, and Mogollon to the Flagstaff area, what did? We propose a less prosaic explanation than either Colton's or Pilles's ideas. We imagine that the spectacle of the erupting Sunset Crater Volcano could have been seen for an extremely long distance. During the day, the plume of smoke would be visible for many miles, perhaps as far away as several modern states. The sunlight may have been temporarily dimmed due to the ash and smoke in the atmosphere. At night, the glow of fire and cooling lava would have been particularly impressive. Those people who were too far away to see and hear the spectacle firsthand would certainly have heard of it from neighbors and travelers. Surely, we believe, the eruption of the Sunset Crater Volcano was the most remarkable event in the lives of the residents of prehistoric Arizona.

It is not far-fetched to speculate that the people also attributed to the erupting volcano incredible supernatural power. People flocked to the area, we suspect, to propitiate the power to which they attributed the eruption, and perhaps to absorb some of it. We note that quests to places of power in order to pray, meditate, and seek visions are common in many Native American religions, and the roots of this practice were probably prehistorical.

In our view of the past, the Hohokam constructed ballcourts in the Flagstaff area to be able to practice their ceremonies in a magical place of power, thus imbuing their rituals with holiness and greater effectiveness. There may even have developed a tradition of pilgrimage to this holiest of places, not unlike the sacred journeys made today by Hopi and Zuni peoples. The Hopi travel to the San Francisco Peaks before important ceremonies, for example, to gather spruce boughs that they will wear and carry in dances, and to pray.

Along similar lines, Christian Downum thinks that the beginning of the Hopi Katsina religion can be traced to this time in the Flagstaff area. Certainly the power lingers there still, where the Katsinam dwell in the San Francisco Peaks. The Hopi believe that the wind god Yaponcha, the spirit of the whirlwind, lives in a crack in the lava flow from Sunset Crater. The deep, even supernatural significance of Sunset Crater Volcano can be felt today.

Whatever happened in prehistory, what followed next is clear. The Elden phase represents the peak of Sinagua Culture beginning some time around 1150 and ending around 1220. A number of relatively large pueblos were built at this time, marking unprecedented population growth in the area, and this construction boom was accompanied by an expansion in agricultural systems that included the building of numerous field houses. The largest, most spectacular, and best known of the Flagstaff sites were built during this phase. These include groups of sites that can be visited today at Walnut Canyon and Wupatki National Monuments.

Walnut Canyon National Monument is a spectacular zone of cliff dwellings tucked into the limestone walls of the canyon. Walnut Canyon was transferred to the National Park Service in 1934, and the trails and visitor facilities at the monument were built by the Civilian Conservation Corps. Today a steep, winding trail with incredible canyon vistas leads the visitor along ledges filled with prehistoric dwellings. Archaeologists have recorded more than 300 rooms beneath the rock overhangs of the canyon. Dwellings, field houses, and agricultural features also are found on the canyon rim. Mostly field houses are found on the south rim, which appears to have experienced little intensive occupation. The most unusual feature of Walnut Canyon is the presence of so-called forts. These buildings are built atop ridges that jut over the rim of the canyon, and each island of land is linked to the rim by a narrow peninsula. There are five forts in the canyon, sites that apparently were the centers of communities and that served defensive functions as well as other needs. Third Fort contains a large community room.

The dense occupation of Walnut Canyon was a product of the Sunset Crater Volcano eruption; the area was sparsely settled before the eruption. Most of the sites, and apparently all of the cliff dwellings, were built during the Elden phase. There are hints that these later residents of the canyon expanded into areas that had previously been little used. An expanding local population seems the likely cause of this growth. Around 1250 to 1300, Walnut Canyon was rapidly abandoned, a process that may have been caused or contributed to by the Great Drought that devastated the Colorado Plateau around this time.

Wupatki was made a national monument in 1924, largely through the efforts of Harold Colton. In the years since its establishment, the Museum of Northern Arizona and the National Park Service have carried out various archaeological investigations there, including survey and excavation. The monument is located northeast of Flagstaff and Sunset Crater and consists of a number of ruins that can be visited. The ruins perch on sandstone mesas, appearing to rise seamlessly from the living rock from which they are built. Some ruins, in particular The Citadel and Crack-in-Rock Pueblo, command spectacular views of the countryside. The Citadel has been described as one of the forts constructed during the Elden phase. Perhaps the most impressive ruin is Wupatki Pueblo itself, where the visitor center is located. Wupatki is a compact, multistoried block of rooms and walled plaza areas. Most interesting are the public facilities that were probably oriented toward community ceremonies. The ballcourt at Wupatki was built of stone masonry, unlike the typical earthen ballcourts of the desert areas. Wupatki also has a large circular "amphitheater" that lacks features of either ballcourts or circular Anasazi kivas and a number of subterranean structures that may represent kivas.

An extraordinary and important discovery dating to this time was made at Ridge Ruin. Archaeologists found the burial of a man who was accompanied by an incredible array of well-preserved wooden artifacts, as well as other offerings. Included were several wands ending in carved deer's feet, human hands, and other shapes, as well as miniature bows and arrows and other mysterious objects. Hopi who viewed the ceremonial offerings identified the man as an important person or leader of the Motswimi, or Warrior society. Perhaps this "magician" derived his power from the events associated with the eruption of the Sunset Crater Volcano. It certainly is striking that modern Hopi would connect this magician of the past with a present Hopi society. Support for Downum's argument for a Sinagua origin of the Katsina religion, the presence of priestly societies among the Sinagua, and a link between the Sinagua and the Hopi are suggested.

The Turkey Hill Phase (A.D. 1220 to 1300) and the Clear Creek Phase (A.D. 1300 to 1450). Beginning around 1220, Sinagua prehistory changed course once again. In the Turkey Hill phase, villages became smaller and many were abandoned. The scale of the agricultural systems was reduced, and ballcourts ceased to be used. This appears to mark a contraction of Sinaguan settlement, which Christian Downum suggests was created by environmental conditions at this time, whether naturally induced or created by Sinagua overuse of their lands. Although this certainly may have been the case, we also think it no coincidence that the exodus of Sinagua and other people from the Flagstaff area took place around the same time that the Sunset Crater Volcano ceased its volcanic activity. The earth no longer trembled and shook; the sky no longer reflected the fires in the bowels of the earth; the magic no longer worked, and the rituals lost their power. The Sinagua and all who had joined them packed up and moved away.

In the following Clear Creek phase, between 1300 and 1450, most of the traditional Sinagua territory was abandoned, and the remaining population concentrated in a few extremely large towns, such as Chavez Pass Pueblo on Anderson Mesa. This is one of the largest towns in the southern part of the Southwest, with an estimated 1,000 rooms. By 1450 even these settlements were abandoned, and the people probably moved northward to the Hopi Mesas, where they live today. Hopi tradition clearly identifies sites such as Chavez Pass Pueblo as the origin point for many of the clans, further evidence linking Hopi and Sinagua. Today's Hopi remember the ancestors who saw the night light up with fire and smoke in 1064 and who left their mark forever on the northern plateau landscape.

Southern Sinagua

We know less about the Southern Sinagua than the Northern Sinagua. Archaeologists have viewed the Verde River valley and the Southern Sinagua Culture as marginal—peripheral geographically and culturally to the great developments of the Anasazi and Hohokam Cultures. Much of what we do know stems primarily from archaeological survey, as little excavation has been carried out. Archaeologists are only beginning to write the prehistory of the Verde Valley.

Colton originally identified the Verde Valley as part of the Sinagua Culture on the basis of its similarities to the culture of the Flagstaff region. In his view, the Hohokam were the first inhabitants of the Verde Valley. Colton speculated that the Sinagua Culture of the north later pushed southward into the Verde Valley, displacing the resident Hohokam—one of the migration theories that was popular at the time. Colton theorized that the Great Drought may have caused the southward movement of the Sinagua and that instead of stopping permanently in the Verde Valley the Sinagua may have continued southward into the Phoenix area. In his 1946 book *The Sinagua,* Colton was adamant that much additional work with the Southern Sinagua would have to be done before their place in southwestern prehistory would be clear. By the mid-1990s we have come only a little further toward achieving this clarity.

The Verde River is the last remaining perennial river in Arizona. Second only to the Salt River in the amount of land it drains, the Verde has its headwaters in the mountains north of the Prescott Valley. It stretches more than a hundred miles southward to empty into the Salt River just north of Phoenix. There is enormous environmental diversity in the valley, which in its length and breadth spans mountains to desert. Such diversity evidently held an appeal for a number of prehistoric peoples who lived in the valley at one time or another.

Named in Spanish el Río de los Reyes—the River of the Kings—the Verde was discovered by Europeans when Antonio de Espejo traveled there in 1583 in search of fabled mines. Later, trappers and mountain men were the first U.S. citizens to explore the Verde and other Arizona rivers. The struggle to harness the waters of the Verde in order to turn Phoenix from desert to paradise began in the late nineteenth century, with ambitious entrepreneurs who founded the Rio Verde Canal Company. Once notorious for its floods, the Verde today is tamed, controlled by Horseshoe and Bartlett Dams along its lower reaches.

Although the river flows sweetly past stands of huge cottonwoods and other trees that choke its banks, the middle Verde Valley is hot and dry. Mesquite and creosote cover the floodplain and hills, and the sun reflects blindingly off the white limestone cliffs. Millions of years ago, geological block faults dammed the ancestral Verde River and created lakes and dry lake beds, or *playas*. Limestone was deposited in the lakes, and salt formed in the playas. Through time, the soft limestone eroded, creating caves and caverns, some of which collapsed to form sinkholes. Prehistoric people later would build their homes in the cliff faces and enlarge the caves to create dwellings in the rock itself. They irrigated their crops with water from the sinkhole lakes and mined the salt and traded it widely.

Early History and the Hohokam Connection

Not much is known of the first residents of the Verde Valley. Doubtless there was Archaic Period occupation and an early occupation by the first people to make and use pottery, but these times are poorly understood because so few sites have been excavated. The Archaic Period is labeled the Dry Creek phase.

The residents of the Verde Valley from A.D. 700 or so are more visible archaeologically. From their houses, pottery, and other material goods, archaeologists suspect that these people were Hohokam or were closely connected to the Hohokam Culture. They built Hohokam-style "houses in pits," cremated their dead, and constructed ballcourts for their ceremonial activities. The arrangement of their houses, trash mounds, and cremation areas indicates a social organization similar to that seen elsewhere in the Hohokam deserts—a good clue to cultural and ethnic similarities. Colonies of immigrant Hohokam may have been established because of the rich natural resources of the valley. Salt, argillite for making jewelry, and high-quality chert and obsidian for fashioning arrowheads and other tools may have drawn the Hohokam northward.

In their close connection with the Hohokam of the Phoenix Basin, the early inhabitants of the middle Verde Valley resemble the occupants of the lower stretches of the river. Indeed, the farther one travels down the Verde

River toward the Salt River, the more Hohokam-like the early occupation becomes. Our understanding of the prehistory of the lower Verde region is quite new. The first major excavation in the area, which was previously known only through archaeological survey, was undertaken in 1992 by archaeologists from Statistical Research, Inc. They discovered a large and impressive site in the Horseshoe Reservoir area, which was occupied from around A.D. 800 to 1000 and which boasted two ballcourts. This site was literally a surprise. Its extent was unknown from surface indications, and we were not expecting to find large Hohokam villages that far north of Phoenix. It was extremely fortunate that Bureau of Reclamation archaeologist Jon Czaplicki directed us to work at what originally appeared to be a small, insignificant hamlet.

At this site, named Scorpion Point Village after a finely made, scorpion-shaped arrowhead that was found there, archaeologists also found evidence for another attraction of the Verde River area for the Hohokam. Cotton seeds were abundant in the excavated houses, suggesting that this crop was grown along the river. Cotton may have been a sort of cash crop that the Verde people exchanged for corn, pottery, or other goods.

Water was brought to the fields along the river through irrigation canals much like those of the Phoenix area, although the system was smaller and less extensive because the valley was relatively narrow. Canals in the area that are today covered by Horseshoe Reservoir were recorded by Frank Midvale in 1945. Midvale has his own remarkable story. Of an immigrant Bohemian background, Midvale was so sensitive about his ethnic identity that he changed his name several times. Growing up in Phoenix, Midvale and his friends played among the archaeological sites of the central city, perhaps using the platform mound at La Ciudad as a coasting hill. He became fascinated with archaeology at an early age, collecting arrowheads and learning what he could about the subject. When Midvale was in high school, Omar Turney, who recorded the Hohokam irrigation systems of Phoenix, became his mentor, and Midvale also became fascinated with Hohokam irrigation. Midvale took classes in archaeology when he could, did extensive survey work and some excavation, and supervised excavations at the site of La Ciudad. He later worked for Gila Pueblo, surveying in Phoenix, the lower Verde Valley, and western Arizona in search of the elusive "red-on-buff culture."

When the lower Verde Valley was to be inundated by Horseshoe Reservoir, Midvale and his friend James Simmons rushed there to record, photograph, and map the canals before they disappeared beneath the lake waters. They were guided by Harry T. McCoy, whom Midvale called "my best guide and an old-timer from the pioneer days." Midvale photographed a wall that was identified later as an aqueduct to carry irrigation water over two washes, perhaps the first such feature identified in Arizona.

Although Midvale never achieved the academic credentials that would have given him professional status, his work in identifying and documenting Hohokam irrigation canals was invaluable. His work demonstrated the valuable contributions that nonprofessionals can make toward understanding the past.

Later History: The Honanki Phase (A.D. 1130 to 1300) and the Tuzigoot Phase (A.D. 1300 to 1400)

By 1100 or so, change was being wrought in the Verde Valley. The upper reaches of the river had been abandoned by the Hohokam population, but Hohokam influence in the middle Verde Valley peaked at this time. Shifts in political and economic connections appear. Imported pottery and other nonlocal goods indicate that, whereas previous connections were with the Hohokam of the south, after this time trading relationships shifted to the Anasazi of the Colorado Plateau.

Colton's hypothesized migration of Northern Sinagua into the area occurred at this time. As we saw in chapter 4, it was around this time that dramatic changes took place in the Hohokam Culture. Originally archaeologists used the same explanation they applied to the Classic Period Hohokam—a migration by puebloan peoples into the southern deserts—to explain the changes in the Verde Valley.

The Honanki and Tuzigoot phases in the Verde Valley reflect these shifts. The population of the area gradually abandoned smaller settlements to come together in just a few, much larger pueblos. Tuzigoot National Monument is one of these. This restored Sinagua pueblo sits on a ridge above the Verde River. Today's visitor can trace the footsteps of the vanished Sinagua through the efforts of Byron Cummings. In 1933, when his fieldwork near Prescott was concluding, Cummings began to seek another site to investigate. With the advice of Earl Jackson, a graduate student who was then surveying the Verde Valley, he chose Tuzigoot as a promising site. "Its excavation," he wrote, "would provide archaeological information in regard to the Upper Verde drainage which has heretofore been entirely lacking, no systematic excavation ever having been carried out in the region."

Tuzigoot was at the time owned by the United Verde Copper Company, which gave permission for excavation. The site was excavated in 1933 with a crew paid out of Federal Emergency Relief Administration funds and continued in 1934 under the Arizona branch of the Civil Works Administration (CWA). The project called for the complete excavation of the ruin, its restoration, and the repair and display of all artifacts that were recovered. The work was supervised by several of Cummings's assistants at the Arizona State Museum. More than 80 rooms and 400 inhumations were excavated. Local citizens worked to have the land, museum, and collections donated to the federal government. On July 25, 1939, Tuzigoot National Monument was established.

In their report on the work at Tuzigoot, Louis R. Caywood and Edward H. Spicer sketched the prehistory of the Verde Valley as it was understood at the time. As others had before them, they noted that kivas were absent, but they thought that a rectangular room with a raised platform at one end may have served as a ceremonial room. The pottery suggested a clear connection with the Northern Sinagua, but there were some differences. Corrugated pottery was absent, and it could not be determined whether the decorated pottery had been locally produced or imported from the Flagstaff region. They concluded that it was not possible to designate an independent culture in the area; Tuzigoot was "obviously a pueblo where cultural influences from various regions were at work."

Two other Southern Sinagua ruins of this period that can be visited today are Montezuma Castle and Montezuma Well. Neither ruin had anything to do with Montezuma; the sites were given these fanciful names in the nineteenth century when every archaeological site was associated with the Aztecs in the public's imagination. Montezuma Castle also was excavated as a CWA project by Cummings's student Earl Jackson in 1933. Montezuma Castle is a cliff dwelling that originally contained five stories and a possible balcony. There were probably about forty-five to sixty rooms in the original pueblo. Some were dug into the limestone and others were

Montezuma Castle, a five-story Sinagua cliff dwelling that, despite its name, had no connection with the Aztec ruler.

built of masonry. Even some of the graves were carved into the living rock. These cist graves were made by digging into the clay underlying a ledge and sealing the open side with large, vertical limestone slabs.

Two other ruins built in cliffs were discovered first by Jesse W. Fewkes many years ago. These are the sites of Palatki (Red House) and Honanki (Bear House). A similar site was excavated in 1933 by an amateur archaeologist. Hidden House, as the site was called, was a small cliff dwelling in Sycamore Canyon that produced a remarkable collection of perishable materials. An adult male was buried in one of the rooms, fully dressed and accompanied by fascinating objects. Two painted cloths covered the man, who was wearing a loincloth, from head to toe. A decorated cloth quiver containing a dozen arrows, a leather quiver with ten unfinished arrows, and a bow suggested that the man was a hunter or warrior. Woven cloth and human-hair bags, baskets, and a feathered prayer stick were among the objects buried with this individual. Colton illustrates the painted blanket in his 1960 book *Black Sand*. Discoveries such as this remind the archaeologist that much of the equipment used by living people, along with the clothing and ornaments that they wore, does not survive the test of time. Such discoveries also remind the nonarchaeologist that much valuable information is all too often lost through vandalism and looting. Think of the loss had this burial been discovered first by careless pothunters rather than a careful amateur archaeologist!

Archaeologists are unsure about how far south to extend the boundaries of the Sinagua Culture. Working today in the lower Verde Valley, archaeologists have documented masonry sites contemporaneous with the Honanki and Tuzigoot phases that are similar in many ways to the culture of the middle Verde Valley but which differ in others. The Roadhouse Ruin near Horseshoe Reservoir is a compact cluster of courtyards, each composed of rectangular rooms, one or more oval rooms, and open "patios." The walls were constructed of black basalt slabs placed vertically and interspersed with horizontal slabs of soft white stone. The people who lived there apparently abandoned the irrigation canals to concentrate on dry farming. Large dry-farming fields are marked by extensive systems of rock alignments to capture and direct rainfall, and by rock piles that held in moisture and protected growing agave and other crops. Not surprisingly, given the nearness of the river, the people also were fishermen. An unusual quantity of fish bones was recovered from the site, along with freshwater mollusk shells and the bones of waterfowl, muskrats, and beaver.

Another difference from the middle Verde Valley is the almost complete lack of decorated pottery in the ruins dating to this period, whereas in previous times the people had made decorated pottery of their own as well as importing it from other areas. Archaeologists are presently seeking an answer to the puzzle of why these Verdeans were isolated. The answer may lie in the so-called forts the pueblos constructed high on mesa tops and ridges commanding a sweeping view of the surrounding country. Many are strengthened with defensive walls and have sealed outside doorways and rooms that hug the edge of cliffs.

Abandonment and the People Today

Like other parts of Arizona, the Flagstaff region and the Verde Valley were abandoned around 1400. The ultimate fate of the Sinagua is unknown. Albert H. Schroeder believed that the Sinagua of the Verde Valley moved southward to join the people living in the Phoenix area. Peter Pilles thinks that at least some Northern Sinagua joined the early Hopi pueblos above the Mogollon Rim, leaving the black sand area unpopulated, although the Hopi continued to make their sacred journeys to the mountains.

There is indeed some evidence linking the Sinagua with the Hopi of historical times. Hopi tradition holds that several clans once lived in a warm, well-watered region to the south in a place of red rocks called Palatkwapi. Clans migrated slowly in a northeasterly direction from Palatkwapi, stopping to build pueblos along the way and eventually arriving at the village of Walpi on First Mesa. Some scholars, and some Hopi, believe that Palatkwapi may have been located in the Verde Valley. The route traveled to First Mesa is marked by large ruined pueblos and has been called by historian James Byrkit "the Palatkwapi Trail." This route was well used by the Hopi to procure salt and mineral ores for pigment from the Verde Valley; it was the Hopi who led Espejo into the Verde Valley for the first time. In historical times, the Palatkwapi Trail was used by soldiers and settlers as they struggled to tame Arizona. We may never be able to link Sinagua and Hopi, but these clues, few and tentative as they are, are nevertheless tantalizing.

The Story Continues

The story of the Sinagua began with Harold S. Colton and a private institution, the Museum of Northern Arizona, and it continues to unfold through a different kind of archaeology and with the assistance of different institutions. We can see reflected in the Sinagua story the sweeping changes that have remade southwestern archaeology over the past sixty years. In the 1930s, most archaeology was carried out by private institutions such as the Museum of Northern Arizona. Today, private cultural resource management firms also conduct much of Arizona archaeology, but under the auspices and with the funding of federal and state agencies such as the Bureau of Reclamation, the Arizona Department of Transportation, the Tonto National Forest, and the Bureau of Land Management. Statistical Research is piecing together the mysteries of lower Verde Valley archaeology, and its studies will benefit not only archaeologists but also the Native Americans who today live along the river and the public as a whole. We will see the remarkable results of these changing trends even more clearly in the chapter that follows, which tells the tale of the Salado Culture.

We close with Colton's own words: "We must think of the inhabitants of the black sand region as people who had problems of population, food and sanitation to meet. They engaged in business and had economic relationships with neighboring tribes. They formed a microcosm, a small world in itself, and so had to meet in one way or another most of the problems that we have to meet today. Perhaps a study of their history will help us meet some of our own problems of urbanization and avoid some of the mistakes made by earlier inhabitants."

9 THE SALADO

Who were the Salado? This is a mystery that archaeologists have struggled with for more than sixty years. We have come full circle in our understanding of the Salado Culture. Ideas that once were prominent but that were later discarded as old-fashioned have been resurrected and supported with new and stronger evidence. Salado stands as a testament to the intractability of the often mute past and the difficulties encountered when we attempt to make it speak. Understanding the history of the Salado Culture helps us to understand archaeology and how archaeologists strive to reconstruct the past.

Although the Salado Culture was originally defined in the Tonto and Phoenix Basins by archaeologists from Gila Pueblo, today the term *Salado* is applied to a much larger area. Salado sites extend in a broad sweep from central Arizona into western New Mexico. When archaeologists speak of the Salado, they generally refer to a complex that includes adobe compound architecture and Pinto, Gila, and Tonto polychrome pottery, and which lasted from around A.D. 1200 until 1450. Salado also may be viewed as a horizon of change, a time of dramatic cultural reorganization in central and southern Arizona that was probably linked to equally dramatic environmental events. In this chapter we focus on the Salado of the Tonto Basin, the region where the most recent work has been done and where the Salado Culture is understood best. In the Tonto Basin, Salado serves as an overarching label for a cultural melting pot where peoples of many different cultures met and merged.

The history of the Salado is intimately connected with that of the Hohokam. As we will see, the two cultures were linked through an accident of history that defined the one in terms of the other. The Salado originally were seen as an immigrant Puebloan group who migrated into the Tonto Basin and southern Arizona to establish homes alongside the Hohokam and who brought with them a complex of new ideas and new things. Disentangling the Salado from the Hohokam has proved an extremely difficult task.

Although our notions about the Salado have changed cyclically in the six decades since the culture was initially recognized, we are today much closer to understanding the way the Salado lived, the problems they faced, and their solutions to these problems than we once were. What follows in this chapter is more than the prehistory of the Salado Culture; it is also a testament to the ongoing process of archaeological discovery.

Land and People

At the heart of central Arizona is the Tonto Basin, a wide expanse of alluvium ringed by mountain ranges lying to the northeast of modern Phoenix. The lifeblood of the basin is the Salt River, after which Harold Gladwin named, in Spanish, the Salado Culture. The Salt River rises in the stately White Mountains, cutting the spectacular Salt River Canyon on its way westward. The river emerges in a natural basin northwest of modern Globe, where it is joined by Tonto Creek. This ideal catchment was selected as the site for Theodore Roosevelt Dam, originally built in 1911 and recently rebuilt by the U.S. Bureau of Reclamation. Today the dammed Salt River forms Roosevelt Lake, a mecca for Phoenix bass fishermen and boaters. Many pieces of the Salado puzzle, we will see, may lie beneath the lake. The Tonto Valley above Roosevelt Lake usually is referred to as the upper Tonto Basin, and the area of the lake is called the lower basin.

Below Theodore Roosevelt Dam, the Salt River winds toward Phoenix, continuing through a series of lakes created by other modern dams along what is known as the Apache Trail, eventually joining the Gila River near Phoenix. Because of these human interventions, the riverbed below the dams typically is dry, holding water only after rainstorms. In prehistoric times, however, the Salt was a free-flowing river that nourished Hohokam irrigation systems and later the lush fields of the historical Pima Indians. It was a natural channel between the Hohokam center and the Tonto Basin, funneling ideas and trade goods. The Salt River made irrigation

Roosevelt Lake, looking northeast to the Sierra Anchas. The ruins that hold the answers to the many questions that surround Salado Culture lie here in the Tonto Basin.

possible for the people who inhabited the Tonto Basin in prehistoric times, but it was not easy to harness for human use. The river flows through one of the steepest gradients in the Southwest. It was subject to severe, destructive floods and was difficult to tap with irrigation canals.

The Tonto Basin is surrounded by a rugged ring of mountain ranges, the most impressive of which are the Mazatzals to the northwest, capped by Mount Ord and Mazatzal Peak, which rises to more than 7,000 feet. Tonto Creek flows along the east side of the Mazatzal Mountains. The rugged Sierra Ancha ("Wide Mountains" in Spanish) northeast of the Tonto Basin are cut by steep canyons. More mountains hold the mining towns of Globe, Miami, and Superior, and to the southwest lie the Superstition Mountains, a rocky wilderness country famed in southwestern legends.

This country truly is transitional. The basin is an arid, low-elevation, Sonoran Desert land dominated by saguaro, mesquite, and other plants that were used extensively by the Hohokam. The bajada and upland slopes of the mountains that surround the basin offer higher-elevation resources such as agave or mescal, juniper, oak, and pinyon, as well as game, all of which would be appreciated by Mogollon hunter-gatherers. Perhaps most significant, the basin once offered diverse possibilities for farmers using different agricultural techniques. Canals could be constructed to divert water from the Salt River and Tonto Creek onto irrigated fields, whereas dry farming and floodwater farming could be carried out in the upland parts of the basin. Some of these methods worked better under particular rainfall and groundwater conditions than others, as we shall see. The environmental mosaic of the Tonto Basin and its strategic position between the Mogollon mountains and the Hohokam desert proved irresistible when the Southwest was languishing during the Great Drought of 1276 to 1299. The considerable diversity of cultures that inhabited the Tonto Basin prehistorically is one factor that has made the Salado Culture so difficult to sort out. We return to this point later.

In historical times, the basin was home to the Southern Tonto Apache, one branch of the Western Apache, and was also occupied by the Yuman-speaking Yavapai. Both practiced a mobile, mixed lifestyle combining hunting and gathering with small-scale farming. Traditionally, the Apache lived in brush structures called *gowa*, or wickiups, and often recycled many of their tools from prehistoric sites. As a consequence, Apache sites are extraordinarily difficult to identify archaeologically. Apache Plain (brown pottery that may have wiped surfaces and fingernail impressions) is occasionally found at prehistoric archaeological sites. We see the Apache presence most often in the huge roasting pits that they used to bake agave.

In the nineteenth century the basin witnessed continuous battles as the U.S. Army grappled with the Western Apache. The army established forts and fought campaigns against the Apache, culminating in 1872 with the surrender of the Southern Tonto Apache. No land was set aside for Apache use in the Tonto Basin. A seven-acre reservation established near Payson about twenty years ago now houses less than a hundred Tonto Apache. The modern San Carlos and White Mountain reservations are located just east of the Tonto Basin.

The historical era was dominated by mining. In the 1890s, copper, silver, and gold were found, leading to a virtual boom, with more than 150 claims filed during the next few years. Ranching was another successful enterprise, although, as occurred so often in the West, disputes between the cattle ranchers and the sheepmen arose. Tonto National Forest was formed in 1905 to help resolve these problems. The forest, which encompasses nearly three million acres of land stretching from the Mogollon Rim to the Superstition Mountains and from Cave Creek to the White Mountain Apache Reservation boundary, completely surrounds the Tonto Basin.

The community of Globe was where in 1928 Harold Gladwin and Winifred MacCurdy built the archaeological research institution of Gila Pueblo on the ruins of a Salado pueblo in Sixshooter Canyon. Their work would define the Salado Culture and launch a debate that continues today.

Discovering the Salado

In perhaps no other area of southwestern prehistory is the human element more important than in telling the fascinating story of the Salado. The story of the discovery of the Salado is a dramatic tale of intrigue, intellectual competition and conflict, and debate made even more striking because—unlike the discovery of the Mogollon, Hohokam, and Anasazi—the tale continues. Although the discovery of Salado began some sixty years ago, the controversy over who the Salado were remains to be resolved in the 1990s. Indeed, much of the evidence archaeologists need to answer these questions is only beginning to be collected.

The fascinating story of the Salado has come full circle. Ideas first articulated by Gila Pueblo archaeologists in the mid-1930s came to dominate southwestern thought in the 1940s, 1950s, and 1960s. After subsequent decades of alternative interpretations, these early ideas were resurrected by the authors of this book in 1982. The Gila Pueblo model was taken up again by other archaeologists in the 1990s, attempting to flesh it out using modern data and techniques. In telling the Salado story, we will trace the evolution of these ideas as they developed through the years.

Four Archaeologists Discover Salado

The initial discovery of the Salado Culture seems to have been either a race between archaeologists vying to report it first or a story of an almost total lack of communication among scholars. Four different archaeologists uncovered the basic evidence that would permit archaeologists to define the Salado Culture and devise a migration theory to explain their presence in the southern deserts. Only one, however—Harold Gladwin—is credited with the discovery.

The story begins with the first explorers in the Tonto Basin. Archaeologists such as Adolf Bandelier described the highly visible masonry ruins, some of which were walled compound ruins and others large "checkerboard" ruins or pueblos. The first systematic investigations at these sites were carried out in the 1920s by Erich Schmidt, who conducted extensive excavations at Togetzoge Pueblo, located between the modern towns of Miami and Superior. This sprawling site included about 120 rooms, a large plaza, and several walled courtyards. Schmidt also carried out limited investigations at other sites, including some of the large platform mound sites that nearly seventy years later would be studied under the sponsorship of the Bureau of Reclamation.

At about the same time that Schmidt was working in the Tonto Basin, Harold Gladwin was investigating the Hohokam site of Casa Grande. As we learned in chapter 4, Gladwin had discovered pottery at Casa Grande from what he believed to be two different cultures, one stratigraphically above the other and therefore later. The earlier culture, represented by red-on-buff pottery, would become known as the Hohokam, and the later one, identified by polychrome pottery, was the Salado Culture. Gladwin believed that the latter was "the result of invasion and therefore alien to the local culture." That Schmidt came to the identical conclusion in his doctoral dissertation has been forgotten by many, as much of Schmidt's work remained unpublished until 1988. It is a tantalizing sidelight to the Salado story that Gladwin tried unsuccessfully to hire Schmidt to work for Gila Pueblo.

Gila Pueblo's investigations in the Tonto Basin soon turned up the same kind of polychrome pottery found in the later stratigraphic units at Casa Grande, and it was associated with aboveground masonry architecture completely unlike Hohokam pit houses. Gladwin believed that these sites in the Tonto Basin represented the source of the culture that apparently had displaced the Hohokam at Casa Grande.

Recall that at this time Gila Pueblo was investing a great deal of energy in tracing the range of the red-on-buff culture across the Southwest. Glad-win assigned Emil Haury to excavate a pit house site overlooking Roose-velt Lake in the Tonto Basin. The report on the site labeled Roosevelt 9:6 established the idea that a Hohokam population initially settled in the Tonto Basin during the Colonial Period. In a curious historical twist, Haury's report of the Colonial Period Hohokam Culture at Roosevelt 9:6 (1932) first defined the Hohokam Culture but outside its home territory.

The contrast between the earlier Hohokam occupation and the later one, characterized by masonry architecture and polychrome pottery, be-came strikingly evident as Gila Pueblo explored the Tonto Basin. Haury carried out small-scale excavations at Rye Creek Ruin in the upper basin. One of the largest sites in the Tonto Basin, Rye Creek contains more than 150 rooms, a large enclosed plaza, and two possible platform mounds. Certainly no less influential in shaping Gladwin's notions of the Salado was the site on which Gila Pueblo itself was built. This large site had been dug unscientifically by the previous owner, a Mrs. Healy, who dressed and painted the human remains removed from the diggings and used the whole thing as a money-making tourist attraction in a way modern archaeolo-gists never would condone. When they acquired the site and Mrs. Healy's collection, the Gladwins began to excavate Gila Pueblo in a more system-atic and scientific fashion, working throughout 1928 and 1929.

The third player to enter the competition to define Salado was Florence Hawley, a young woman whose father worked as a chemist for the Globe mines. Later known by her married name of Ellis, Florence Hawley was one of the first and best-known women archaeologists working in the Southwest. She explored some of the later pueblo sites in the Globe area, such as Inspiration I. In 1932, Hawley published the theory that the Salado migrated from the upper Gila River area, and that another migration from the Little Colorado River region took place slightly later. Her no-tions were based primarily on ceramic evidence. The pottery styles of the two immigrant groups merged in Pinto Polychrome, the earliest of the polychrome pottery associated with the Salado Culture. As we will see shortly, Gladwin published the identical theory.

Although Schmidt and Hawley had proposed the same theories, Har-old Gladwin is associated with the discovery of the Salado Culture. In 1935 the definition of the Salado Culture appeared in a publication that was

Pinto (left) and Tonto Polychrome bowls of the Salado Culture.

devoted to the red-on-buff culture. Gladwin listed the artifacts and the architecture of the Salado people and devised a phase system to describe the changes in material culture that he recognized. In the theoretical framework of the day, migration was a pervasive and common explanation for cultural change, so it was not unexpected that Gladwin would seek the origins of the Salado outside the Tonto Basin, in the Little Colorado River region of northeastern Arizona. Leaving the area around modern Springerville, the people who became the Salado crossed the Mogollon Rim and traveled southward through the rugged mountain country cut by Canyon, Carrizo, Cherry, and Cibecue Creeks. The farther south they traveled, the more distinctive their material culture became, and they eventually arrived in the Tonto Basin with a unique set of traits, which included masonry rooms surrounded by a compound wall, black-on-white and polychrome pottery, inhumation, and turquoise jewelry. Gladwin labeled the traits and the time in which they occurred the Roosevelt phase.

Why did he believe the Little Colorado region was the source of the Salado Culture? Quite simply, it was because of the marked similarity in the designs of the ceramic types labeled Roosevelt Black-on-white and Pinto Polychrome, which were found in Tonto Basin, and the Little Colorado area ceramic types of Tularosa Black-on-white and St. Johns Polychrome.

Gladwin's case for the migration—and the notions of Hawley and Schmidt as well—were based in large part on what was presumed to be a hiatus in occupation between the Hohokam occupation and the Salado occupation. Although there was abundant evidence for a Colonial Period Hohokam occupation, as at Roosevelt 9:6, no trace of Sedentary Period occupation of the Tonto Basin had been found at that time. Therefore, it was assumed that the basin was abandoned during the Sedentary Period, when the Hohokam were thought to have mysteriously withdrawn. This notion of abandonment during the Sedentary Period persisted for many years.

Gladwin also posited another migration around A.D. 1300, when a group of people from the Kayenta region moved into the Tonto Basin, bringing with them more formalized pueblos and Gila Polychrome pottery. Because of similarity in the designs on Gila Polychrome and Kayenta orange ware pottery, Gladwin proposed that the migrants were Anasazi from the Kayenta region. This migration established the Gila phase in the Tonto Basin.

Gladwin also linked the Salado Culture to developments in the desert around Phoenix. He proposed that the Salado invaded the Hohokam home territory during the Classic Period, bringing with them polychrome pottery, inhumation burial of the dead, and multistoried pueblos. "These factors have been definitely associated with the people who were responsible for the Middle Gila phase of the Salado culture," Gladwin wrote.

Haury and the Salado Invasion

The fourth archaeologist to be associated with the discovery of the Salado Culture was Emil Haury. Haury fully articulated the "Salado invasion" hypothesis in 1934 in his doctoral dissertation, published by Harvard University's Peabody Museum in 1945. In this study, which preceded the 1935 definition of the Salado Culture by Gladwin, Haury reworked the late

1880s excavations of Frank H. Cushing at the important Classic Period site of Los Muertos in the Phoenix area. Haury stamped this work with his own interpretations of the Hohokam gleaned from the excavations at Roosevelt 9:6 and from his knowledge of the archaeology of the Tonto Basin. Haury's migration theory proposed that the Salado represented an immigrant group of Puebloan people who arrived in the Tonto and Phoenix basins and established homes alongside the Hohokam. Haury believed that the two cultures coexisted on friendly terms yet maintained separate cultural identities. There was no evidence of a "hybridization" of the two cultures.

The Salado migration hypothesis was a brilliantly conceived theory that accounted for the facts of the archaeological record as they were known at the time. With its publication, the first conception of the Salado Culture was in place. Salado had been discovered, defined, and explained. This theory would reign for thirty years, after which a new generation of archaeologists would turn the notion on its head and devise revolutionary new ideas about Salado.

Salado: The Hohokam Revision

Little professional work was accomplished in the Tonto Basin during the three decades following the discovery and definition of the Salado Culture. Some stabilization and excavation was conducted at Tonto National Monument, although the work was not published until 1962. Largely ignored was a series of papers published during this time by Erik Reed, who argued forcefully that the Salado Culture represented one variant of a pueblo culture that was strongly Mogollon in character and that could be readily distinguished from the Anasazi. He called it the Western Pueblo. The stage was set for the revolution in Salado archaeology: the notion that Salado was not a distinct culture but merely the Classic Period expression of the Hohokam Culture.

Three phenomena contributed to this revolution in thought and theory. First was a set of ideas about the Classic Period Hohokam generated by William Wasley. Wasley, who served as the highway salvage archaeologist with the Arizona State Museum, was a University of Arizona Ph.D. who studied with Haury. In 1966 he wrote a paper in which he articulated several striking new ideas. The thrust of these ideas was that there was cultural and demographic continuity between the pit–house–dwelling, pre–Classic Period population and the adobe–compound–building people of the Classic Period. Salado did not represent a migration of pueblo peoples southward into the desert but was instead an indigenous development from local *Hohokam* populations. How this notion must have struck Wasley's mentor, Haury, we shall never know.

Second, Wasley's new theory appealed tremendously to archaeologists who were seeking to develop fresh explanations for past human behavior. The viewpoint that archaeology was anthropology was taking hold during the late 1960s and early 1970s, and the profession was becoming aware of the need to conduct archaeology within the broader framework established by cultural anthropology. There was little room in anthropological archaeology for traditional models of migration and diffusion.

The third impetus for acceptance of Wasley's new ideas came from contract archaeology. As we noted in chapter 1, the 1970s were years of development for cultural resource management, and it was especially important in the desert. Archaeologists working under the auspices of the Arizona Department of Transportation, federal agencies, and other sponsors began to conduct the first long-term, intensive investigations of Hohokam sites since Snaketown. Arizona archaeology was becoming Hohokam archaeology, and the new work supplied evidence to give Wasley's theories credence in the archaeological community.

To explain the striking changes in architecture, ceramics, and burial patterns that took place during the Classic Period, Wasley and other Hohokam archaeologists sought to trace the origin of these traits as far back into pre-Classic times as possible. Thus they argued, for example, that red-slipped pottery, one of the ceramic wares that characterized the Classic Period in the Phoenix area, actually began to be produced during the pre-Classic period, therefore assigning it to Hohokam, not Salado, origins.

Further connections between Hohokam and Salado were sought by proposing "transitional" phases that were thought to bridge the gap between the pre-Classic and Classic Periods. For example, David Doyel defined the Miami phase for the Tonto Basin. He proposed that most of the so-called Salado traits, such as aboveground masonry architecture, were contemporaneous with presumed Hohokam ceramics, but because the diagnostic polychrome pottery that identified the Salado Culture was absent, these traits therefore must be Hohokam. Subsequent work demonstrated that the mixture of traits was actually the product of mixed deposits at archaeological sites—Salado with Hohokam.

In the 1980s the view that the Salado represented an in-place evolution of Hohokam Culture crystallized, taking on the status of an accepted fact. Archaeologists working in the Phoenix area, in the Tucson Basin, and in more distant regions such as the Tonto Basin generally accepted these revolutionary notions. Not only was Salado viewed as the Classic Period Hohokam Culture but the culture history of the Tonto Basin, as a peripheral Hohokam region, was seen to parallel that of the Phoenix core area. The original definers and describers of the Salado Culture, Haury and Gladwin, would scarcely have recognized the Salado in this new guise.

Nevertheless, a few archaeologists maintained a minority opinion. They were not satisfied with the concept of Salado-as-Hohokam, and were frustrated especially by the absence of a causal mechanism for the dramatic changes of the Classic Period. These archaeologists argued that, although there was evidence for Hohokam colonization of the Tonto Basin during pre-Classic times, there also were data suggesting that local people of essentially Mogollon affiliation occupied the region as well. Most telling, they argued that many different people lived in the Tonto Basin during the Classic Period and that there was little evidence for continuity between the pre–Classic Period Hohokam people and the basin residents who followed them in time. In support of this view was the relatively sudden appearance of many Classic Period characteristics. There was no lengthy time of experimentation and evolution.

Beginning in 1977, one of the first large contract projects in the Tonto Basin amassed evidence in support of this minority view. The Cholla Project, which we directed, demonstrated that many so-called Classic Period Hohokam sites in the Tonto Basin closely resembled mountain Mogollon sites in architecture and material culture. Small compound sites with enclosing walls were identical to contemporary sites such as Chodistaas Pueblo, and many large pueblos were indistinguishable from pueblo towns such as Grasshopper Pueblo (see chapter 6). Non-Hohokam pottery such as corrugated ware also was abundant at many Classic Period sites, and mortuary practices were similar to those of the Mogollon. In short, we

argued in 1982 a point of view similar to that of Erik Reed—that the Salado Culture stemmed essentially from the mountain pueblo tradition
and that there was considerable cultural diversity within what had been
called Salado.

Thus, archaeologists concerned with the Salado Culture found themselves in two warring camps. The prevailing notion of the Salado as Classic Period Hohokam was accepted by Hohokam archaeologists and was
fueled largely by research projects carried out at Arizona State University.
The minority view, promoted by archaeologists experienced in mountain
as well as desert archaeology, saw the Salado as the product of many cultures, not just one, and the Tonto Basin as a virtual melting pot of people.
Not surprisingly, this view was held by archaeologists trained at the University of Arizona. The traditional rivalry of the football field and basket-
ball court carried over into intellectual debate as well.

A new twist was added to the debate in the 1980s as archaeologists began to discuss the nature of Hohokam and Salado social organization as
well as cultural affiliation. At Arizona State University, archaeologists began to explore the idea of incipient social complexity among the Classic
Period Hohokam. Chiefdoms and states developed as a consequence of
the bounty the Sonoran Desert produced when it was exploited by Hohokam irrigation systems. At the University of Arizona, archaeologists held
to the view that Classic Period Hohokam and Salado, although certainly
representing a sophisticated and complicated culture, nevertheless were
not complex in terms of the power relations and political authority that
anthropologists use to define chiefdoms and states.

Intellectually exciting though this controversy was, it could not be resolved on the basis of available evidence. There was, simply, insufficient
data. Prior to the 1980s, archaeology in the basin also was plagued by a
number of seemingly intractable problems—the dating of sites and the
chronological sequence, the lack of excavation data from large habitation
sites, and extensive vandalism. It was time, as Haury often said, to argue
with a shovel instead of words. The opportunity came with the Central
Arizona Project, sponsored by the Bureau of Reclamation. The bureau
proposed a number of modifications to the Theodore Roosevelt Dam,
and millions of dollars were spent on archaeology to mitigate the impact
that proposed construction would have on cultural resources.

The Bureau of Reclamation divided the archaeological investigations among three institutions: a university and two private consulting firms. Each focused on a different but related facet of the study, examining large and small sites, platform mound and agricultural sites, and early and late sites. This mixture of different viewpoints, intellectual histories, and theories proved to be extremely fertile ground for the development of new interpretations. These investigations would bring our ideas of Salado prehistory back to earlier points of view. Notions of population movement, cultural diversity, and ethnic coresidence would be resurrected and bolstered by the tremendous body of data that had been collected. Archaeologists would eschew the idea of complexity and would even admit that Haury and Gladwin had been right after all.

But can we finally put the Salado controversy to rest? The Bureau of Reclamation convened an advanced seminar in May 1995 to synthesize and discuss the results of the work in the Tonto Basin. As one might predict, there was little consensus among the group as to who and what the Salado were. Some argued forcefully that there was no distinct Salado Culture and that the term should be dropped. Others countered with good evidence supporting the notion that a mixture of different cultures formed Salado. We can foresee that the debate may continue well into the twenty-first century. Yet this controversy, although sometimes frustrating, is always exhilarating and clearly is a signal of intellectual health and well-being. It has been said that science does not prove but probes, and in probing the Salado Culture we are building on the past and laying a foundation for the future.

Pre-Classic Times: Setting the Stage for Salado

To consider the Salado, we must set the stage. The Tonto Basin was home to a variety of people, hailing from various regions, long before the Salado built their platform mounds and pueblos. It certainly was not uninhabited even before the arrival of Hohokam colonists around A.D. 800. The population of the Tonto Basin during the Archaic Period was undoubtedly small. Indeed, if we follow the conclusions of Michael Berry and Claudia Berry and of R. G. Matson, the basin may have been settled at this time by Archaic people moving northward from southern Arizona. As elsewhere in Arizona, the Archaic population consisted of small groups of people who pursued hunting, gathering, and some farming and who probably moved fairly frequently across the landscape in their quest for food.

Some time between A.D. 100 and 200 these people began to manufacture pottery. The earliest pottery is much like that made by other pottery-producing people at this time. It was tempered with sand and was gray to brown in color, and the most common vessel form was a neckless or "seed" jar. The ceramic-making people lived in small pit houses that were made of brush and mud and that were often bean-shaped in plan view. They built large communal houses that probably served as the venue for ceremonial activities. They continued to subsist on a combination of farming, hunting, and collecting wild plant foods. In these respects the earliest pottery-making population of the Tonto Basin was similar to, indeed nearly indistinguishable from, the early Mogollon people who lived at Bluff Village in the Forestdale Valley, the inhabitants of the Flattop site in the Petrified Forest region, and the early pottery-making people of the Tucson Basin. We are beginning to understand that the earliest ceramic-producing farmers shared similar lifestyles and similar technologies regardless of where they lived. Only later did distinctions begin to emerge that separated the Hohokam, Mogollon, and Anasazi. If we label their culture, it must be considered essentially Mogollon, however.

Some time around A.D. 700 or 800, the Tonto Basin became the cultural melting pot that would characterize it throughout its occupation. Small groups of Hohokam began moving north out of the Phoenix Basin in search of new lands. The environment of the Tonto Basin was sufficiently like that of the Hohokam homeland so that the immigrants had little difficulty in establishing themselves. They could build canals to bring water from the Salt River and Tonto Creek to irrigate their cornfields, and they could collect saguaro and mesquite.

Why would the Hohokam seek colonies outside their home territory? Some of the ideas put forth include pressure from a continually expanding population, deteriorating environmental conditions that affected crops and wild plant foods, the desire to enlarge their resource base, and the need to seek new frontiers for trade. Cotton may have been an important part of this process. Archaeologists working in other "peripheral" regions, such as the lower Verde Valley, have discovered that cotton was an extremely important resource in these areas. Perhaps the Hohokam actively sought to bring new lands under cultivation for cotton production. The Hohokam colonization of the Tonto Basin coincided with a time when the climate was variable but moderate. It was possible for the Hohokam to farm the floodplains successfully throughout the Colonial Period.

Sites such as Roosevelt 9:6 are interpreted as settlements that housed the Hohokam colonists. Indeed, the resemblance of these sites to those of the Phoenix area is striking in many ways. The formal structure of the sites is similar, suggesting that the same type of family and household organization existed. Instead of the more-or-less random, dispersed placement of houses that characterizes early Mogollon villages, these sites have a clustered arrangement of houses around open courtyards, and each courtyard group was associated with discrete cremation cemeteries and trash mounds. At least two such groups, probably representing extended households, are present at Roosevelt 9:6. There was imported red-on-buff pottery in relatively high frequencies, slate palettes, and other ritual paraphernalia at these sites.

Hohokam settlements were established along the Salt River. Although closely resembling their counterparts, the Tonto Basin Hohokam settlements never reached the scale of those in the Phoenix and Tucson Basins. Villages were much smaller in size, and, although we presume that these folk irrigated their fields, the extensive canal systems that characterized the Phoenix area also are missing. Whether this reflects the smaller size of the Tonto Basin and the many topographic obstructions to large irrigation systems that it presents, or whether the evidence for irrigation now lies under the waters of Roosevelt Lake, remains unknown. We do know that the Tonto Basin has much less irrigable land than the Phoenix Basin, as a glance at any map will show. Perhaps most important, no ballcourts have been discovered in the Tonto Basin. As we saw in chapter 4, the ballcourt game, along with cremation burial and associated ritual objects and ideology, formed the core of Hohokam religious life. The lack of ballcourts in the Tonto Basin suggests that the population was not completely integrated into the Hohokam regional system. Although some archaeologists continue to believe that ballcourts eventually will be found as the scope of archaeological work expands, this seems unlikely, given the intensive excavation that has been conducted recently.

At the same time that Hohokam people began to farm in the lower Tonto Basin along the Salt River, other people living in the upper basin along Tonto Creek were developing their own unique cultural tradition. At the Deer Creek site, for example, an unusual type of cremation ritual was practiced that involved rectangular wooden platforms on which the deceased were placed. This ritual was different from the cremation practices of the Hohokam yet also stood out from the typical burial practices of the Mogollon. The pottery used for cooking and food storage at this settlement was like Mogollon ceramics in shape and manufacture, and the ritual objects we associate with the Hohokam Culture were absent. Some decorated pottery from the Phoenix Basin was present, but not in the quantities seen in the lower basin. In short, it appears that the Tonto Basin was home to at least two distinct cultural traditions, one more like Hohokam and one resembling Mogollon more closely. No doubt others will be discovered as the result of ongoing archaeological research.

The Gladwin and Haury models of Salado prehistory posited that the Tonto Basin was abandoned during the Sedentary Period, which began some time around A.D. 950, paving the way for the influx of settlers moving down from the north. We now know that this did not occur, but we also know that considerable changes did take place in the distribution of settlements across the landscape. The population seems to have moved around a great deal, living in a number of small settlements that were occupied only briefly. Permanent settlements appear to have been restricted to the Salt River portion of the basin. No large villages that date to this period have yet been reported, although such sites may yet be discovered. In cases where previously occupied settlements continued to be inhabited, the occupation that dates to the Sedentary Period was less substantial than the previous one. For the first time, people began to experiment with growing crops in the higher-elevation areas surrounding the floodplain. The unusually good climatic conditions of this time period, with abundant and predictable rainfall, probably were responsible for the expansion of settlement into upland areas and experimentation with dry-farming methods.

By the end of the Sedentary Period, connections with the Phoenix Basin appear to have been severed. Hohokam decorated pottery disappeared from the ceramic inventory, to be replaced by black-on-white pottery made on the Colorado Plateau. The changes we see at this time probably were related to the collapse and reorganization of the Hohokam regional system, although the dynamics of this phenomenon are poorly understood.

By the Miami phase, around A.D. 1150 to 1250, considerable change had taken place. The local folk began to build above-ground masonry houses instead of the pit houses of pre-Classic times but still used the plain ware and red ware pottery of their local tradition. Unfortunately, most Miami phase sites have later, more substantial occupations superimposed upon them, so it is difficult to sort out the earlier and later settlements. We think, however, that there probably developed a vigorous and unique local tradition that was distinct from the previous Hohokam cultural system. Although the phase refers to a specific period of time during which changes in architecture and lifestyle took place, we no longer view the time as one of transition between two essentially Hohokam occupations. Miami phase sites are especially abundant in the upper Tonto Basin and the slopes of the Mazatzal Mountains.

Salado Culture of the Roosevelt Phase

The stage set for the Salado Culture includes an environmentally diverse region that had been populated throughout its history by a mixture of local and nonlocal peoples. They apparently forged a successful adaptation that, although borrowing from its cultural antecedents, nevertheless remained distinctive. The Roosevelt phase, which began around A.D. 1250, was a time of unprecedented social and economic change. The lifestyle that had operated successfully for more than a thousand years ended. Instead of small, dispersed settlements whose inhabitants practiced a relatively mobile strategy combining some farming with a good deal of gathering and hunting, a system of large, permanent villages whose inhabitants invested heavily in irrigation agriculture was established. Completely new ceremonial structures—platform mounds—lacking local precedents began to be built. There is evidence that puebloan peoples from the Colorado Plateau and mountain zone began to move into the basin in increasing numbers. What archaeologists label the Salado Culture emerged, and life in the Tonto Basin would never again be the same.

To what can we attribute these dramatic and enduring changes? Carla

A cliff dwelling at Tonto National Monument in about 1910. It was probably built by pueblo people from north of the Mogollon Rim, one element in the short-lived mixing of peoples and ways of life that we define as the Salado Culture.

Pueblo rooms at Besh Ba Gowah Archaeological Park, a partially restored
Salado pueblo in Globe, Arizona.

Van West and Jeffrey Altschul consider that climatic and demographic
events on the Colorado Plateau—the aftermath of the Great Drought—
were responsible in large part for the changes we see in the Tonto Basin.
The late thirteenth century was a time of widespread environmental uncertainty coupled with equally broad shifts in regional populations. Farmers on the Colorado Plateau were faced with a drought of unprecedented
severity. They fled the plateau for the better-watered regions below the
Mogollon Rim. The Tonto Basin, with its arable land and irrigable rivers,
obviously was attractive. Although the Great Drought did affect the Tonto
Basin, it was less disastrous to farmers than on the Colorado Plateau. The
Salt River was unpredictable and subject to disastrous floods that could
devastate irrigation systems, farmlands, and crops. Paradoxically, the river
would have been much easier to control with prehistoric technology during the drought years. In short, the Tonto Basin was an attractive place to
be during the Great Drought.

The influx of settlers had several impacts. On the one hand, the greater number of people may have placed restrictions on mobility, curtailing the seasonal movements to which people were accustomed and restricting the amount of available farmland. The larger population may have depleted local resources, such as mesquite, used for food as well as fuel. Competition and conflict no doubt arose. On the other hand, the increased population made it possible to invest more energy in irrigation agriculture. This apparently is what took place; the Roosevelt phase Salado focused more intensively on irrigation than ever before, growing cotton as well as corn and other crops. At the same time, they also increased cultivation of dry-land crops such as agave.

The changes heralded by the Roosevelt phase in economy, social organization, and ritual life created a need to forge ties between the members of these large, ethnically diverse communities. A village-based organization with a stronger political orientation served the needs of these kinds of communities better than the kinship-based organization of earlier times. The platform mound system arose as the symbol of integration in the Tonto Basin and the focus of religious life.

Compounds and Villages

The basic residential unit was a small settlement consisting of a few rooms surrounded by a compound wall. Each compound, which was built of adobe reinforced by cobbles or posts, probably was occupied by one or two families, each of which used several rooms. The central plaza of the compound was used for outdoor activities and usually included one or more granaries. These beehive-shaped storage features were made of coarsely woven basketry material that was plastered over with mud to provide secure, dry protection for the foodstuffs inside. The base of the granary was formed of relatively flat stone cobbles, which typically are the only thing that remains for the archaeologist to find. We know details about the construction of the granaries from one or two examples that have been preserved in protected sites. These granaries were used to store corn, squash, and other foodstuffs, and their capacity suggests communal use.

Outside of the compound there often was a large, rock-ringed roasting pit that probably was used by the residents for communal feasts. Instead of cremation cemeteries, the deceased were placed in simple graves either inside rooms or in the outdoor areas.

The villages were composed of numerous residential compounds, each housing a few families. The compounds were loosely arranged around the core of the village, which was a platform mound surrounded by a compound wall. The platform mounds were all built at about the same time, around 1280. Most of the mounds resemble those of the Phoenix Basin, and the majority apparently were specialized ceremonial precincts that were not used for residential or other secular purposes. One excavated mound supported two large masonry rooms that apparently were not used for habitation. Most mounds contained filled cells resembling rooms that were constructed to provide stability and support. Some mounds also have huge adobe and rock pillars that supported the upper story.

What sort of activities took place at the platform mounds? Gladwin provided a rather thrilling interpretation of these activities at the Rye Creek site in his book *A History of the Ancient Southwest.* In addition to the platform mound, the site also had an unusual room with an inlaid sherd mosaic floor. Gladwin correlated the mound, mosaic floor, and a large chert blade that was found there in a most distinctive interpretation: "The combination in the same site of a platform which *may* have been an altar, a deep room with a sherd-mosaic floor which *could* have been a sort of dungeon, and a flint blade which *might* have been a sacrificial knife has made me wonder if human sacrifice may not have been practiced at the Rye Creek Ruin" (italics in original). Gladwin was quick to point out, however, that his suspicions may have been ill founded and that "probably a more pleasant and satisfying explanation could be advanced."

Many years after Gladwin published this idea in 1957, archaeologists also would correlate platform mounds with ritual activities, but they did not stretch their imagination so far as Gladwin did to include human sacrifice. We cannot say with certainty, but we believe that mounds were the focus of the community's ritual life. Ceremonies may have been conducted on top of the mounds, watched by the villagers crowded into the courtyard below. We have no evidence that sacrifice of any kind took place and no data to suggest that the mounds were the residences of chiefs or priests.

Not all the mounds functioned in the same way, however. Some mounds served different purposes, although their function is still controversial. One "mound" actually appears to be an elevated tower that may have served signaling or other communication purposes. Other mounds resemble the typical ritual type of mound but were not associated with residential compounds. Although the concept of the platform mound was readily accepted by the Salado, they incorporated the mound notion into their culture in varying ways.

Immigration and Ethnicity

The Tonto Basin was a magnet drawing ethnically diverse populations from many regions. People abandoned the driest areas of the Colorado Plateau during the Great Drought, and it was inevitable that their movements would displace many already-established communities. Some of these Anasazi immigrants appear to have fled southward to the Grasshopper region, and the displaced Mogollon, as well as the Anasazi, found their way to the Tonto Basin. During the Roosevelt phase, at least some of the people who moved into the basin were Puebloan. There is a clear mixture of architectural styles and ceramics, suggesting that various groups occupied the basin. Some sites display a distinctly puebloan style of architecture that contrasts markedly with the typical compounds that were scattered across the landscape. Instead of growing larger by adding new, separate compounds, the sites marked by the pueblo type of construction were enlarged by adding rooms and compounds to existing features. The result is a larger number of contiguous rooms and less open space than in more typical compounds. A high percentage of corrugated pottery also was recovered from many of these sites, whereas the people living in compounds used more plain ware and red ware pottery.

In previous years, the moist climate had made it possible for people to expand into the upland areas adjacent to the Tonto Basin where dry farming was possible. During the Roosevelt phase, these areas were abandoned, as the drought precluded farming without irrigation. These people joined the folk already dwelling in the Tonto Basin.

At the same time, the population within the basin must also have been growing naturally. The increase in population through migration and natural population growth may have created intense competition for land. Good, irrigable farmland no doubt was at a premium, and there were far more people competing for the land than ever before. The appearance of field houses, agricultural features, and other improvements to the land where none were present previously suggests that the people were becoming increasingly concerned with land ownership. In earlier times, when an agricultural field failed because of insufficient rainfall or other reasons, the people simply moved to another area where conditions were better. Now, during the drought years of the Roosevelt phase, they did not have this option; they were tied to the river and to land that could be irrigated with river water.

One result of this competition was, inevitably, conflict. There is evidence for raiding, including burned rooms at many settlements. At one recently excavated site, archaeologists uncovered the bodies of men who were flung, haphazardly and without burial, onto the floors of burned rooms. These men had injuries that occurred around the time of death, suggesting that they did not die of natural causes.

Richard Ciolek-Torrello posits that the village and platform-mound system arose as a means of coping with increasing social and economic uncertainties created by the large, ethnically disparate population and by climatic stress on farming. Among Puebloan peoples of the historical Southwest who also farmed primarily by irrigation, such as the Pueblos along the Rio Grande in New Mexico, similar kinds of village organizations arose. The entire community cooperated in clearing land, building irrigation ditches, and maintaining the irrigation system. A village structure, often divided into two parts, or moieties, controlled the political, religious, and economic life of the community, rather than the kinship-based units that performed these functions among Puebloans who did not farm by irrigation. The people of the Tonto Basin seem to have turned to the ceremonial system associated with platform mounds as a spiritual means of coping with the uncertainties of the times. The ceremonies that took place on the mounds probably were designed to bring good crops, and the storage areas that are often associated with the mounds could have served as community reserves in case of crop failure. The platform mound served as a method of integrating the ethnically diverse community and easing the apparent discord and strife.

It is evident that cooperative effort was required to build the platform mounds. Recent estimates suggest that platform mounds could have been built by as few as thirty-six able-bodied men in two years, a figure that is consistent with the estimated population of the residential compounds associated with these mounds. Nevertheless, building platform mounds required considerable effort and cooperation among all the residents of a village. This is especially so given that the dirt, rocks, and adobe forming the mounds had to be dug with wooden or stone tools and moved without benefit of draft animals, wheelbarrows, or wagons.

Some aspects of the platform mound complex may have originated in the region around Casas Grandes in Chihuahua, which also is called Paquimé. The adobe columns or pillars and the storage granaries of Roosevelt phase sites are architectural details that occur primarily in the Casas Grandes region. Platform mounds also are present there. The Casas Grandes system was expanding at this time, although we do not have good correlations between the chronologies of the two regions. This is an avenue of research for archaeologists to pursue.

Salado Culture of the Gila Phase

The Gila phase, which began around A.D. 1350, was a second time of rapid and unprecedented change in the Tonto Basin. Just as rapidly as they were constructed, the platform mounds fell into disuse and were either abandoned or converted to other types of uses. The population deliberately abandoned their previous settlements and united at one or two large pueblos. These villages are large agglomerations of hundreds of rooms. At the same time, cliff dwellings were built in the basin, suggesting an increasing concern with protection and defense. We think that these changes again can be linked to climatic and environmental uncertainties. The closing years of the Roosevelt phase were marked by increasing rainfall. According to Van West and Altschul, the irrigation systems, which would have functioned so well during the preceding dry years, would have been damaged and probably were abandoned. A complete restructuring of social and economic organization was the result.

Besh Ba Gowah Pueblo in the city of Globe, first excavated in 1935 by Irene Vickery, originally was a massive pueblo that may have had as many as 450 rooms. Today only a portion of it remains, the rest having been disturbed by modern activities. Archaeologists returned to Besh Ba Gowah in the 1980s to excavate and reconstruct portions of the site. Visitors to the site and museum, which is open to the public, can gain a feel for what life must have been like in the large, aggregated pueblos. Another large Gila phase site recently was excavated for the Bureau of Reclamation by Arizona State University. The Schoolhouse Point site contained about a hundred rooms. At the core of the site was a series of protected storage rooms, with many granaries and storage vessels. It is evident that great attention was paid to the security of stored food, for whatever reason such care was necessary.

Another indication of the need for security for people and food, as well as being a reflection of the varied ethnic origins of the Tonto Basin population, is the presence of cliff dwellings along the margins of the basin. Tonto National Monument is a group of well-preserved cliff dwellings built in caves in cliffs far above the desert floor. The rooms were built of unshaped masonry blocks with adobe mortar and plaster, and many have T-shaped doorways like those of Anasazi cliff dwellings. Many details of the perishable material culture of the ancient cliff dwellers, usually not preserved in open archaeological sites, were obtained from the excavations at the monument. Sandals, basketry, cradleboards for carrying infants, arrows, yucca string skirts, and many food remains were found. Although finely woven and embroidered cotton cloth, cotton remains, and weaving tools were recovered, archaeologists found no evidence of looms, such as the anchoring holes that are often found on the floors of kivas. Tonto National Monument lies west of the city of Globe, and a tour of the site is an excellent introduction to prehistoric culture for those who are hardy enough to hike the steep trail.

It is curious that, although we have speculated that Puebloan folk migrated into the Tonto Basin, some important features of Pueblo villages are absent. Chief among these are kivas and great kivas. To date, no kivas have been identified in the Tonto Basin. Although some may speculate that this is due to the low level of archaeological excavation in the basin, we suggest a different reason. We think that by the 1300s the kivas and great kivas of the Mogollon and Anasazi areas were probably involved in the religion centering on rainfall and fertility that archaeologists label the Katsina cult, after the Hopi belief system. For whatever reason—perhaps because the irrigation systems of the preceding years made it unnecessary, perhaps because other ritual systems were already in place—the Salado people did not adopt the Katsina cult. They clearly did not build the kind of architectural features in which its ceremonies were carried out in other areas.

Like other parts of the Arizona desert, the Tonto Basin was abandoned completely some time after A.D. 1400. It should come as no surprise that we do not know the reasons why this happened. We can speculate, however, and some recently acquired clues to the mystery may aid us. Donald Graybill connected the tree-ring records of the late prehistoric and modern periods that showed two remarkable climatic events during the late fourteenth century. The first of these was an unprecedented series of floods between 1380 and 1385 that would have literally washed away villages and farmland. At the same time, groundwater levels dropped to disastrous lows. Geomorphologists tell us that the combination of high precipitation and low groundwater produces severe erosion, which would have radically affected farmers. The floods were followed by equally disastrous drought years between 1385 and 1390, preventing the Salado from recouping their losses and employing the dry-farming methods that were productive in less dry years. Faced with this climatic one-two punch, the Salado had no choice but to leave. Many of them may have fled southward along the Gila and San Pedro Rivers. These river valleys are dotted with large Salado ruins, although because few have been investigated professionally it is not possible to say at this time whether these villages were occupied before or after the Tonto Basin was abandoned.

A Concluding Thought

We have almost come to the end of the Salado story without answering the question with which we started: Who were the Salado? The simplest answer is that they were no one and everyone. We see in the Salado a clear parallel with the situation that we have drawn for the Sinagua. Throughout its history the Tonto Basin has been home to a diverse population who intermarried, interacted, and traded with people of other cultures and who borrowed those elements of cultures that they found useful and discarded the rest. The culture we call Salado was the high point of this complicated history, created by the mixture of peoples pushed from their homelands by drought and strife and drawn to this well-watered region, bringing with them new ideas and new beliefs. Ethnically diverse and culturally syncretic, the Salado Culture, which emerged in the Roosevelt phase, was unique and unparalleled.

What seems clear is that the Salado were not a regional variant of the Hohokam Culture. The people of the Tonto Basin did not simply follow the trajectory of the Hohokam living in the Phoenix area, although parallels do exist. The people of the Tonto Basin—all of them, as it is evident that they did not represent a single culture—were independent folk with their own ideas about the way things should be, their own methods of coping with life, and their own beliefs. What we seek to do now is not simply to classify and label these people but to reconstruct their history and understand their story. Why did they take the paths they chose? Who were their leaders? What disasters befell them? And why did they leave, relegating the land to the hawk, the coyote, and all the silent wild creatures?

We have seen that the story of the Salado reflects the ongoing nature of archaeological research and the process of discovering the past. The questions change, and so do the answers, as more information is gathered and our knowledge grows. Today we are on the verge of painting a picture of the Salado Culture that is as detailed and understandable as those we have created for the other prehistoric cultures of Arizona. The Salado have proved our most intractable piece of the past, difficult to pigeonhole into the neat categories of which we are so fond, their culture a complicated and rich tapestry. The spirit of the Salado remains in the land and in the fragments of pottery, worn stone tools, and bits of frayed sandals they left behind. These things speak to the archaeologist, and because they do, the true story of the Salado will eventually be known much as it must have happened.

10 CORONADO ENDS PREHISTORY

American history—contrasted with Native American prehistory—began with the arrival of Europeans from Spain. Long before Englishmen landed on the shores of Virginia and the rocky coast of Plymouth, Spanish explorers had already traversed the Atlantic coast from Labrador to the Straits of Magellan and had determined the extent of North America from Florida to California. Between 1539 and 1543, three Spanish expeditions explored the interior and the western coast of the present United States: one was led by Hernando de Soto and traveled from Florida to the Mississippi River and beyond; another, led by Francisco Vásquez de Coronado, went from the Mexican west coast to central Kansas; and the last, led by Juan Rodríguez Cabrillo, traveled northward from Matanchel on the Mexican west coast to possibly as far as the Rogue River in Oregon. These expeditions collectively determined the vastness of North America and assessed its copious natural resources. Within this enormous and rich land lived many Native American cultural groups, which the Spanish described in writing for the first time. Prehistory had ended, and history had begun.

Coronado led the first European expedition to explore what today forms the greater American Southwest. Within forty-eight years after Columbus's landing, Coronado's men stood on the edge of Arizona's Grand Canyon and visited the pueblos occupied by Native American peoples at Zuni, Hopi, Acoma, Pecos, and along the Río Grande. From New Mexico they went east toward the Great Plains, where they explored parts of Texas and saw and described the large buffalo herds. Moving north, the Coronado Expedition crossed Oklahoma and traversed southern Kansas as far as the Great Bend of the Arkansas River before reaching Native American villages in central Kansas. Thus, the Coronado Expedition became one of the great stories of the second Age of Discovery.

Coronado was the leader of this enterprise of courage and defiance. He was born in 1510 in Salamanca, Spain, to the nobleman Juan Vásquez de Coronado and Doña Isabel de Lujan. In 1512, Juan Vásquez was appointed *corregidor* (mayor) of Burgos in northern Spain. Because of legal entanglements, he created a *mayorazgo,* or entailed estate, in 1520, in which he assigned his estate to his oldest son Gonzalo. The mayorazgo prescribed that the estate would be passed down through Gonzalo's first-born male descendants. Thus Francisco, along with Gonzalo's other two brothers, would have to seek their own positions in life. With his social fate decided by the mayorazgo, Coronado bided his time, waiting for an opportunity. It came in 1535, when the newly appointed viceroy of Mexico, Antonio de Mendoza, sailed from Spain to his position in the New World. With him he took along twenty-five-year-old Francisco Vásquez de Coronado as a member of his retinue.

With Viceroy Mendoza's political friendship and patronage, Coronado's prominence rose in Mexico City. By summer of 1538 he had been appointed a member of Mexico City's city council and a charter member of the Brotherhood of the Blessed Sacrament for Charity, a charitable society founded to aid the needy and educate orphan girls. Soon after, he married a wealthy heiress, Beatriz de Estrada, daughter of the deceased royal treasurer. His mother-in-law, Doña Marina, presented the newlyweds with a large country estate. Francisco himself acquired the lands of Juan de Burgos, who had returned to Spain. In a few short years Francisco Vásquez had climbed the political and social ladder of colonial New Spain. With the imprisonment of Nuño de Guzmán, governor of the province of Nueva Galicia, north of Mexico City, Viceroy Mendoza appointed Coronado to the vacant governorship in 1539.

Meanwhile, Alvar Núñez Cabeza de Vaca and his three companions, survivors of the ill-fated Narvaez expedition to Florida, had been rescued in 1536 after walking to Sonora. In Mexico City they reported on their shipwreck in the Gulf of Mexico and what they had seen in their eight years of wandering between the Texas coast and Sonora. Their incredible stories would inspire a series of expeditions northward.

Viceroy Mendoza sought an experienced explorer to mount an expedition to the north on a quest to verify stories of rich civilizations and cities built of gold. He selected Marcos de Niza, a French Franciscan monk who had previously been assigned to Peru and Guatemala. By spring of 1539, Fray Marcos de Niza began traveling north on an exploring venture following tales of the famed Seven Cities of Cibola. The small party was composed mainly of Native American guides and escorted by Estevan Dorantes, also known as Estevan the Moor, who had accompanied Cabeza de Vaca on his doomed voyage. In autumn 1539, Fray Marcos returned to report his travails and the death of Estevan. His accounts of Cibola were written carefully and do not seem particularly misleading with regard to his having seen any cities of gold. Although little in his writing suggests such treasure, what he *told* people apparently was a different story indeed.

Viceroy Mendoza, confident that the unexplored territory north of Mexico was vast and rich, ordered that a large expedition be organized to explore and verify the existence of the fabled kingdom of Quivira, which was thought possibly to lie just beyond Cibola. Because of his rivalry with Hernán Cortés, who had petitioned to lead the expedition, Viceroy Mendoza was anxious to appoint one of his own trusted followers. He selected Coronado to lead the expedition to Cibola.

The Road to Cibola

Royal approval for the expedition arrived on January 6, 1540, and by late February Viceroy Mendoza had reviewed the final preparations at Compostela, on the west coast of Mexico in the modern state of Nayarit. More than 230 mounted men and 62 foot soldiers formed the main body of the Spanish troops, with others scheduled to join them on the way. By the end of February, the main body—with over 800 Native American allies, a number that would later swell to just over 1,000—prepared to leave Compostela for Culiacán, the next staging area. The march from Compostela to Culiacán, located in modern Sinaloa and the last Spanish frontier outpost in the north, took almost a month. The process of moving the large, unwieldy expedition northward was slowed by thickly forested mountains and hostile Indians, who had felt the devastating blows of the Spanish conquest. The slow pace was not surprising. Not only did Coronado's men have to herd a thousand head of horses, they also had to tend 600

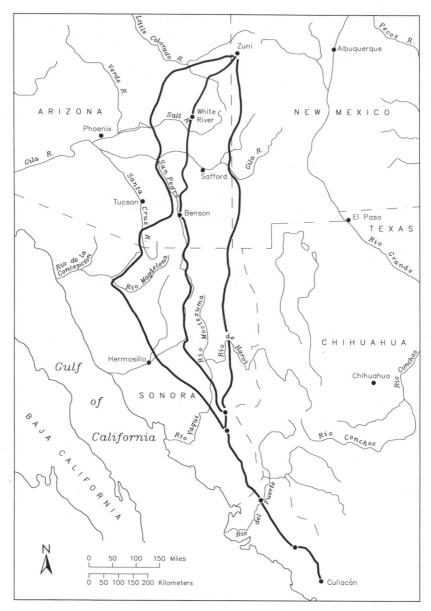

Possible routes of the Coronado Expedition through Arizona. From west to east, they are the routes proposed by Albert Schroeder, Herbert Bolton and Stewart Udall, and Charles Di Peso.

pack animals and other stock that included sheep, goats, and cattle—supplies on the hoof. After reaching Culiacán, Coronado decided to advance with about seventy-five horsemen and twenty-five foot soldiers, some native allies, and a small herd of cattle. The main army would advance to Cibola at a slower pace.

Led by native guides and accompanied by Fray Marcos de Niza, Coronado and his vanguard army crossed one river valley after another through Sonora, heading north to wealth and glory. The traditionally accepted route is that, after leaving Culiacán, the expedition passed near Pericos, an ancient settlement in country that opens into broad, flat coastal plains. North beyond Pericos, the guides led them through a series of rivers and into a narrow canyon that they followed for some distance before reaching Corazones, "pueblo of the hearts," so named for the hundreds of deer hearts that the residents offered to the expedition.

From Corazones the expedition went northward, and after reaching a place called Chichilticale, or the Red House, thought to be somewhere in Arizona, the fatigued men and animals rested for two days to prepare for their march through the mountainous, unpopulated country ahead. The march across the despoblado that lay beyond Chichilticale was long and arduous, crossing difficult terrain made more perilous by a lack of provisions and the bone-weary fatigue of the men and animals. Coronado wrote that they found no grass and that the horses were so exhausted that they perished. Finally, after crossing impassable mountains, they found "fresh rivers and grass like that of Castile." Their relief was short-lived. They camped somewhere beyond the river that they named the Frio because it was cold, and there three men died from eating poisonous plants because they were so hungry.

Despite their fatigue and hunger, the expedition moved northward until they were a day's march from the first Zuni village. Zuni warriors attacked an encamped advance guard of the expedition led by García López de Cárdenas on July 6, 1540. The next day, at Cibola (probably the Zuni village of Hawikuh), the exhausted and starving men attempted to persuade the Zuni of their friendly intentions. When they failed to do this, Coronado, believing he and his men might perish from a lack of food and water, decided to attack the village. Initially the Spaniards were at a distinct disadvantage. The pueblo fortress, lacking outside doors and having rooftops from which arrows and stones could be rained down on the attackers, was readily defensible. During the fracas Coronado was hit by stones and received an arrow in the foot as he attempted to scale a ladder at one of the houses, but Cárdenas came to his rescue. The tale grows curiously ambiguous here. Historian Herbert Bolton writes that "Coronado was carried as dead to a tent where for a long time he lay unconscious; and when he revived he was told the welcome news that the pueblo had been captured and that in it a large supply of provisions had been found." How the tide was turned and the Spanish prevailed, we probably will never know. Having taken the Zuni pueblos, the expedition camped there for the summer.

Cibola was the first of many great disappointments. The streets and the buildings of the city were not paved with gold but were of ordinary stone. The accuracy and veracity of Fray Marcos's statements were questioned sorely. When the soldiers first set eyes on Cibola, Pedro de Castañeda, the chronicler of the expedition, wrote that "such were the curses which some of them hurled at Fray Marcos that I pray God to protect him from them."

Cibola served as a base of operations for sending out small exploring parties. Pedro de Tovar, as we have already discussed, reached the Hopi village of Awat'ovi and brought an end to Hisatsinom Anasazi prehistory. García López de Cárdenas traveled to the Grand Canyon and peered into its depths to view the Colorado River far below, and Hernando de Alvarado attained the edge of the Great Plains.

Coronado and a portion of his army moved toward the Río Grande Valley in New Mexico and by fall of 1540 had established a winter camp at Tiguex, a pueblo near present-day Bernalillo, north of Albuquerque. The situation at Tiguex, although at first friendly, soon turned antagonistic, and a full-scale war broke out between the natives and the explorers. The Spanish fought the Native Americans at several pueblos along the Río Grande and the Pecos River farther to the east. Later, Mexican royal officials investigating the causes of the Tiguex War held Coronado and other officers responsible for their actions against friendly natives. García López de Cárdenas received a fine and a seven-year prison sentence for his abuse of military power. Coronado was exonerated.

By spring of 1541, Tristan de Luna y Arrellano had brought the main army up from Corazones, and Coronado prepared to depart for Quivira, about which tales of priceless treasure continued to circulate. He proceeded to Pecos Pueblo, where he made an uneasy peace before departing for the Great Plains. At Pecos he was offered a guide whom the Spaniards named El Turco (The Turk), a Plains Indian with tales of gold who may have been instructed to lead the Spaniards as far away as possible and lose them on the plains. Heading across the plains, Coronado encountered canyons and decided that he and thirty horsemen and a few foot soldiers would proceed to Quivira, the rest returning to the Río Grande. Once out of the canyons, the expedition crossed into Oklahoma and finally arrived, we now believe, at the Great Bend of the Arkansas River. Having found no gold for the Spanish, The Turk was executed for lying about the route and the existence of Quivira.

Coronado proceeded some distance beyond the Great Bend, possibly reaching central Kansas before he turned back to the Río Grande by way of a more direct route. After returning to Tiguex, Coronado suffered a head injury while racing his horse with Captain Rodrigo de Maldonado. Apparently his saddle girth broke, and he fell face first and suffered a concussion when trampled by Maldonado's horse. Later, Coronado would report to his superiors that he had turned back because of his injuries, although his men believed he had exaggerated them in order to force the return of the entire expedition. In retreat they retraced their trail back to Mexico City, where they reported their failure to find gold to Viceroy Mendoza.

Like other pioneering efforts, the Coronado Expedition was part of an historical process that marked the New World with its distinct European character. The expedition was significant in several ways. It prepared the way for eventual Spanish settlement by blazing new trails northward. The expedition established a historical archive based on reconnaissance, correspondence, and reports that contributed geographical knowledge of North America and its animals and plants. Perhaps most significant to our story, the expedition observed Native American cultures for the first time. For the native people of Arizona and the Southwest, the Coronado Expedition signaled the end of prehistory and the beginning of a new era of cultural change. New World peoples, isolated from the technological advances as well as the conflicts and strife of the Old World, began to take part in global culture.

Cultures at Contact

At one time or another, almost everyone has wondered about the radical difference in technological achievement so evident in the clash between Europeans and Native Americans. The question has two parts. The first concerns the factors that bring about cultural change and whether such change is rapid or gradual, which we discussed earlier in chapter 2. The second part involves the perspective that modern industrial society brings to evaluating other peoples and cultures.

Let us consider first our gadget-ridden, consumer-oriented modern society. We tend to measure our social position and happiness, as well as that of others, by material goods, especially brand-name products and symbols of affluence. (The first draft of these words, for example, was written with a German-made fountain pen bearing a French name that became affordable to an archaeologist only when a discount chain went bankrupt.) Our modern society measures individuals and other societies by the standards of our modern material culture, and although this measure is wholly appropriate for some purposes, it is not appropriate for all. How, for example, do we compare languages, or religions, or artistic expression? This is the point precisely. When we move beyond material culture and technology, the cross-cultural measurements of achievement and excellence are less certain. Because of this, archaeologists are careful about using modern industrial society's standards in making judgments about all aspects of preindustrial or nonindustrial peoples. What the Clovis people, for example, may have lacked in hunting technology was amply compensated for by physical skill, mental alertness, and sheer guts. The people of the past must be seen in the context of their own time and place.

If the New World Clovis people were at the same technological level as their Old World contemporaries, then what happened to give the Europeans such a commanding lead by the contact year of 1492? The most satisfying answer to this question comes from the physiologist Jared Diamond. He takes a global perspective in drawing attention to the rather obvious fact that the New World is oriented north–south and the Euro-Asian land mass is oriented east–west. Whereas Old Worlders could move rather freely from east to west, mingling people and ideas along a well-populated, temperate environmental zone, this was not possible in the

New World because of natural barriers created by radically different environmental zones. The result of these major geographic differences was that less interaction and idea exchange took place in the Americas than in Europe and Asia. Add to this the absence in the Americas of large animals that were suited to domestication—such as horses, cattle, sheep, goats, and pigs—and one begins to see some of the natural environmental factors behind differences in the rate of technological change.

It is no surprise, therefore, that Coronado's horsemen and foot soldiers—armed with metal swords, pikes, and guns and protected by armor—encountered little resistance from native peoples as they marched through Arizona to Zuni and then back again to Mexico.

Coronado's Trail through Arizona

Coronado's expedition changed the course of southwestern history irrevocably, and thus we naturally are curious about the trail that it followed. Because the map drawn in Coronado's own hand has been misplaced, the true route has been shrouded in mystery and dispute. The route is unquestionably crucial for what its location can tell us about Native American peoples at the last moment of prehistoric time.

Volumes have been written tracing the route of the Coronado Expedition, and as with virtually all other historical and archaeological enterprises, the issue is fraught with controversy and clashing opinions. The first speculations began with the movement of Anglo Americans into Arizona and New Mexico in the mid nineteenth century. As early as 1848 a location for Chichilticale was suggested, and the one favored at that time identified it with the Hohokam Big House at Casa Grande. In 1892 Adolph Bandelier first described the route that later would be discussed by the geographer Carl O. Sauer and that has become the most widely accepted version. This route was the one favored by Herbert Eugene Bolton, the historian most closely connected with the problem of identifying the Coronado Trail. His volume on Coronado, first published in 1949, is not only a biography and history but also a detailed reconstruction of the route that Coronado traveled on his monumental foray into the American Southwest. Bolton's version of the Coronado Trail has been accepted by most historians and has become entrenched in public interpretations.

Museum exhibits show the trail as Bolton originally defined it. A recent book by Stewart L. Udall presents the Bolton route with only minor deviations. In short, the Bolton route has been accepted as the Coronado Expedition route.

Bolton broke new ground in showing the way that history and archaeology could combine to verify the expedition's route. He believed, first, that to verify the trail it was necessary to get out of the library and into the field to retrace the route on the ground. Second, he wanted an archaeologist to accompany him, and he asked the most eminent scientist he could find—Emil W. Haury. Third, Bolton steered his investigations by the best available physiographic markers—the sequence of rivers encountered by the Coronado Expedition as recorded by Captain Juan Jaramillo, who traveled with the vanguard army forging the way through the wilderness.

We agree with Bolton that Jaramillo's rivers are crucial markers, for two reasons. First, water would have been a major concern of Coronado's horsemen as they crossed the Sonoran Desert in June 1540—in the hottest and driest month of the desert year. The men of the vanguard and the main army were mounted, and those of us who maintain horses know full well their daily demand for water. Second, the rivers described by Jaramillo are an excellent source of new data. Unlike other trail markers, such as vegetation, which may have changed character greatly within the past five hundred years, the rivers remain little altered in their courses. Most important, their hydrologic character can be reconstructed, as pioneered by Donald Graybill of the Laboratory of Tree-Ring Research at the University of Arizona. It should be possible to determine precisely how much water flowed in Arizona's rivers during the summer of 1540, thus giving us an important tool in discovering the expedition's route.

Although Bolton clearly was on the right research tack, we must disagree with the specifics of his route reconstruction. The characteristics of the modern rivers Bolton identifies with those described by members of the expedition do not agree. Our familiarity with the White Mountain Apache Reservation, and in particular with the White River, has led us to question Bolton's identification of the White River as Jaramillo's Río de las Balsas. This, in turn, has led us to question the trail as Bolton identified it.

Jaramillo's narrative concerning the rivers flowing through Arizona begins with the expedition leaving a native settlement called Ispa. Beyond this village, usually identified as modern Arizpe in Sonora, lay a depopulated area, which took about four days to cross. On the other side of this small despoblado was a river called the Nexpa. Jaramillo writes, "We went down this stream for two days, and then left the stream, going toward the right to the foot of the mountain chain. . . . Crossing the mountains, we came to a deep and reedy river, where we found water and forage for the horses."

Bolton identified the Río Nexpa as today's San Pedro River. The mountain chain he believed to be the Pinaleño and Santa Teresa Mountains, and he suggested that Coronado crossed there in the pass that separates the two ranges. Jaramillo's "deep and reedy river" was for Bolton the Gila River. Bolton suggested that the vanguard crossed the Gila around present Bylas, then began the ascent that would lead them into the great despoblado where horses and men alike would perish.

The next river after Jaramillo's "deep and reedy river" was reached on San Juan's day (June 24) after three days' travel, and it was named in that saint's honor. Bolton identified the Río San Juan as the Salt River, which he believed the vanguard forded near the mouth of Bonito Creek.

Jaramillo's account records that, on leaving the San Juan, "we went to another river, through a somewhat rough country, more toward the north, to a river which we called the Rafts (de las Balsas), because we had to cross on these, as it was rising." "This stream," according to Bolton, "was White River, and was reached by Coronado just below the site of Fort Apache. In much of its course White River flows through deep gorges or barrancas, but here, near the old fort, there is a shallow place where it was feasible to use rafts for transporting men and baggage."

Our field inspection leads us to think that not only would it have been unnecessary to use rafts to cross the White River at Fort Apache, it would have been impossible. The river is shallow there, less than two feet deep, and flows over large boulders. Horses and men could easily ford the river, whereas rafts would run aground. The modern White River has not been altered significantly by dams or agricultural use. Summer thunderstorms might indeed cause the river to rise, but the rain-swollen river would have subsided in less time than it would have taken to build rafts to cross it. We believe, then, that Bolton's identification of the White River at Fort Apache as the Río de las Balsas is incorrect.

From the Río de las Balsas the members of the vanguard traveled two short days to another river that they named the Río de la Barranca, suggesting that it flowed through a steep and narrow gorge. Bolton identifies the Río de la Barranca as a branch of the White River that runs through Post Office Canyon. Our field research suggests another problem with this portion of the river sequence. According to Jaramillo, it was two short days' travel from the Río de las Balsas to La Barranca. By today's road, Post Office Canyon is less than fourteen miles from the river crossing at Fort Apache, a short two days' travel indeed even for exhausted horses and men.

After crossing La Barranca, the vanguard traveled in another day's journey to El Río Frio, named because its waters were cold. Bolton identifies the Río Frio as "one of the small streams in the vicinity of McNary, ten miles northward of La Barranca." We suggest, however, that a small stream that today is unnamed would scarcely be equated in Jaramillo's narrative with rivers such as La Barranca and the Río de Las Balsas, which were sufficiently impressive to be given names in his narrative.

The final river encountered by the expedition was the Río Bermejo, four days' journey beyond the Río Frio. Here, according to Jaramillo, the vanguard began to see "an Indian or two." The despoblado was ended, and Cibola was at hand. Castañeda and Jaramillo both wrote of the river, and their descriptions are similar. It was a river "about 8 leagues from Cibola, which they called Red River, because its waters were muddy and reddish. In this river they found mullets like those of Spain. The first Indians from that country were seen here." The Río Bermejo undoubtedly was the Little Colorado River, whose waters today run muddy and red after summer rains. Tired and hungry, Coronado and his men arrived at the Zuni village of Hawikuh in early July 1540.

It seems to us that Bolton's river sequence is in error. The key point of the sequence appears to be Jaramillo's Río de las Balsas. If a better choice for this river can be found than the unacceptable White River, the rest of the river sequence may fall into place using the Little Colorado River as the Río Bermejo to anchor the end of the sequence. Identifying the best candidate for the Río de las Balsas will require additional work in the field.

We leave Jaramillo's rivers to consider the location of Chichilticale, mentioned in the chronicles as a port, a people, a mountain chain, a mountain pass, and a ruined pueblo that became the famous route marker called the Red House. It was remembered well by the chroniclers, for at Chichilticale the great despoblado began. Oddly, the men who documented the Coronado Expedition wrote different accounts of the Red House. Although Jaramillo is precise and descriptive concerning the rivers, he writes little concerning Chichilticale. Castañeda, on the other hand, provides a detailed description of Chichilticale and writes little about the rivers. Imagine the fame and success awaiting the archaeologist who can locate this ruin and recover the Spanish colonial artifacts that no doubt are buried there!

Bolton attempted to mesh the two disparate accounts and to locate Chichilticale along the river sequence. Like Bandelier and Sauer before him, Bolton placed Chichilticale at the foot of Eagle Pass, the gateway to the Gila River between the Pinaleño and Santa Teresa Mountains. Bolton's candidate for the Red House is a ruin on the 76 Ranch in the foothills of the Pinaleños to the east of Aravaipa Creek and some distance to the southeast of Eagle Pass. Bolton's identification of Chichilticale apparently was inspired by Jaramillo, who writes that, leaving the Río Nexpa, the vanguard traveled to the east "to the foot of the mountain chain in two days' journey, where we heard news of what is called Chichiltic Calli."

Was this the mysterious Red House? Unfortunately, we think not. Although there are some areas of red soil in the vicinity of the 76 Ranch, in other respects Bolton's location of the Red House conflicts with observations on the physiography of the despoblado region. Castañeda writes that "the country rises continually from the beginning of the wilderness until Cibola is reached." This does not describe well the topography of the area beyond the 76 Ranch, which includes a hilly and often steep rise across the pass between the mountain ranges, a gradual descent into the low, broad valley of the Gila River, which lies beyond the mountains, and then a difficult ascent into the Gila Mountains beyond the valley. Moreover, Castañeda's bucolic description of the country surrounding Chichilticale suggests a higher, more mountainous location than that around Eagle Pass: "The rest of the country is all wilderness, covered with pine forests." There were oaks with sweet acorns, wild rosebushes, many springs, rivers, and mountain lions. Historian Carroll Riley has pointed out that unfortunately this description serves equally well for virtually all of the mountain country south of the Mogollon Rim and eastward to the upper Gila River drainage.

Clearly, the Red House is the most likely route marker that can be identified archaeologically. Castañeda's description of the structure itself and the area surrounding it is lengthy and detailed. The pueblo, already ruined when the Spanish first saw it, is likely to remain visible today. The fact that armies of mounted men—with their tack, weapons, armor, and equipment—and support personnel camped for long periods of time at the Red House increases the likelihood that recoverable remains would be present.

Other routes and other locations for Chichilticale have been suggested, but none fits the descriptions of the Spanish journals any better than Bolton's reconstruction. Albert Schroeder, for example, thought that the Nexpa was the Salt River and that Chichilticale was one of the large sites now buried under the waters of Roosevelt Lake, that the mountains that the expedition crossed were the Sierra Ancha, and that the San Juan River was present-day Cherry Creek. Schroeder believed that the "barbarous" natives encountered by the Spanish in the area around Chichilticale were the highly mobile, nonagricultural Yavapai. Other accounts identify Chichilticale with the Tonto Cliff Dwellings, which seems unlikely as none of the Spanish chronicles mention that Chichilticale was a house in a cave. We personally like the idea that Chichilticale may have been Kinishba Pueblo on the White Mountain Apache Reservation near White River, excavated and reconstructed by Dean Byron Cummings in the 1930s and now falling into ruin for the second time. This location certainly fits the description of the narratives well.

Coronado returned to Culiacán by the same route he had used to discover Cibola. Writing of the return journey, Castañeda is uncharacteristically terse: "The wilderness," he writes, "was crossed without opposition." Perhaps the way was well marked by then, considering all the troops and animals that had marched across the land during the time Coronado was seeking Quivira. Nevertheless, the apparent ease with which the return trip was made contrasts strongly and oddly with Coronado's own tale of hardship and misfortune on the journey toward Cibola, as documented in his letter to Viceroy Mendoza of August 1540. One can also question why the general chose to return across the despoblado when he had recently wintered on the Río Grande—surely a more promising avenue southward than the central Arizona mountains.

We close with another issue. We have noted that the Coronado Expedition was accompanied by Native American guides who were charged with finding the route to Cibola. There is considerable evidence to suggest that these guides were unfamiliar with the country, with ways in which it could be traversed and how to live off the land. The expedition crossed the central Arizona mountains in the most haphazard and arduous way possible. Along the way, the men and horses starved, driven indeed to eating poisonous herbs—a peculiar state to be in, in well-watered, green mountains teeming with deer and other game. We suspect that the guides, and indeed the expedition, were in fact lost. This is an important bit of information for the prehistorian, for a lack of familiarity on the part of Coronado's native allies with north-south routes of travel indicates that these routes must have been disrupted for some time before the arrival of the Spanish. The abandonment of central Arizona by prehistoric peoples apparently was not fiction but fact.

A Concluding Thought

It is not our intent to denigrate the significance of Bolton's work or to deny that the trail taken by Coronado through Arizona can ever be documented scientifically. Rather, the reverse is true. Bolton's study provides the research agenda for verifying the route, and archaeological techniques will supply the necessary tools.

Coronado's journey into Arizona was an event with major cultural consequences. It brought a sudden and dramatic end to southwestern prehistory. Pueblo culture would assume a new trajectory. The search for Coronado's trail symbolizes a special opportunity for archaeologists, historians, and Arizonans to join together in forging a deeper understanding of Arizona's Native American and Spanish heritage. The rivers of Jaramillo remain. It is now our task to decode the message they hold and pierce the mist that still hides Coronado's footsteps along the trail.

EPILOGUE

Writing this book has been a labor of love. We have sketched a highly personal prehistory of Arizona, one that means a great deal to us as individuals as well as professional archaeologists. Here we summarize some of the more important reasons why the prehistory of Arizona is personally meaningful, and in so doing, touch upon several themes that thread through these pages.

First, prehistory is all about people. People have made the past by their eccentric and astounding and saddening behavior. People have also discovered the past, as we have seen, and have brought to its interpretation the great variety of their individual personalities, training, and skills. It is not possible to separate the account of the Mogollon Culture, for example, from that of the man who discovered it, Emil Haury. And it is with people that the responsibility for discovering, unlocking, and preserving the past lies. We have stressed throughout these chapters that the discovery of the past is not restricted to archaeologists but is the prerogative of all Arizonans. Astonishing discoveries await, and the interested and enlightened public, along with professional archaeologists, form the best possible team for making these discoveries. In the same way, the responsibility for preserving the past also lies with the public, for professionals alone cannot accomplish what must be done.

A second theme, related to the first, is that of discovery. Many have asked us if there is anything left to discover, and the answer to that is a resounding "You bet!" As we have seen in the previous chapters, our knowledge of the past is uneven. Some cultures, especially those that archaeologists have studied long and intensively, such as the Anasazi, are understood well, but in many cases, much research remains to be done before we can do more than sketch prehistory. The Patayan Culture is a good example of this need to continue the search. Our book also has stressed the changing nature of archaeological research. The Salado Culture stands as a prime example of how our understanding of the past changes along with our theoretical perspectives and methods. Discoveries are made as new information is collected and new techniques for studying the past are developed. Recall that we have been doing archaeology in the Southwest only for slightly more than a century. The past remains a rich store of information waiting to be discovered and studied.

Third, we note that one of the many things that has changed in archaeology is the nature of the people who do it. Virtually all of the major players in southwestern archaeology have been, and are, men. We have a father of southwestern archaeology, but no mother. Fortunately, this is changing, and as more women join the ranks of professional archaeologists, so too will our perspectives on the past change. In these pages we have sought to engender the past whenever possible, and this remains a goal toward which we strive.

A fourth theme is the involvement of Native Americans in the study of their own past. One of the more important issues to emerge in the past few years is the voice of southwestern Indians in decisions concerning the treatment and disposition of prehistoric remains and the reconstruction of prehistory. We acknowledge their prerogative to reconstruct the past as they see it and have strived to present the Native American views of prehistory when these are known and appropriate. We have tried to merge the many paths to the past and orchestrate the many voices presenting prehistory.

Last, we hope to have underscored the vital theme of preservation and conservation. No discoveries can be made, no reconstructions of past history can be created, if archaeological resources are destroyed by thoughtless actions or vandalism. We are asked often why we do what we do. What is the point of archaeology? To this we answer that archaeology is a tool for preserving the past for the future. Archaeological resources are nonrenewable; when the last Hohokam site has been excavated, no more will ever be created. Preserving historical and prehistoric resources for future study and for future enjoyment by all Arizonans is vitally important, for the past belongs to us all. Archaeological resources in our state are protected by a number of state and federal laws. All of us must respect these laws. We saw in chapter 1 that the history of Arizona archaeology is as much a story of legislation and the protection of archaeological resources as it is a tale of changing research goals. Although the first protective act was passed in 1906, we are still fighting the battle to preserve our heritage, as contemporary debates over archaeological resource protection continue to be waged in the Arizona legislature. In this area as elsewhere, we call upon the interested public to help professional archaeologists by talking to your children about the importance of archaeology, by reporting vandalism, and by respecting our state and federal laws.

The future of prehistory in Arizona remains bright. With cooperation from all, there is much to be done, discovered, and learned. We hope that this book has provided our readers with a basic knowledge of Arizona archaeology, and if it has also kindled interest, stimulated thought, and promoted preservation, we can ask no more. Our task has been well done if we have conveyed to our readers some of the excitement and fulfillment that we have shared in discovering Arizona's past.

Glossary

archaeomagnetic dating. A dating technique that matches the direction of magnetized iron particles in fired clay with the position of the earth's magnetic pole in the past to derive dates in calendar years.

adobe. Mud used as a wall plaster or as a wall construction material poured directly into a form or into molds for making bricks.

agave. A wild-occurring desert plant cultivated by the Hohokam for food and fiber, also called mescal and century plant.

ak-chin (O'odham). Floodwater farming in the alluvial outwash fan of an arroyo.

archaeology. The study of material objects regardless of time or space in order to describe and explain human behavior and culture.

artifact. Any item manufactured or modified by people; roughly synonymous with *material culture.*

atlatl. A hand-held implement used to hurl a spear with increased force.

bajada. A desert foothill slope.

ballcourt. An elliptical field defined by earthen or stone embankments and used by the Hohokam for a version of the Mesoamerican ball game, as well as other public ceremonies and activities.

barrio (Spanish). Neighborhood.

branch. A subdivision of a prehistoric culture, as in the Forestdale Branch of the Mogollon.

caliche. A seemingly impenetrable layer of calcium carbonate not far below the surface of the desert.

ceramic. Artifacts, usually containers, made from clay and temper and produced by firing; used interchangeably with *pottery* in the Southwest.

chronology. Arranging past events or objects according to the sequence of occurrence. Absolute chronologies are in calendar years, whereas relative chronologies employ ordinal scales of measure, such as early, middle, and late.

cliff dwelling. A pueblo built into a rockshelter or against a cliff face.

coil and scrape. A method of thinning and finishing pottery used throughout most of the central and northern Southwest. Clay coils are bonded together by pinching, then a scraper made from a gourd or potsherd is used to smooth the surface and thin the vessel walls.

compound. A walled enclosure defining domestic and/or public ceremonial space.

corrugation. A method of finishing pottery that leaves the coils partially smoothed, providing a textured exterior surface.

cranial deformation. Unintentional and often almost imperceptible flattening of the skull produced by the pressure of restraining an infant's head in a cradleboard.

cremation. The burial of burned human remains in place (primary cremation) or removed to another location (secondary cremation).

culture. The collective knowledge of a people and the rules and regulations for transforming knowledge into appropriate social action.

Culture. A term used by archaeologists to label a distinct collection of material traits, behavior, and organization in prehistory, as in the Mogollon Culture.

dendrochronology. The technique devised by A. E. Douglass that matches patterns of variation in the annual ring width of a single tree-ring specimen against a master sequence to permit the specimen to be dated in calendar years.

despoblado (Spanish). An unpopulated area.

flaked stone tools. Tools manufactured by removing flakes or chips by percussion or pressure.

Great Kiva. A large structure used for communal ceremonial and social activities.

ground stone tools. Tools—such as metates, manos, and axes—shaped by grinding and polishing rather than by flaking.

hematite. An iron ore ground to produce red paint.

inhumation. The burial of a fully articulated body (primary inhumation) or of a disarticulated body, usually of skeletal remains after disintegration or removal of the flesh (secondary inhumation).

intaglio. Images formed on the desert floor by scraping away the darker stone pavement to reveal the light-colored soil beneath.

jacal. Wall construction of upright poles interlaced with twigs and plastered with adobe.

kachina. A portable wooden figure depicting a Katsina; often called a kachina doll.

Katsina (plural: Katsinam). A supernatural being in Pueblo religion, personified in masked dancers.

kiva. A Pueblo ceremonial chamber often built below ground and frequently detached from habitation rooms.

lithics. Stone artifacts, commonly flaked stone tools.

macaw. A large, brightly colored tropical parrot traded for its feathers and its ritual value.

mano (Spanish for "hand"). A stone held in the hand for use in grinding seeds and grains on a metate.

masonry. A technique of wall construction using stones, often laid in horizontal courses.

material culture. Any tool, construction, or alteration of the environment by human beings.

metate. A flat, basin- or trough-shaped stone on which corn and seeds are ground with a mano.

midden. A trash deposit, often piled in a heap.

olla (Spanish). A pottery jar with a narrow opening, commonly used for water storage.

paddle-and-anvil. A pottery-thinning technique used by the Hohokam and Patayan to bond coils by striking the vessel's exterior with a paddle against an anvil, usually a smooth stone, held against the interior.

palynology. The scientific study of plant pollen.

petroglyph. An image hammered, pecked, or scratched on rock.

Period. The largest time unit of cultural classification, usually further divided into phases.

phase. The smallest unit of culture history, representing a prehistoric culture at a specific point in time and identified by pottery types, house construction, mortuary practices, and other traits.

phyllite. A tabular metamorphic rock with a dull gray opaque color.

pictograph. An image painted on a rock.

pit house. A semisubterranean habitation structure.

plain ware. Pottery that has not been slipped, painted, or textured.

platform mound. An earthen tumulus associated with Hohokam ceremonialism, derived ultimately from Mesoamerica.

polychrome pottery. Pottery decorated with three or more colors.

preceramic. The time before the use of pottery.

prehistory. The archaeological study of the past before writing. In the American Southwest, prehistory is the time from the initial peopling of the Americas until A.D. 1540.

projectile point. A spear point, dart point, or arrowhead.

protohistorical period. The time following European arrival in 1492 but before Europeans came to live in sustained contact with native peoples. In Arizona, the protohistorical period is generally considered to have ended around 1700 or 1750.

provenance. The place of origin, or the location where an artifact is produced.

provenience. The location at a site where an artifact is recovered.

pueblo. A single or multistory village built of stone or adobe.

ramada (Spanish). A domestic structure made of four upright posts supporting a roof of branches or brush, also called a shade.

ranchería. A settlement pattern of widely spaced households.

sherd. A piece of a broken pot, also called a shard or potsherd.

Sipapu (Hopi). The hole in a kiva floor symbolizing the origin place of the Pueblo people.

site. The archaeological term for the location of past human activity as identified by material remains.

slip. A thin wash of clay and water applied to the surface of a pottery vessel as an over-all color.

smudging. A method of surface treatment in pottery that uses polishing and sooting together to form a glossy black interior surface.

stratigraphy. The archaeological study of stratification, which is the deposition or ac-cumulation of sediments and cultural material. In an orderly sequence, the lowest deposits are the oldest.

temper. Any nonclay material (sand, crushed rock, crushed sherds, etc.) added to clay to provide strength and prevent cracking when forming ceramic vessels.

trincheras (Spanish for "terraces"). Dry-laid rock terraces along hill slopes in south-ern Arizona and northern Sonora and Chihuahua, Mexico.

Selected Readings

CHAPTER 1. From Clovis to Coronado

Cheek, Lawrence W.
   1994   A.D. 1250, Ancient Peoples of the Southwest. Phoenix: Arizona Department of
          Transportation.
Chronic, Halka
   1983   Roadside Geology of Arizona. Missoula: Mountain Press.
Cordell, Linda S.
   1984   Prehistory of the Southwest. New York: Academic Press.
Cordell, Linda S., and George J. Gumerman, eds.
   1989   Dynamics of Southwest Prehistory. Washington, D.C.: Smithsonian Institu-
          tion Press.
Lowe, Charles H.
   1964   Arizona's Natural Environment. Tucson: University of Arizona Press.
Nabhan, Gary Paul
   1985   Gathering the Desert. Tucson: University of Arizona Press.
Noble, David Grant
   1981   Ancient Ruins of the Southwest: An Archaeological Guide. Flagstaff: North-
          land Publishing.
Reid, J. Jefferson, and David E. Doyel, eds.
   1986   Emil W. Haury's Prehistory of the American Southwest. Tucson: University of
          Arizona Press.
Sheridan, Thomas E.
   1995   Arizona: A History. Tucson: University of Arizona Press.
Woodbury, Richard B.
   1993   Sixty Years of Southwestern Archaeology: A History of the Pecos Conference.
          Albuquerque: University of New Mexico Press.

CHAPTER 2. Clovis Hunters Discover America

Folsom, Franklin
   1992   Black Cowboy: The Life and Legend of George McJunkin. Nowot, Colorado:
          Roberts Rinehart.

Greenberg, Joseph H., Christy G. Turner II, and Stephen L. Zegura
  1986   The Settlement of the Americas: A Comparison of the Linguistic, Dental, and Genetic Evidence. *Current Anthropology* 27 (5): 477–497.
Martin, Paul S., and Richard G. Klein
  1984   *Quaternary Extinctions: A Prehistoric Revolution.* Tucson: University of Arizona Press.
Meltzer, David J.
  1993   *Search for the First Americans.* Washington, D.C.: Smithsonian Institution.

CHAPTER 3. Archaic Ancestors

Haury, Emil W.
  1950   *The Stratigraphy and Archaeology of Ventana Cave.* Tucson: University of Arizona Press.
Jennings, Jesse D.
  1957   *Danger Cave.* University of Utah Anthropological Papers 27. Salt Lake City: University of Utah Press.
Matson, R. G.
  1991   *The Origins of Southwestern Agriculture.* Tucson: University of Arizona Press.
Sayles, E. B.
  1983   *The Cochise Cultural Sequence in Southeastern Arizona.* Anthropological Papers of the University of Arizona, no. 42. Tucson: University of Arizona Press.
Waters, Michael R.
  1986   *The Geoarchaeology of Whitewater Draw, Arizona.* Anthropological Papers of the University of Arizona, no. 45. Tucson: University of Arizona Press.
Wills, W. H.
  1988   *Early Prehistoric Agriculture in the American Southwest.* Santa Fe: School of American Research Press.

CHAPTER 4. The Hohokam

Downum, Christian E.
  1993   *Between Desert and River: Hohokam Settlement and Land Use in the Los Robles Community.* Anthropological Papers of the University of Arizona, no. 57. Tucson: University of Arizona Press.
Fish, Suzanne K., Paul R. Fish, and John H. Madsen, eds.
  1992   *The Marana Community in the Hohokam World.* Anthropological Papers of the University of Arizona, no. 56. Tucson: University of Arizona Press.
Gumerman, George J., ed.
  1991   *Exploring the Hohokam: Prehistoric Desert Peoples of the American Southwest.* Albuquerque: University of New Mexico Press.

Haury, Emil W.

1976   *The Hohokam: Desert Farmers and Craftsmen.* Tucson: University of Arizona Press.

Houck, Rose

1992   *Hohokam.* Tucson: Southwest Parks and Monuments Association.

Kelly, Isabell T.

1978   *The Hodges Ruin: A Hohokam Community in the Tucson Basin.* Anthropological Papers of the University of Arizona, no. 30. Tucson: University of Arizona Press.

Whittlesey, Stephanie M., Richard S. Ciolek-Torrello, and Matthew A. Sterner

1994   *Southern Arizona: The Last 12,000 Years.* Technical Series No. 48. Tucson: Statistical Research, Inc.

Woosley, Anne I., and John C. Ravesloot

1993   *Culture and Contact: Charles Di Peso's Gran Chichimeca.* Albuquerque: University of New Mexico Press.

CHAPTER 5. The Patayan

McGuire, Randall H., and Michael B. Schiffer, eds.

1982   *Hohokam and Patayan: Prehistory of Southwestern Arizona.* New York: Academic Press.

CHAPTER 6. The Mogollon

Haury, Emil W.

1985   *Mogollon Culture in the Forestdale Valley, East-Central Arizona.* Tucson: University of Arizona Press.

Haury, Emil W.

1989   *Point of Pines, Arizona: A History of the University of Arizona Archaeological Field School.* Anthropological Papers of the University of Arizona, no. 50. Tucson: University of Arizona Press.

Houck, Rose

1992   *Mogollon.* Tucson: Southwest Parks and Monuments Association.

Longacre, William A., Sally J. Holbrook, and Michael W. Graves

1982   *Multidisciplinary Research at Grasshopper Pueblo, Arizona.* Anthropological Papers of the University of Arizona, no. 40. Tucson: University of Arizona Press.

Lowell, Julie C.

1991   *Prehistoric Households at Turkey Creek Pueblo, Arizona.* Anthropological Papers of the University of Arizona, no. 54. Tucson: University of Arizona Press.

Reid, J. Jefferson

1989   A Grasshopper Perspective on the Mogollon of the Arizona Mountains. In *Dynamics of Southwest Prehistory,* edited by Linda S. Cordell and George J. Gumerman, pp. 65–97. Washington, D.C.: Smithsonian Institution Press.

Zedeño, María Nieves

1994   *Sourcing Prehistoric Ceramics at Chodistaas Pueblo, Arizona: The Circulation of People and Pots in the Grasshopper Region.* Anthropological Papers of the University of Arizona, no. 58. Tucson: University of Arizona Press.

CHAPTER 7. The Anasazi

Adams, E. Charles

1991   *The Origin and Development of the Pueblo Katsina Cult.* Tucson: University of Arizona Press.

Adams, E. Charles, and Kelley Ann Hays

1991   *Homol'ovi II: Archaeology of an Ancestral Hopi Village, Arizona.* Anthropological Papers of the University of Arizona, no. 55. Tucson: University of Arizona Press.

Ferguson, William M., and Arthur H. Rohn

1987   *Anasazi Ruins of the Southwest in Color.* Albuquerque: University of New Mexico Press.

Givens, Douglas R.

1992   *Alfred Vincent Kidder and the Development of Americanist Archaeology.* Albuquerque: University of New Mexico Press.

Gumerman, George J.

1984   *A View from Black Mesa: The Changing Face of Archaeology.* Tucson: University of Arizona Press.

Houck, Rose

1992   *Anasazi.* Tucson: Southwest Parks and Monuments Association.

McNitt, Frank

1966   *Richard Wetherill: Anasazi.* Albuquerque: University of New Mexico Press.

Vivian, R. Gwinn

1990   *The Chacoan Prehistory of the San Juan Basin.* New York: Academic Press.

Webb, Ernest G.

1983   *Tree Rings and Telescopes: The Scientific Career of A. E. Douglass.* Tucson: University of Arizona Press.

CHAPTER 8. The Sinagua

Downum, Christian E.

1992   The Sinagua. *Plateau* 63 (1).

Houck, Rose
 1992 *Sinagua.* Tucson: Southwest Parks and Monuments Association.
Trimble, Stephen
 1981 People of the Verde Valley. *Plateau* 53 (1).

CHAPTER 9. The Salado

Crown, Patricia L.
 1994 *Ceramics and Ideology: Salado Polychrome Pottery.* Albuquerque: University
   of New Mexico Press.
Houck, Rose
 1992 *Salado.* Tucson: Southwest Parks and Monuments Association.

CHAPTER 10. Coronado Ends Prehistory

Bolton, Herbert E.
 1949 *Coronado: Knight of Pueblos and Plains.* Albuquerque: University of New
   Mexico Press.
Fontana, Bernard L.
 1994 *Entrada: The Legacy of Spain and Mexico in the United States.* Tucson: South-
   west Parks and Monuments Association.
Nentvig, Juan
 1980 *Rudo Ensayo: A Description of Sonora and Arizona in 1765.* Ed. and trans.
   Alberto Francisco Pradeau and Robert R. Rasmussen. Tucson: University of
   Arizona Press.
Pfefferkorn, Ignaz
 1989 *Sonora: A Description of the Province.* Trans. Theodore E. Treutlein. Tucson:
   University of Arizona Press.
Udall, Stewart L.
 1987 *To the Inland Empire: Coronado and Our Spanish Legacy.* Garden City, New
   York: Doubleday and Company, Inc.
Winship, George P., trans. and ed.
 1990 *The Journey of Coronado, 1540–1542.* Golden, Colo.: Fulcrum Publishing.

Figure Credits

99   Hohokam figurines. Photograph by Helga Teiwes; courtesy of the Arizona State Museum; neg. no. 81041.

102   Map of Los Muertos. Drawing by Charles R. Riggs.

103   Casa Grande. Courtesy of the Arizona Historical Society; neg. no. 26711.

128   Intaglios at the Ripley Geoglyph Complex. Courtesy of Statistical Research, Inc.

129   Damaged intaglios. Courtesy of the U.S. Bureau of Reclamation.

135   Forestdale Valley and Tla Kii Ruin. Photograph by Emil Haury; courtesy of the Arizona State Museum; neg. no. 543.

139   Map of Bear Village. Drawing by Charles R. Riggs; adapted from Haury 1985:150, fig. 3.

140   Cleaning an Anasazi jar. Photograph by E. B. Sayles; courtesy of the Arizona State Museum; neg. no. 3241.

146   Corrugated and plain Mogollon pottery. Photograph by Emil Haury; courtesy of the Arizona State Museum; neg. no. 3037.

148   Map of Turkey Creek Pueblo. Drawing by Charles R. Riggs.

153   Map of Grasshopper Pueblo. Drawing by Charles R. Riggs.

154   Excavating at Grasshopper Pueblo. Courtesy of the *Tucson Citizen*.

162   Kinishba Pueblo. Photograph by Chuck Abbott; courtesy of the Arizona Historical Society; Cummings Collection, box 4, file 3.

168   Second Mesa. Photograph by Helga Teiwes; courtesy of the Arizona State Museum; neg. no. 37704/37705.

172   White House and Chaco great house. Photograph provided by the National Park Service, Western Archeological and Conservation Center, Tucson.

181   A. E. Douglass. Photograph by Emil Haury; courtesy of the Arizona State Museum; neg. no. 660.

188   Black-on-white Anasazi pottery. Photograph by Helga Teiwes; courtesy of the Arizona State Museum; neg. no. 18820.

192   Tusayan Village. Drawing by Charles R. Riggs.

195   Betatakin. Photograph provided by the National Park Service, Western Archeological and Conservation Center, Tucson.

210   Wupatki Ruin. Photograph provided by the National Park Service, Western Archeological and Conservation Center, Tucson.

213   San Francisco Peaks. Photograph by Jefferson Reid.

226   Montezuma Castle. Photograph provided by the National Park Service, Western Archeological and Conservation Center, Tucson.

232   Roosevelt Lake and Sierra Anchas. Photograph by Jefferson Reid.

237   Pinto and Tonto Polychrome bowls. Photograph by Helga Teiwes; courtesy of the Arizona State Museum; neg. no. 38652.

248   Tonto National Monument cliff dwelling. Courtesy of the Arizona Historical Society; neg. no. 17904.

250   Besh Ba Gowah. Photograph by Jefferson Reid.

262   Coronado Expedition routes. Drawing by Charles R. Riggs.

Index

About the Authors

Jefferson Reid is a southwestern archaeologist and a professor in the Department of Anthropology at the University of Arizona, from which he received his Ph.D. in 1973. He has been director (1979–1992) of the University's Archaeological Field School at Grasshopper on the White Mountain Apache Reservation and editor (1990–1993) of *American Antiquity*, the scholarly journal of anthropological archaeology in the Americas. His thirty seasons of fieldwork range from large prehistoric pueblo ruins of the American Southwest to temple mounds in the Southeast and Mayan pyramids in the Mexican jungle. His research interests include the method, theory, and philosophy of reconstructing past human behavior and culture; the organization of southwestern village farming communities; the Mogollon Culture of the Arizona mountains; and especially the fascinating history of southwestern archaeology.

Stephanie Whittlesey holds a Ph.D. in anthropology from the University of Arizona (1978). She was associated for many years with the Archaeological Field School at Grasshopper. She became immersed in the emerging field of cultural resource management and has since dedicated her career to melding the goals of preservation and reconstructing the past. Along the way she discovered the vital importance of involving the public in archaeology to protect and preserve the past. Since 1989 she has worked for Statistical Research, Inc., a private cultural resource management consulting firm based in Tucson, where she now serves as senior principal investigator and director of research. Her research interests include ceramics, early farming communities, social organization, and the prehistoric cultures of the central Arizona mountains and deserts.